# EXPANDING
# THE
# STRIKE
# ZONE

# EXPANDING THE STRIKE ZONE

## Baseball in the Age of Free Agency

### DANIEL A. GILBERT

University of Massachusetts Press
*Amherst & Boston*

Copyright © 2013 by University of Massachusetts Press
Printed in the United States of America

ISBN 978-1-55849-997-3 (paper); 996-6 (hardcover)

Designed by Jack Harrison
Set in Adobe Minion Pro
Printed and bound by Thomson-Shore, Inc.

Library of Congress Cataloging-in-Publication Data

Gilbert, Daniel A.
Expanding the strike zone : baseball in the age of free agency / Daniel A. Gilbert.
pages cm
Includes bibliographical references and index.
ISBN 978-1-55849-997-3 (pbk. : alk. paper) — ISBN 978-1-55849-996-6 (hardcover : alk. paper)
1. Baseball—Economic aspects—United States.    2. Baseball players—Salaries, etc.—United States.
3. Free agents (Sports)—United States. I. Title.
GV880.G55 2013
338.4'3796357640973—dc23
2013017810

British Library Cataloguing in Publication Data
A catalogue record for this book is available from the British Library.

*For my mother and father*
AND FOR
*Amanda*

# CONTENTS

# ACKNOWLEDGMENTS

It is a pleasure to acknowledge the extraordinary amount of help I received while working on this book. I began researching the history of baseball in the American studies program at Yale University, where I had the opportunity to learn from a great group of teachers. I owe a world of thanks to Michael Denning, for the depth and generosity of his engagement with my work. Jean-Christophe Agnew and Matthew Frye Jacobson helped me find a voice as a cultural historian. Mary Lui offered detailed comments on the initial version of the manuscript. Thanks also to Roberto González Echevarría, Seth Fein, Jonathan Holloway, William Kelly, Jennifer Klein, and Stephen Pitti for advice and encouragement early on. I am grateful, as well, to Vicki Shepard, Jean Cherniavsky, and Brenda Crocker for all they did to support the project.

While in New Haven I had the great fortune to be part of two collectives that profoundly shaped my understanding of the practices and politics of cultural work. I first developed many of the book's arguments through conversations and collaborations in the Working Group on Globalization and Culture, which in those years included Amanda Ciafone, Michael Denning, Rossen Djagalov, Amina El-Annan, Sumanth Gopinath, Myra Jones-Taylor, Nazima Kadir, Christina Moon, Bethany Moreton, Naomi Paik, Ariana Paulson, Olga Sooudi, Laura Trice, Van Truong, Charlie Veric, and Kirsten Weld. My comrades in the Graduate Employees and Students Organization organized me, inspired me, and put up with me through thick and thin. I owe special thanks to Carlos Aramayo, Jeffrey Boyd, Brenda Carter, Amanda Ciafone, Sarah Haley, Drew Hannon, David Huyssen, Amanda Izzo, Mandi Isaacs Jackson, Ben Looker, Ariana Paulson, Shana Redmond, Mary Reynolds, Anita Seth, Annemarie Strassel, and Brendan Walsh.

Colleagues at Macalester College, where I taught for three years while working on the book, made St. Paul, Minnesota, the warmest of intellectual environments. Thanks, especially, to Karin Aguilar-San Juan, Ernesto Capello, Duchess Harris, Peter Rachleff, Jane Rhodes, Paul Schadewald, Kathie Scott, and Scott Shoemaker. I finished the book at the University of Illinois, among colleagues in the School of Labor and Employment Relations who could not have been more generous with their support and good cheer. Thanks in particular to Steven Ashby, Monica Bielski Boris, Robert Bruno, Joel Cutcher-Gershenfeld, Alison Dickson Quesada, Martha Glotzhober, Ed Hertenstein, Emily LaBarbera Twarog, Jennifer Lee, Michael LeRoy, Joseph Martocchio, and Ronald Peters. The sisters and brothers of the Campus Labor Coalition and the Campus Faculty Association helped make Urbana an inspiring place to write about labor history. I am also grateful to the students in the 2011 and 2012 IBEW Arbitration Institutes and the 2012 United Steelworkers Summer School, who offered valuable feedback on my presentations about ballplayer unionism.

The Yale and Macalester students who took my seminars on baseball history deserve special recognition. They engaged enthusiastically and forgivingly with early versions of the book's arguments, and taught me a great deal along the way. Two excellent research assistants, Andrew Berger and Alex Schmidt, provided critical help in the book's final stages. Conversations with many other friends and colleagues over the years helped shape my thinking about baseball in the age of free agency. I want especially to acknowledge the insights of Andrew Friedman, Stetson Hines, Eli Jelly-Shapiro, Seth Kertzer, Mark Krasovic, Jake Lundberg, Adam Machado, Bob Morrissey, Carmen Parrotta, Rachel Perlmeter, Isaac Reed, and Kevin Strait. Josh Rosenblatt graciously hosted me during my research in Austin, and Barbara Stevens and Rufus King welcomed me into their home in Washington, D.C., sustaining me with great food and conversation every night of my lengthy stay.

I would like to offer a special word of appreciation to all of the journalists and scholars of baseball whose work informed and inspired my own—I could never have written this book without the benefit of their publications. I also wish to thank the archivists and librarians whose labor and expertise I relied on, especially the staffs of Yale's Sterling Memorial Library, the National Baseball Hall of Fame, the Tamiment Library, the Library of Congress, the Seattle Municipal Archives, and the Center for American History in Austin. Special thanks to Mike Mashon, who helped me throughout my research in Washington, to Laurie Martínez, who was a terrific guide to Campo Las Palmas, and to Raúl Martínez, who spoke with me at the Liga Mexicana's academy in El Carmen. Carlos José Lugo was incredibly generous with his time and wisdom on several occasions, both during my research in the Dominican Republic and subsequently. Carlos also invited me to tag along to a game in Santiago, so that I could interview his broadcast partner, one of the greatest pitchers in baseball history. I am deeply indebted to Juan Marichal, Jim Bouton, Houston Jiménez, and Marvin Miller for sharing their personal memories with me.

While revising the manuscript I had the benefit of the sharp insights and warm camaraderie of my fellow members of the New Americanist Working Group—Aaron Carico, Amanda Ciafone, Sarah Haley, Naomi Paik, Shana Redmond, and Jason Ruiz. I am grateful particularly to Jason for all he did to organize the group, and to the Institute for Scholarship in the Liberal Arts at the University of Notre Dame for providing funding for our meetings. I want also to say a special word of thanks to George Lipsitz for joining us over multiple days in the fall of 2011, and for his generous comments on our projects.

Co-panelists and audience members at the American Studies Association, the American Historical Association, and the Tepoztlán Institute for Transnational History of the Americas offered helpful feedback on earlier versions of chapters, and I thank especially Jose Alamillo, Amy Bass, Annie Gilbert Coleman, Dana Frank, Sayuri Guthrie-Shimizu, David Kazanjian, Theresa Runstedtler, Nancy Struna, and Kerry Taylor for theirs. I benefited a great deal from the chance to present a version of chapter 4 as part of the Chicago Seminar on Sport and Culture at the Newberry Library, and am grateful to Steven Reiss and Gerald Gems for making that opportunity possible. Alan Klein and Rob Ruck both graciously read sections of the book, and offered much-appreciated feedback and encouragement. The full manuscript had the benefit of careful readings by two other All-Stars of baseball history: Adrian Burgos Jr. and Daniel Nathan. I could not be more grateful for their input and advice.

I gratefully acknowledge the funding I received from the Library of Congress Coca-Cola Fellowship for the Study of Advertising and World Culture, and the Robert M. Leylan Dissertation Fellowship at Yale. Generous support from the School of Labor and Employment Relations at the University of Illinois allowed me to complete the book and secure photograph permissions.

It has been a privilege to work with the great team at the University of Massachusetts Press. I thank David Blight for his suggestion that Clark

Dougan would be the ideal editor for my book. As a first-time author I was fortunate to work with someone as wise and as good-humored as Clark—every historian should be so lucky. Carol Betsch skillfully shepherded the book through multiple stages of the process, and Amanda Heller's meticulous copyediting improved my prose and sharpened my arguments. Jack Harrison did a great job designing the book, and Karen Fisk is making sure it finds an audience. Jan Williams prepared the index, and Maria Wieromiejczyk proofread the final draft.

My parents and sister have endured various manifestations of my baseball obsession for more than three decades. Somehow, after all this time, Peggy, Tom, and Carrie Gilbert find it in their hearts to remain enthusiastic supporters. For that, and for so much more, they have my love and my thanks. The Ciafones—Judy, Russ, C.C., and Joanna—welcomed me into their wonderful family, and supported this book in countless ways. Two relatives who inspired me from a young age to care about both baseball and history are no longer with us. The Honorable John Mason, a lifelong Bostonian who somehow managed to get away with being an Orioles fan, showered me with trading cards and encouraged me to become a writer. My grandmother Helen Homans Gilbert told me stories about Ted Williams, took me to my first game at Fenway Park, and otherwise gave me no choice but to fall in love with her Boston Red Sox.

I could never have written this book without my partner, Amanda Ciafone. Passing along readings and inspiration as we embarked together on transnational cultural history projects, taking endless excursions to familiar and far-flung ballparks, and carving out time to read draft upon draft with boundless insight and care, Amanda lived and labored with every word on these pages. For all that we have shared, and for all that lies ahead, she has my heart.

# EXPANDING
# THE
# STRIKE
# ZONE

# Introduction

WHY DOES BASEBALL MATTER? Why do we care so deeply about the teams we follow? How do we manage to turn games into consequential events? These are the sorts of fundamental philosophical questions that many of us have been forced to ask ourselves—or our loved ones—in states of baseball-inspired despair. I found myself doing this kind of soul searching in late October 2003, grasping for clues that might explain the depth of my depression in the wake of the Red Sox' defeat at the hands of the Yankees in the seventh game of that year's American League Championship Series. For readers fortunate enough to be unaware of the events of that bleak autumn, Boston's noble nine had held a late-game lead over their archrivals from New York, only to have a string of otherworldly misfortunes bring the Evil Empire roaring back to an improbable extra-inning victory. Like many Sox fans, I spent the next several days in a fog, staring blankly at friends, family members, and not a few mirrors, working through my solemn grief. I hit bottom in a Dunkin' Donuts in Hartford, Connecticut, where I had sought refuge from the annual meeting of the American Studies Association, convinced that there was little point in listening to presentations on new approaches to cultural history when the present felt so bad and the future looked so hopeless. Thankfully, this pathetic story of existential crisis has a happy ending. One year later I found myself on Boylston Street in Boston, standing with my family and millions of other ecstatic Red Sox fans at the parade in honor of the team's first World Series championship since 1918. If you had asked me that day why baseball matters, I probably would have just held up the sign that we made for the occasion: "Dreams Come True."

But in the years since 2004, as my identity as a fan gave way to a growing interest in the history of baseball as a culture industry, the issue of the

1

sport's larger significance came up again and again, and it lies at the heart of this book. Why should baseball matter to those interested in broader questions of historical change and cultural meaning? What can the game's history teach us about the world? What wisdom might that heartbroken Red Sox fan be able to offer his colleagues in the American Studies Association? Strangely enough, the experience of hopeless fans like myself is an important part of the answer to these larger historical questions. Ultimately, baseball matters because we collectively insist that it does. Along with journalists, broadcasters, and other observers, fans help make baseball into a dynamic form of storytelling. We invest meaning in what happens on the field, creating characters out of athletes and narratives out of their games. An overwhelming amount of baseball storytelling involves two complex and intertwined themes: work and place. In the world of modern mass spectatorship, ballplayers' struggles and triumphs on the diamond—and increasingly at the negotiating table—have become shared stories about work. And, as fans, we derive special significance from the labors of teams that represent the places we imagine ourselves to be from.

Baseball terminology is full of allusions to labor and craft. Sportswriters and broadcasters frequently comment on players' work habits, either praising or scorning the way they "go about their business" on the field. Even the most highly paid athletes who always hustle, who play with reckless abandon, or who otherwise exhibit a selfless dedication to their jobs earn the label "blue collar." When a hitter extends an at-bat, forcing the pitcher to throw a hittable pitch or else surrender a walk, he is praised for "working the count." Expertly handling a tough offering, the batter might be credited with a "nice piece of hitting," as if his ground-rule double were the display-quality work of a master carpenter. Teams that score via the sound execution of basic fundamentals like bunting are praised for their ability to "manufacture runs." Pitchers simply "work" (as in "Pedro Martínez works a fastball up and in to Derek Jeter"). When they show signs of fatigue, however, pitchers appear to be "laboring." Through the sport's vernacular terms of description and evaluation, commentators and fans construct an idealized work ethic. Expressions of virtue and valor developed in reference to athletes often resonate beyond the diamond, with phrases like "team player" having currency in a multitude of workplaces.

As baseball's everyday language of labor reveals, the sport mediates between work and play.[1] Like other forms of mass-produced culture that took shape in the age of modern industrial capitalism, from amusement rides to feature films, baseball games have always promised spectators a measure of freedom within otherwise oppressive or alienating circumstances.[2] Whether gathering with friends to watch a game during a hard-earned weekend, or tuning in to a radio broadcast to make the working hours pass faster, baseball fans place the sport in a dynamic dialogue with the world of work. Furthermore, as a number of writers have remarked, the sport's lack of a clock and expansive, irregular playing fields create a temporal and spatial distance from the regimentation of our working lives.[3] The cultural historian Warren Susman wonderfully captures baseball's mediation between labor and leisure in his classic analysis of Babe Ruth as a "heroic producer in the mechanized world of play."[4] Susman argues that Ruth's immense popularity in the 1920s stemmed from the fact that he both embodied and transcended the contradictions of the world in which he lived. Spectators could delight in the slugger's unprecedented statistical successes, achievements that drew considerable cultural power from the period's general obsession with quantification and evaluation. At the same time, the larger-than-life Ruth broke the rules of his increasingly regimented society, allowing his fans to transcend its strictures vicariously. This dynamic by no means retired with the Sultan of Swat. Generations of athletes who followed Ruth onto baseball's playing fields have served in similar mediating positions.

Throughout the professional history of the sport, team owners have drawn on baseball's exceptional status as idealized play to enforce unique forms of exploitation. For decades, owners defended the reserve clause, the centerpiece of baseball's longtime labor regime that prevented players from entertaining competing offers from other clubs, as essential to the stability and fairness of the sport. Ballplayers' special status has also shaped the broader impact of baseball's industrial relations. Because of their prominent cultural positions, athletes' labor struggles have been among the most visible of any workers in recent memory. Indeed, ballplayers' individual and collective contract battles have figured prominently in both journalism and popular fiction about the sport. Baseball's labor history, then, is simultaneously one of struggles over wages and conditions for workers in a particular industry, and one of battles over ideas *about* work that matter to millions more.[5]

In addition to being about labor, baseball—like every sport—is fundamentally about territory. Baseball games involve a number of spatial struggles, from the stealth act of base stealing to that most electrifying form of territorial defiance, the home run. One of the sport's most subtle forms of struggle over turf involves the strike zone, the boundaries of which are the subject of constant negotiation, despite their seemingly unambiguous rule-book definition. Baseball's greatest pitchers are capable, with pinpoint accuracy, of "expanding the strike zone"—forcing opponents and umpires alike to offer at "bad" pitches. The aces of the 1990s Atlanta Braves, for example, became legendary for their abilities in this regard. On their best days, Greg Maddux and Tom Glavine would work farther and farther outside, starting at the edge of the official boundary and gradually moving considerably beyond. By consistently hitting their catcher's target, Maddux and Glavine could coax umpires to grant them a progressively wider strike zone, a practice that left opposing hitters with the pitiable choice of either swinging at an untouchable pitch or being sent back to the dugout with their bat still on their shoulder.

Issues of territory extend from action on the diamond itself to the role of the sport within the larger geography of cities, regions, and nations. Collective notions of local identity lie at the center of both the political economy and the cultural meaning of professional baseball. The sport traffics in the powerful fiction that corporate franchises can represent communities. Teams' success at the box office, their ability to win public support for new stadiums, and their broader cultural relevance, all depend on a sense of civic belonging. Individual players play critical roles in the construction of affiliation so central to the sport. Throughout baseball history, teams have sought out stars for their representational potential among desirable communities of fans. For example, the Yankees won generations of Italian American supporters, both in New York City and beyond, with the success of their great center fielder Joe DiMaggio in the late 1930s and 1940s.[6] Over the second half of the twentieth century, the representational potential of individual athletes would become ever more important both to the business of baseball, as team owners sought increased profits through new forms of broadcasting and marketing, and to the sport's broader symbolic meaning, as new communities of fans cheered for teams performing on far away diamonds. The corporate construction and manipulation of local identity has not gone unchallenged in baseball; the industry has been shaped and reshaped by collective dissent from team owners' agendas. Indeed, territorial claims stand among the game's most contested elements.

One of baseball's distinguishing territorial features is its transnational geography. With a history in countries such as Japan and Cuba extending back to the nineteenth century, baseball has long been something much more than national and much less than global, mapping a distinct set of connections both within and between East Asia and the Americas. The particularity of the sport's cultural terrain is signaled in a phrase that journalists and other commentators have used for generations: "the baseball world." The expression often appears as shorthand for the sport's imagined community. For example, when in 2011 the Los Angeles Angels signed first baseman Albert Pujols to a ten-year contract worth $250 million, a headline on ESPN.com proclaimed, "Angels Shock the Baseball World."[7] When applied to the game's geography (and not simply its constituents), the phrase also serves to differentiate baseball's idiosyncratic transnational configuration from those of other sports and culture industries.[8]

The final third of the twentieth century saw significant transformations in the structure of both work and territory in the baseball world. As players in Major League Baseball (MLB) won new power in their industry through collective bargaining, team owners responded by creating more flexible modes of control over the recruitment and development of future generations of athletes. Exercising territorial power derived from their position atop the sport's hierarchy of professional leagues, MLB executives significantly expanded their teams' geographic reach, in search of top players and new fans from Latin America and East Asia. The period was also defined by teams' adoption of increasingly flexible positions with respect to their "home" cities, as owners and league officials threatened to relocate franchises in order to win public subsidies for ballpark development. These new forms of labor and territorial flexibility became defining elements of a new era in baseball: the age of free agency.

The seeds for this period of transformation were planted in the years following World War II, when MLB team owners and league officials expanded their power and influence across a newly integrated baseball world. Racial integration of formerly segregated professional leagues formed one part of a massive reconfiguration of baseball in the Americas, as circuits that once operated on the far side of the color line came to represent untapped scouting and development sites in the eyes of MLB team owners. Baseball officials in the United States also negotiated new agreements governing the mutual recognition of player contracts with recently revived professional leagues in Japan, further integrating baseball relations across the Pacific. In addition, as MLB executives sought new markets, they moved franchises into new territories across the continental United States. Central to this period of massive territorial reorganization in the baseball industry were emerging forms of cultural representation, including new styles of print journalism and the powerful new medium of television. These interrelated developments form the subject of chapter 1, which examines the era of integration and expansion—the period out of which the age of free agency emerged.

By the mid-1960s, players on major league teams found themselves left out of their sport's growing profits. Their collective response, which came in the form of a remarkably successful union movement, would transform the business of baseball. Although the Major League Baseball Players Association (MLBPA) had existed for several years, it did not wield much power until players reorganized it with the help of a new executive director, former United Steelworkers of America economist Marvin J. Miller. Over the course of Miller's first decade with the MLBPA the players won significant improvements in basic salaries and benefits and, even more important, a new system of contractual free agency. The union's victories at the bargaining table were part of a larger transformation, marked by new forms of player power and self-representation, both on the field and in popular culture more broadly. From Curt Flood, the African American star of the St. Louis Cardinals who fought Major League Baseball's power structure all the way to the Supreme Court, to Jim Bouton, the rebellious pitcher-turned-author whose controversial memoir *Ball Four* broke from the sport's conventional styles of storytelling, a generation of big league ballplayers enacted a new cultural politics of representation. These developments, the making and meaning of free agency, constitute the subject of chapter 2.

The MLBPA's stunning success from the 1960s onward depended on the union's successful mobilization of star power. The players built their union by asserting control over their own commodification (insisting, for example, on a fair share of revenue from baseball cards and television broadcasts), and proved that Major League Baseball could not exist without their own popular appeal. As the age of free agency unfolded, players' potential to attract new fans became an increasingly important consideration for their teams. The role of star power came into sharp relief in 1981 with the tremendous success that the Mexican pitcher Fernando Valenzuela enjoyed with the Los Angeles Dodgers. Valenzuela became a breakthrough transnational sensation in the midst of a moment of remarkable labor upheaval, marked by tumultuous strikes in both Major League Baseball and Mexico's top professional circuit, the Liga Mexicana. Chapter 3 considers the linked histories of these two strikes as evidence of the divergent forms of agency at work in the baseball industry of the early 1980s. As players on MLB teams succeeded in defending their hard-won system of free agency, athletes in Mexico struggled to secure measures of professional autonomy and collective power through their union, the Asociación Nacional de Beisbolistas (ANABE), and ultimately their own players' league.

As the Mexican players' movement demonstrates, free agency in Major League Baseball was only one development in a larger period of change in the industry's organization of labor. More and more, as MLB players flexed their star power, the owners of their teams invested in talent development strategies designed to produce a cheap, flexible, and ever-replaceable pool of talent. Among the age of free agency's most central institutions are the so-called baseball academies of the Dominican Republic, in which MLB teams have trained expanding numbers of young prospects. The academies brought a dramatic transformation to Dominican baseball, as older, nationally directed structures were reimagined and replaced. Chapter 4 examines the rise of the academies within the longer arc of Dominican baseball history, focusing in particular on the ways in which the new talent development model worked to reposition the nation and its ballplayers within the larger configuration of power and agency in the baseball world.

Together with the Dominican academies, Major League Baseball's stadiums and ballparks stand as signal territorial forms of the age of free agency. Securing massive public subsidies, team executives erected a new generation of facilities that became entry points into expanding networks of advertising and broadcasting, while looming ever larger in the built environments of major league cities. The national identities of the players hired to perform on these diamonds also became essential elements of teams' territorial flexibility, as clubs sought out stars capable of attracting broader communities of fans. The final chapter examines the complex territorial history of the Seattle Mariners, a franchise that in the first years of the twenty-first century became one of Major League Baseball's most important global brands, thanks to the trans-Pacific popularity of star outfielder Ichiro Suzuki. The history of Ichiro's Mariners, however, is inseparable from that of the International District, downtown Seattle's working-class Asian American community. The Mariners' two stadiums—the Kingdome, which opened in 1976, and Safeco Field, which replaced it in 1999—were built in close proximity to the International District's residences and family businesses. Organizing in opposition to plans for the Kingdome galvanized the neighborhood beginning in the early 1970s, and the district's history of community formation over the succeeding decades developed in counterpoint to the Mariners' corporate staging of local identity. It was this contested territory that Ichiro Suzuki, one of his sport's most captivating athletes, stepped into when he made his MLB debut in the spring of 2001. Along with the millions who watched him play, Ichiro brought new meaning to baseball's age of free agency.

The transformations in the baseball world's organization of work and territory in the final decades of the twentieth century were significant parts of a broader historical shift. Whether the outcome of that shift is defined as "post-Fordism," "the new economy," "neoliberalism," or "globalization," it has become increasingly clear that, as the geographer David Harvey succinctly argues, there has been "a sea-change in cultural as well as in political-economic practices" since the early 1970s.[9] The contours of this "sea-change" include the decline of the business-state-labor compacts of the mid-twentieth century, the rise of just-in-time assembly and other "flexible" forms of global production, the increasing predominance of free market forces in the experience of daily life, and the consolidation of capital and power in the hands of a small transnational elite.

The history of baseball in the age of free agency is that of a single industry within the much larger development of neoliberal globalization. Taken together, baseball's new practices of work and territory embody both "flexible accumulation," as Harvey and others have termed the distinguishing characteristics of capitalist production since the 1970s, and "flexible citizenship," as the cultural theorist Aihwa Ong has named the fluid affiliations and identities that came to define contemporary daily life by the turn of the twenty-first century.[10] Cultural forms like baseball have constituted critical sites of encounter and engagement with the period's dramatic social transformations. If we are to understand the changes in the organization and meaning of work and territory in our recent past, we must look to the fields where such matters have been struggled over and played with, including the diamonds of the baseball world.

# 1

# The Roots of Free Agency

## Integration and Expansion in the Baseball World

O PENING DAY is always a special occasion, containing all the hope and possibility of a new season for players and fans alike. The start of the 1964 National League campaign had a particular significance in New York City, marking the debut of a state-of-the-art home for the local club. On April 17, over fifty thousand New Yorkers made their way to Shea Stadium in Queens to see the Mets christen their diamond with a 4–3 loss to the Pittsburgh Pirates. The Mets had been born two years earlier, playing in the Polo Grounds in upper Manhattan, where the New York Giants had labored for years before departing for San Francisco following the 1957 season. The team's new facility, with its expansive parking lots, movable stands, and twenty-one escalators, stood in sharp contrast to the Polo Grounds and Brooklyn's Ebbets Field, cozy neighborhood ballparks built along streetcar and subway lines and abandoned with the rise of the interstates.

Shea Stadium was designed for the age of the highway, but the facility's debut quickly became a story about the limits of urban automobility. Leonard Koppett's account of the game in the next day's *New York Times,* appearing under the headline "Shea Stadium Opens with Big Traffic Jam," noted that the roads were so choked that city traffic commissioner Henry A. Barnes took to the skies in a helicopter to help "unscramble post-game jams" spreading out past Flushing Meadow on the Van Wyck Expressway. Still, many observers celebrated Shea's gleaming modernity, even as the finishing touches were still being applied on opening day. "Certain items connected with the ball park are incomplete—including the Mets," wrote Arthur Daley of the *Times.* "But it has to be rated as close to perfection in all of its glittering modern appurtenances."[1]

Shea was part of a larger landscape taking shape in Flushing Meadow in the spring of 1964. The home of the Mets stood directly adjacent to the site of the New York World's Fair, which itself opened to the public just days later. Both the fair and the stadium were the work of New York City's "master builder," Robert Moses, and together marked the latest articulation of his enormous imprint on the postwar metropolis.[2] The stadium, while technically a distinct construction project, was in practice a central element of the exhibition experience, as fairgoers were encouraged to make time for the Mets in between viewing marvels like the U.S. Steel Unisphere and Ford Motor Company's Magic Skyway. Fair designers implemented a system of ultraviolet hand stamps at the exit gates, making it possible to return free of charge after a few hours spent taking in a ballgame.[3] Shea Stadium thus established Major League Baseball's place within the larger cultural vision that the fair projected, one that championed the United States as an engine of capitalist democracy in an age of unprecedented affluence— "Man's Achievement on a Shrinking Globe in an Expanding Universe," as the event's theme declared.

At the official dedication on April 22, President Lyndon Johnson proclaimed: "This fair represents the most promising of our hopes. It gathers together, from 80 countries, the achievements of industry, the health of nations, the creations of man." Not missing the opportunity to make a campaign speech with the 1964 election season under way, Johnson went on to outline his vision for what he would soon brand the Great Society, a nation "unwilling to accept public deprivation in the midst of private satisfaction." Like the larger political moment that the fair represented, the exhibition presented an opportunity for movements to voice claims for social justice. The day of Johnson's dedication, activists from the Congress of Racial Equality (CORE) organized an automobile "stall-in" to draw fairgoers' attention to the racialized inequality on display every day in the city, outside the utopian confines of the fair.[4]

The baseball world of 1964, like the expanse of cultural marvels that spread out beyond Shea Stadium, exhibited its own processes of contradictory global change. In the two decades following World War II, baseball saw transformations that rank among the most celebrated and analyzed in the history of sport, the two best known of which were the racial integration of formerly segregated major and minor league teams, and the expansion of Major League Baseball across the United States, beyond the industrial and commercial centers of the Northeast and Midwest. Integration and expansion have become key chapters of a familiar narrative, with events

Opening day at Shea Stadium, alongside the New York World's Fair, April 17, 1964. (*Meyer Liebowitz/The New York Times/Redux*)

such as Jackie Robinson's 1947 debut with the Brooklyn Dodgers and the team's departure for Los Angeles a decade later looming large in many accounts of the so-called national pastime. Integration and expansion, however, were fundamentally transnational developments, and were central to the deepening of Major League Baseball's influence beyond the borders of the United States. In the two decades after World War II, as MLB teams integrated and moved to new locations, league officials also brokered new agreements with Latin American and Japanese counterparts. At the same time, emerging forms of writing and broadcasting brought new dimensions to the production and interpretation of baseball's meaning. Taken together, the changes of the postwar era created the conditions out of which the age of free agency would grow.

## The Formation of the Modern Baseball World

Developing from a variety of bat-and-ball games with their origins in the British sporting tradition, baseball was first formalized into codified rules, clubs, and leagues in the United States in the mid-nineteenth century. The sport took shape in the sphere of fraternal organizations in New York City in the 1840s, expanding nationally through the Civil War years, and by the 1870s the first professional baseball teams and leagues had been formed.[5] While these developments were unfolding in the United States, baseball also took root in other parts of the world. Two locations in particular were central to the game's international development: Cuba and Japan.

Cuban students who learned the game in the United States brought it home with them, and by the late 1860s the sport was gaining popularity there. Growing numbers of players and supporters made baseball into a form of Cuban national culture, defining the sport in opposition to the Spanish colonial pastime of bullfighting.[6] The rise of baseball as a national sport in Cuba was echoed in Japan in the final decades of the nineteenth century. Although, as the historian Donald Roden recounts, international sailors and businessmen were the first to play baseball in the country, an ultimately more important development occurred when U.S. educators in Japanese secondary schools began teaching the game to their students in the early 1870s. Roden argues, "While Americans in Yokohama played baseball to be more American, Japanese students, especially in the higher schools, turned to baseball in an effort to reify traditional values and to establish a new basis for national pride."[7] In the years of baseball's early development in both Cuba and Japan, and in the decades that followed, the sport would provide space for the construction of competing and complex national and transnational identities.

Cuban and Japanese players, coaches, and supporters not only made baseball a popular sport in their respective nations but also served as key conduits in further disseminating the sport regionally. Cuban baseball enthusiasts were largely responsible for spreading the game throughout the Caribbean. For example, the thousands of Cubans who fled to the Dominican Republic during the Ten Years' War (1868–1878) brought baseball along with the capital that would help create their new home country's modern sugar industry.[8] In East Asia, Japanese individuals and institutions similarly served as key conduits of baseball's regional development at the turn of the century. Although a U.S. missionary, Philip Gillett, is credited with first introducing baseball to Korea, the soldiers and officials of the occupying Japanese army facilitated the sport's further development as a rich and contested form of Korean culture.[9]

By the first years of the twentieth century, the basic outlines of the modern baseball world were in place, with teams and leagues established throughout regions of North America, the Caribbean Basin, and the Pacific Rim.[10] Despite the history of transnational subjects—from students and teachers to businessmen and soldiers—spreading and remaking the sport, some in the United States claimed ownership, championing baseball in nationalist terms. Chief among such figures was the prominent sporting goods magnate A. G. Spalding, himself a former star ballplayer, who argued in one of the first histories of baseball (published in 1911) that the sport had "followed the flag."[11] While U.S. interests and institutions—including the military— played central roles in building the baseball world, the sport's transnational development was not a simple function of one nation's global power. As the Dominican and Korean cases suggest, the pervasive characterization of baseball as "America's game" fails to account for the regional networks of capital and culture that shaped its history around the world.

In the twentieth century, the period between the two world wars, which saw the emergence of professional leagues in a number of countries, marked a new stage in the sport's development. As organized circuits grew in several nations, baseball enjoyed ever greater popularity in the United States, becoming a major modern culture industry. New superstar players like Babe Ruth enjoyed comprehensive coverage in daily newspapers and, by the late 1920s, on radio. Ruth's mass mediated heroics came on the heels of the "Black Sox" scandal of 1919, in which several members of the Chicago White Sox were banned from Major League Baseball for conspiring to "fix" World Series games against the Cincinnati Reds. As one of the most charismatic and celebrated athletes to ever play the game, Ruth helped to rescue MLB's popularity in the wake of this industry-shaking controversy, leaving a cultural imprint rivaled by few athletes in the history of any sport.[12] White players by no means held a monopoly on celebrity status. African American athletes such as catcher Josh Gibson and pitcher Satchel Paige were mass culture sensations as well, their exploits receiving comprehensive coverage in the black press.[13]

The interwar period also saw the further development of transnational connections and exchanges across the baseball world. One particularly significant example was the practice of off-season barnstorming, in which players formed touring teams to play in front of new audiences. Ruth and other U.S. stars made several international barnstorming tours, including one to Japan that played a key role in stimulating the formation of that nation's professional leagues.[14] Baseball in the Americas in the era of racial exclusion consisted of overlapping networks of leagues and barnstorming circuits. Many players barred from white professional ball played year-round, often in the United States and Canada in the summer and in the Caribbean during the winter. Havana, the capital of Latin American professional baseball until the Cuban Revolution, was as central a baseball hub as New York or Chicago.[15]

As the modern baseball industry took shape at the turn of the twentieth century, lasting forms of organizational hierarchy developed. The term "organized baseball" has its roots in the late 1800s, when league officials in the United States came to a series of key accords—known as "national agreements"—over the mutual recognition of player contracts and territorial rights.[16] As the historian Jules Tygiel notes, signatories to the pacts "referred to their operations as 'organized baseball' and labeled all others 'outlaw' leagues' " in order to "distinguish themselves from lesser pretenders."[17] With the color line dividing the sport into separate and unequal spheres of action, the expression "organized baseball" was deeply racialized. In the second half of the twentieth century the term took on a more explicitly international dimension, and an aura of nationalist chauvinism, as MLB officials and team owners exercised new territorial power throughout the baseball world.

Another important hierarchical divide in professional baseball has been the distinction between "major" and "minor" leagues. The sport's early history saw multiple competing circuits, and the frequent practice of rivals "raiding" their competitors' rosters. The leaders of two especially powerful bodies, the established National League and the upstart American League, resolved a long-running dispute by signing the pivotal National Agreement of 1903, creating a partnership known from that point forward as "the major leagues." Two years before the 1903 agreement, feeling threats to their own ability to retain players and attract fans posed by the ongoing power struggle between the NL and the AL, representatives of other professional baseball leagues operating in the United States formed the National Association of Professional Baseball Clubs (NAPBL, or simply the National Association). Designed to protect shared interests in the face of growing National and American League power, from its founding in 1901 the National Association became the collective voice of the minor leagues. The National Agreement of 1903 formalized relations between the majors and their subordinates, establishing a hierarchy of circuits (with the minors ranked as class A, B, C, or D) and further cementing the universal system of player contracts and other provisions that the minor league officials had adopted in forming the NAPBL two years earlier.[18]

Over the course of the first four decades of the twentieth century, the relation between major and minor league teams was transformed, most significantly, through a new approach to player development: the farm system. The most influential figure in this history was Branch Rickey, who pioneered the model with the St. Louis Cardinals beginning in the early 1920s, before later stints as general manager of the Brooklyn Dodgers (1943–1950) and the Pittsburgh Pirates (1950–1955). Under Rickey's system, which other executives soon copied, the Cardinals owned the contracts of players distributed across a large network of affiliated "farm" clubs. Rather than requiring a team to purchase a player's contract from an independently operated National Association affiliate, the farm system made it possible to summon players to the majors (or trade them to another club) whenever the need or opportunity arose. By the end of the 1930s, Rickey's system was an established standard, with most minor league affiliates serving as farms for the majors.[19] The emergence of the farm system effectively redefined the National Association as a subsidiary organization of the major leagues.

Distinctions between major and minor carry deep implications of the power relations at work in the baseball world. Major League Baseball derives its identity from the conceit that its teams and games represent the very pinnacle of the sport, and that, for example, the annual competition between the best NL and AL teams can legitimately be called the World Series. Even as Major League Baseball gained more and more power and influence in the second half of the twentieth century, and treated increasing numbers of leagues in other parts of the world as "minor" circuits (by using them for player development purposes), many in those "other" places employed more nuanced categorizations. For generations of fans, players, and team owners in the winter professional leagues of the Caribbean, for example, the enterprise has always amounted to something much more than "minor."

## The Racial Integration of "Organized Baseball"

World War II brought sweeping change to the baseball world. Although play continued in most top circuits (a key exception being Japan, where professional competition ceased entirely during 1945), the massive worldwide investment of capital and labor in the war effort altered the operations of many leagues.[20] Images of MLB stars like Joe DiMaggio and Ted Williams trading their baseball jerseys for military uniforms have become iconic scenes in baseball history. The war's effect on baseball went far beyond moving top players from the diamond to the battlefield. In the United States, the wartime migration of African American southerners to industrial cities, combined with the concurrent mobilization for national sacrifice in the name of defending democracy around the world, helped to create the conditions for a successful assault on baseball's color line. As African American athletes, writers, and fans exposed the hypocrisy of segregated white baseball, MLB owners slowly gave in to integration.

Beginning with Jackie Robinson's debut in April 1946 as a member of the Brooklyn Dodgers' top farm team, the Montreal Royals, a generation of formerly excluded athletes transformed old playing fields of white privilege into central stages in the struggle for racial justice. Though African American players like Robinson are often remembered within a national framework, justifiably seen as pioneers in the modern U.S. civil rights movement, the struggles and changes of the postwar decades took shape across an entire transnational system that had grown up around the color line. Indeed, as Adrian Burgos Jr. shows in *Playing America's Game: Baseball, Latinos, and the Color Line*, the full integration of "organized baseball" and the concurrent decline of the Negro leagues were transformational developments both for Latino athletes and for the relationship of Latin American circuits to MLB.[21]

The integration era saw major league team owners exercise new forms of power over other baseball interests, both within the United States and across other territories of the baseball-playing Americas. Some of the first signs of this new dynamic appeared in MLB officials' dismissive attitude toward existing Negro league contracts. Seeking to benefit from what he viewed as a vast untapped resource, Brooklyn Dodgers general manager Branch Rickey quietly began scouting players across the color line. When the Dodgers signed Jackie Robinson, the Kansas City Monarchs cried foul. Tom Baird, one of the Monarchs' owners, declared: "We won't take it lying down. Robinson signed a contract with us last year and I feel he is our property." Neither Rickey nor Robinson put much stock in Baird's position. Rickey claimed that irregularities in the black leagues' contract system made it possible for players like Robinson to ignore their existing deals and sign with MLB suitors.[22]

In the wake of the Robinson signing, officials of the Negro American League and Negro National League adopted MLB's contractual language and attempted formal affiliation. They were refused. MLB commissioner Happy Chandler lectured them: "You must clean out the gamblers. You must establish your game on a fair and honest footing and develop your umpires to the levels of high respect which the decision callers hold in Organized Baseball." Nothing more came of the affiliation attempt, as MLB teams continued in large part to dictate the terms under which they could recruit and sign Negro league players.[23]

Arguments among MLB team owners and league officials over plans for racial integration were often cast in terms of the perceived viability and legitimacy (or lack thereof) of the black leagues. Burgos notes that Clark Griffith, the owner of the Washington Senators, who made a substantial amount of money in rent from the Homestead Grays, insisted that the Negro leagues should be supported and their contracts respected, and that his fellow MLB executives shouldn't "act like outlaws in taking their stars." Rickey, by contrast, maintained: "The Negro organizations in baseball are not leagues, nor, in my opinion, do they have even organization. As at present administered they are in the nature of a racket."[24]

Many watched the subsequent decline of the Negro leagues with concern for the future of African American ballplayers. Some commentators, like *Pittsburgh Courier* writer Jack Saunders, feared that once MLB teams took their pick of those players already active, "major league baseball will revert to the national pastime of those Americans with white skins."[25] Such fears reflected, among other things, the fact that a significant proportion of MLB farm teams operated in southern states where the Jim Crow racial regime remained entrenched, both in the law and in the ever-present threat of extralegal violence. Other commentators saw baseball integration as a deadly blow to one of the most visible and viable forms of African American capitalism. These concerns had grounds as well. Black professional ball lost much of its fan base beginning in the late 1940s, as stars like Jackie Robinson brought millions of African American supporters with them into the imagined community—and paying fan base—of Major League Baseball.[26]

Some black teams did manage to hang on until the early 1960s. Those that survived saw more and more of their business devoted to providing talent for Major League Baseball. According to Negro American League official Sonny Webb, in the late 1950s, "basically, what they were trying to do was sell . . . ballplayers to major league franchises."[27] Adrian Burgos Jr. explores the integration era's shifting terrain of talent development in his analysis of Alejandro "Alex" Pompez, the owner of the Negro National League's New York Cubans, an enterprise whose business was fundamentally changed by MLB's integration. Ultimately, Pompez "maximized the opportunities created by

integration," negotiating a partnership with the New York Giants and becoming one of the leading talent developers for Major League Baseball in
the postwar period.[28]

In 1961 Branch Rickey noted in a memo to the management of the just-
founded New York Mets (preparing for their inaugural MLB season the
following year): "[Negro American League president J. B. Martin] needs
money to keep going. I believe a deal could be made very soon whereby
a sponsoring club or clubs could get the entire production of this Negro
league. This would be a very valuable asset to New York."[29] As Rickey's
memo reveals, one of the enduring meanings of MLB's racial integration,
significant as it was in the struggle for social justice and equality in the
United States, was that MLB owners brought under their contractual control a group of highly prized, previously excluded athletes.

For the athletes themselves, the integration era brought both new opportunities and new challenges. In barnstorming tours and in organized
league play, African American players, along with their Latino teammates,
had for decades been central figures in professional baseball circuits from
New England to the Caribbean. Many players described their experiences
in foreign leagues as being among the richest and most rewarding of their
careers. "We live in the best hotels, we eat in the best restaurants and can
go anyplace we care to," African American infielder Willie Wells said of his
experience playing in Veracruz, Mexico, in 1942. "I've found freedom and
democracy here."[30] In the postwar period ballplayers continued to negotiate transnational differences in racial and other hierarchies, bringing their
labor to new formations of teams and leagues. Indeed, for athletes of color
and white players alike, the integration of formerly segregated circuits in
the United States and Canada represented only one aspect of a period of
broader change in the baseball industry.

### Major League Baseball and the Liga Mexicana

In early 1946 Jorge Pasquel, the most powerful team owner in the Liga Mexicana (Mexican League), created chaos in the baseball world by attempting to compete for talent with MLB clubs, signing players for higher salaries than they had been earning in the United States. In previous seasons
Pasquel and other Liga Mexicana team owners had recruited top African
American stars such as Willie Wells, a practice that barely registered with
MLB officials. The 1946 attempt to lure away white players was another
matter entirely. Commissioner Chandler responded by banning anyone

who "jumped" to play south of the border, an action that, in turn, brought lawsuits from multiple players. Most of the "jumpers" dropped their legal challenges after Chandler offered them a chance at reinstatement, but one player continued his fight through the summer of 1949—former New York Giants outfielder Danny Gardella, who alleged that MLB's restrictive system of player contracts violated U.S. antitrust law. The so-called reserve clause, which allowed teams to retain exclusive rights to players upon the expiration of their contracts, had been a defining element of Major League Baseball from the beginning. Although the U.S. Supreme Court had previously ruled that the Sherman Antitrust Act did not apply to the industry, establishing an anomalous legal status that reinforced the ability of MLB clubs to abide by their own rules, many saw Gardella's case as an opportunity to chip away at team owners' monopoly power. The reserve clause would remain intact, however, when Gardella dropped his legal challenge in October 1949, later indicating that MLB officials had paid him a $60,000 out-of-court settlement to do so.[31]

Through the late 1940s and early 1950s there were several occurrences of cross-border talent raiding between Liga Mexicana clubs and U.S. minor league teams, despite the existence of a verbal agreement designed to limit such activity after the 1946 crisis. As a summer circuit, the Liga Mexicana posed a special challenge, running concurrently with the MLB-affiliated minor leagues. In January 1955, after years of cross-border disputes, officials from the Liga Mexicana signed an agreement that admitted their circuit to the ranks of "organized baseball."[32] Under the terms of the arrangement, teams on both sides of the border agreed to respect contractual rights, and the Mexican circuit accepted official status as a minor league. Unlike in other Latin American countries, where MLB scouts could offer contracts to young players at their own discretion, the rights to all baseball prospects in Mexico remained the province of the Liga Mexicana.[33] The territorial control of "native" talent secured in the 1955 accord would play a defining role in shaping MLB teams' approach to future generations of Mexican athletes. The fact that, by the end of the twentieth century, Major League Baseball featured many more players from the Dominican Republic and Venezuela than from Mexico can be traced to the events that culminated in 1955.

## Major League Baseball and the Caribbean Winter Leagues

Happy Chandler's ban on players like Danny Gardella was only one element of MLB's response to the Liga Mexicana's 1946 challenge. Almost immediately,

MLB officials moved to establish relationships with Latin American leagues in order to forestall the possibility of future threats. The circuit that U.S. baseball officials were most eager to bring under their influence was the Liga Cubana (Cuban League). This league had long been the centerpiece of winter baseball in the Americas and home to some of the top competition anywhere, since elite players could compete against one another outside the restrictions of U.S. racial codes.

As Roberto González Echevarría explains in his detailed history of Cuban baseball, *The Pride of Havana*, MLB owners were motivated in particular by a desire to limit player mobility beyond their jurisdiction. The Cuban circuit had what González Echevarría terms a "dangerously intimate" relationship with the Liga Mexicana—many of its stars had played in the outlaw Mexican circuit. For Cuban team owners and fans the prospect of affiliation with MLB was a complex matter, offering stability and a shot at additional elite international players, but at the expense of national autonomy. The terms offered by MLB officials included a ban on all athletes and managers who had remained involved with the Liga Mexicana, including revered national figures such as players Roberto Ortiz and Napoleón Reyes, and managers Miguel Angel González and Adolfo Luque. Despite this significant cost in local talent and independence, Liga Cubana officials gave in to MLB pressure.[34] On June 10, 1947, the league became an official MLB affiliate. A rival circuit, the Liga Nacional, quickly formed, filling its rosters with athletes and managers branded as "outlaws" by MLB officials. The Liga Cubana won out when the Liga Nacional failed to last beyond one season, its sponsors eventually abandoning the circuit.[35]

In the wake of the Liga Cubana's agreement with MLB, other Caribbean leagues followed suit. At a meeting in Miami in late 1947, George Trautman, the president of the National Association, reached tentative accords with representatives of professional winter leagues in Panama, Venezuela, and Puerto Rico. The *Sporting News* ran a lengthy editorial praising the new "open-door policy" and "good-neighborliness" evidenced in the talks, and trumpeting the notion that the new relationship "not only will strengthen the game throughout Latin-America and cement the tieup with Organized Ball, but also will further Pan-American solidarity in international relations."[36] What was touted as solidarity was in reality new territorial power, as MLB owners succeeded in extending considerable influence throughout the vast majority of professional baseball activity in the Americas. By late 1948, when National Association representative Robert Finch toured affiliated Caribbean leagues, he came away assured that "cesspools of ineligibility" had been eliminated.[37]

As an offshoot of the agreements between Latin American leagues and MLB officials, an organization of affiliated winter circuits, the Confederación de Béisbol Profesional del Caribe (CBPC, usually termed the Caribbean Confederation in the English-language press), formed and became a central body in the industry. Representatives of the CBPC, consisting of officials from member leagues, would meet annually with National Association officials to deliberate on the terms of MLB–winter league relations. Additionally, the CBPC organized the annual Serie del Caribe (Caribbean Series), pitting the top teams from participating leagues against one another. Beginning in 1948 the CBPC and corresponding annual series included the winter leagues of Cuba, Puerto Rico, Venezuela, and Panama. This configuration remained in place through 1960. The Cuban Revolution, which brought a new national amateur system in place of the old Liga Cubana, also precipitated a major break in the CBPC's history. The Serie del Caribe was not reconstituted until 1970, with teams from the winter leagues of the Dominican Republic, Venezuela, and Puerto Rico competing against one another. Mexico's winter professional circuit, the Liga Mexicana del Pacífico, joined in 1971, completing a lineup that would last into the twenty-first century.[38]

The Serie del Caribe's decade-long hiatus after 1960 is just one indication of Cuba's historical importance to the organization of professional baseball in the Americas more broadly. Even before the integration of Major League Baseball, the country had been an important territory for MLB talent development, with the Washington Senators in particular (through their legendary scout Joe Cambria) signing a number of Cuban players. Amid the realignments of the postwar period, Cuba held a central place in Major League Baseball's expanding network of affiliates and partnerships, through the success of the Liga Cubana as well as that of the Havana Sugar Kings of the International League, a top minor circuit with other franchises in such cities as Toronto and Miami. Cuba's revolutionary government not only ended the operation of professional teams based in the country but also restricted MLB clubs from signing amateur Cuban players. Despite these policies, Cuban athletes—many of whom were already members of major and minor league teams in the United States—played leading roles in Major League Baseball in the decades following the revolution. One index of Cuba's centrality to major league talent development before the revolution is the fact that for a decade after the country's rejection of capitalist baseball, more Cubans appeared in MLB games than did players from any other territory outside the continental United States.[39]

The transition to nationalized amateur baseball was one part of a broader reconfiguration of Cuban sport. Established in early 1961, the Instituto Nacional de Deportes, Educación Fisica y Recreación (INDER, the National Institute of Sport, Physical Education, and Recreation) led a range of efforts to build national athletic institutions and bolster Cuba's profile on the world sporting stage. Cuba's new approach to baseball had its international debut later that spring, at the Serie Mundial Amateur in San José, Costa Rica. The Cuban team's impressive victory at the 1961 international amateur series, which happened to coincide almost to the day with the Bay of Pigs invasion, showcased the vitality of revolutionary baseball. The new national league, the Serie Nacional de Béisbol, began play in early 1962, becoming one of Cuba's most prominent cultural institutions. Key figures in the league's early going included a number of players and coaches who had participated in various capacities in MLB-affiliated baseball in previous years. For example, Antonio Castaño, who had managed the Havana Sugar Kings in 1960 before the franchise moved to Jersey City in the wake of the revolution, served as the first skipper for the new Azucareros club. The league's most prominent propagandist, Fidel Castro, proclaimed the 1962 season to be "the triumph of free baseball over slave baseball."[40] In the decades that followed, Cuban ball would remain a powerful "exception" within the baseball world, with an orientation that could not have been more distinct from that of Major League Baseball.

Over the postwar decades a number of MLB teams developed robust Latin American scouting programs. For teams like the White Sox, Pirates, Dodgers, and Giants, "working agreement" arrangements with winter league clubs became their major institutional relationship to Latin America. Such partnerships allowed MLB teams to gain access to their affiliates' top athletes and—just as important—local scouts, who often worked on the coaching staffs of Caribbean clubs. In return, winter league teams received limited access to MLB players and coaches, some of whom possessed valuable international star power, and thus the potential to draw local fans. Some MLB teams shifted their working agreements regularly, while others developed lasting associations. For example, the New York (and later San Francisco) Giants shared an especially long relationship with the Escogido club of the Dominican winter league, thanks to the work of key individuals: one of the Giants' most important "bird dog" scouts in the 1950s, Horacio Martínez, was an Escogido coach and former player.[41]

In annual discussions with MLB and National Association representatives, Caribbean baseball officials consistently pressed for terms that would allow their circuits to function as much like local "major" leagues as possible. The breakdown of "native" versus "imported" players (as the two categories have been termed throughout the history of the winter leagues) was a particularly contested matter. Whereas MLB officials were most interested in exploiting the Caribbean circuits as development opportunities for players (both native and imported) who had yet to prove themselves at a high level (or who needed extra work in one area or another), winter league officials advocated for the increased participation of established MLB stars who could attract large numbers of fans. Of special interest were top native players who had achieved fame in Major League Baseball, and who thus offered the surest route to box office success.

In 1955, the same year as the Liga Mexicana affiliation accord, MLB and Caribbean baseball officials reached a comprehensive agreement over the terms of player participation in the winter leagues. Caribbean officials accomplished one primary goal: players would be allowed to participate in the winter leagues of their native countries, regardless of their MLB service time. In exchange, MLB officials secured a series of measures that served to enhance their territorial power. The agreement limited eligible "imports" to those with less than two years of MLB experience, and further stipulated that winter league clubs could only hire affiliated players—native or imported—by contacting the MLB team that owned their contract. Some Caribbean officials had pushed for a system of direct negotiations with individual players, a form of seasonal freedom of contract that MLB clubs were not willing to allow. Most importantly, the agreement eliminated the so-called dual-contract system, under which Caribbean teams had retained first rights to any player whose first winter league deal predated his signing with a major league club. Though all previously negotiated "dual-contract" arrangements remained valid, MLB executives were intent on eliminating the possibility that other club owners could challenge their claims to future generations of top Caribbean ballplayers. Going forward, winter league teams would have to work through MLB clubs to secure access to the best established players, even though their own coaches were often the very scouts identifying top Caribbean prospects in the first place.[42]

As relations with winter affiliates became increasingly important components of scouting and talent development, MLB owners found it in their
interest to establish an official liaison to their Latin American partners, particularly in the years following the Cuban Revolution and the resulting dis-
integration of the first configuration of the Confederación de Béisbol Profesional del Caribe. In December 1965, MLB commissioner William Eckert
tapped former Havana Sugar Kings owner Bobby Maduro as baseball's first
director of inter-American relations.[43] Commentators across the baseball
world took note of the significance of Maduro's new role. Writing in Caracas's *El Universal,* Pedro Galiana (like Maduro, a Cuban émigré) greeted the
appointment as a major development in Caribbean-MLB relations, hailing
it as "not just any" position. Shirley Povich of the *Washington Post* declared,
"the baseball commissioner's office now has its own State Department."[44]

Even with Maduro in place to oversee "inter-American relations," dis-
agreements persisted between the winter leagues and their MLB partners.
Two incidents that occurred in the Dominican Republic (in the Liga Dominicana de Béisbol Profesional, or LIDOM) during the 1967–68 season,
and the controversy that ensued, exemplified the tense relationship. On
November 30, 1967, LIDOM officials fired an MLB-affiliated umpire, Stuart
Northrup, for what the league deemed poor performance. Then, on December 16, LIDOM officials suspended imported player Steve Demeter for
the rest of the season on the basis of reports that the player had "attacked"
a Dominican umpire, Francisco "Fiquito" Suárez, during an on-field argument. Northrup and Demeter appealed their firings to the National Association, which quickly awarded both men compensation for their lost time,
paying Northrup $1,250 and Demeter $500. When the National Association
drew these payments from funds placed on deposit by LIDOM, Dominican league officials and team owners strongly objected.[45] LIDOM president
Juan Tomás Mejía Feliú, voicing the anger felt by many throughout the
Dominican baseball community, announced plans to prevent all imported
players from participating in the league, and threatened to disaffiliate entirely from MLB. Maduro responded with a request—to which LIDOM officials agreed—that the matter be tabled until the annual conference of U.S.
and Caribbean baseball officials, scheduled for August 1968.[46]

What ultimately emerged from the August meeting was an internal divide between President Mejía Feliú and LIDOM team owners. Mejía Feliú
announced that he would quit in protest if teams broke from the principles
he had articulated and hired imported players. When it became clear that

his colleagues would indeed go against his wishes, Mejía Feliú resigned. Another official, Manfredo Moore, took over as the league's new president on September 15.[47] In the weeks leading up to the August meeting, Alvaro Arvelo, a columnist for the Dominican daily *El Caribe*, had articulated the position that ultimately won out: cutting ties with MLB was simply not realistic if there was to be a viable Dominican professional league. For Arvelo, LIDOM relied on MLB for so much that the league had little leverage. "We need more [from them]," he argued, "than they need from us."[48]

Commentators elsewhere watched LIDOM's 1968 disaffiliation threat with great interest. Venezuelan sports columnist Duilio Digiacomo lamented the fact that in the years since the Cuban Revolution, the winter leagues had come to act individually, rather than speaking with one voice in confronting the growing power of MLB officials. Digiacomo noted that the Puerto Rican and Venezuelan leagues had not rushed to LIDOM's defense, and lamented the fact that some officials had expressed hopes that the league would disaffiliate simply so that top players who had played in the Dominican Republic the previous winter might now be available for their own teams. "Commissioner Eckert," Digiacomo wrote, "should leave the meetings convinced that Venezuela, Puerto Rico, the Dominican Republic, and Nicaragua form a solid team of mutual support."[49] It would prove difficult, however, for Latin American interests to mount major collective challenges to the status quo, even as many shared the sentiments behind Digiacomo's plea for new solidarity. Nonetheless, the winter leagues would remain home to frequent contestation over the terms of Major League Baseball's territorial power.

### Major League Baseball and Nippon Professional Baseball

Close relations between MLB and Japanese baseball officials developed soon after the end of World War II. The postwar resumption of professional baseball was a top cultural priority of the U.S. occupation of Japan under General Douglas MacArthur.[50] One member of MacArthur's staff, Tsuneo "Cappy" Harada, became a critical liaison between the professional baseball systems of Japan and North America. After receiving an official commendation for his efforts in 1946 from the United States Congress, Harada went on to hold a variety of important positions with teams on both sides of the Pacific, and became one of the most influential transnational facilitators in baseball history.[51] Harada was particularly instrumental in setting up tours of Japan by MLB players, whose regular postseason visits became a prominent example of international baseball exchange in the decades following World War II.

The Japanese Central and Pacific Leagues (together known as Nippon Professional Baseball, or NPB) began play in 1950 and soon came to represent a viable career path for players from other regions as well. Beginning with Wally Yonamine, who debuted with the Yomiuri Giants in 1951, a number of Japanese American ballplayers from Hawaii and California enjoyed successful careers in NPB. And as Japanese teams were able to offer salaries competitive with those available in the United States, the opportunity to play professionally in Japan became an attractive option for more ballplayers from the Americas.

By the early 1960s, NPB's growing stature had begun to complicate life for MLB executives, threatening their largely unchecked ability to control contractual rights to players in their own hemisphere. A revealing international controversy erupted in 1961, concerning former Chicago White Sox pitcher Joe Stanka. As a minor leaguer, Stanka had heard Cappy Harada make a presentation about the viability of a professional baseball career in Japan. After the 1959 season, while embroiled in a contract dispute with Chicago, Stanka decided to take Harada's advice. He informed the White Sox of his retirement from Major League Baseball and made arrangements to join the Nankai Hawks of the Japanese Pacific League. After Stanka enjoyed a successful 1960 season with the Hawks, the White Sox made an issue of the pitcher's contract status. White Sox vice president Hank Greenberg notified commissioner Ford Frick, who then pressed Japanese league officials to get the Hawks' ownership to pay the White Sox a fee for the rights to Stanka's services. According to Stanka, his former MLB employers had simply assumed that he was using a retirement threat as leverage in his contract dispute and were later stunned to learn of his success across the Pacific. After considerable negotiation, the parties finally resolved the situation before the 1962 season, when Stanka paid the White Sox a fee to secure his official release. He continued to pitch in Japan for the next several years.[52]

In late 1962, in the wake of the Stanka affair, MLB and NPB officials came to what was termed a gentlemen's agreement, requiring that all trans-Pacific transactions be approved by the two bodies' commissioners' offices.[53] The agreement did nothing, however, to head off the biggest conflict yet in the history of MLB-NPB relations, which again involved the Nankai Hawks,

Masanori Murakami at Shea Stadium, soon after his call-up to the San Francisco Giants, September 1964. (*Associated Press*)

and concerned the contractual status of pitcher Masanori Murakami. In the spring of 1964, Murakami and two of his fellow Hawks (catcher Hiroshi Takahashi and third baseman Tatsuhiko Tanaka) came to the United States through an arrangement between their team and the San Francisco Giants. Under the terms of the agreement, which Cappy Harada helped to negotiate, the three players received minor league assignments. However, the deal also stipulated that should one of the players be brought up to the major leagues, the Giants would have the option to purchase his contract from the Hawks for a fee of $10,000. As it turned out, Murakami pitched exceedingly well in the minors, prompting the Giants to call him up to their major league roster for his debut against the New York Mets at Shea Stadium on September 1, 1964.[54]

Upon arriving at the ballpark for the game, Murakami was presented with a major league contract, which he at first refused to sign. "I was used to the Japanese way, where you only sign a contract once a year," he later recalled. "Also, my parents back home had told me to be very careful about contracts, and it was in English so I couldn't understand what it said."[55] As Murakami remembers it, a team representative frantically located a fan in Shea Stadium's stands who could translate the document, allowing barely enough time before the game for the Giants to make it official with a phone call to the commissioner's office.[56] A few hours later, with his new team trailing the Mets, Murakami made history. "The decades of Japanese growth and devotion were made worth it all," Bob Stevens of the *San Francisco Chronicle* wrote, "when southpaw Masanori Murakami, the first of his nationality ever to pitch in the major leagues, worked one impressive inning, striking out two in the eighth, as the Giants bowed in lesser grandeur to the New York Mets, 4–1."[57] Though some baseball writers like Stevens reached for sarcasm and stereotype to convey its meaning, the reliever's late-inning debut was a moment of great significance.

Murakami continued to pitch well over the final month of the 1964 season—a true bright spot in a disappointing end to the Giants' year. In fifteen innings he struck out fifteen batters, walked just one, and allowed only three runs. Murakami's success caught the management of the Nankai Hawks by surprise and occasioned one of the most significant international incidents in baseball history. The San Francisco front office wired $10,000 to their Hawks counterparts and signed Murakami to a contract for the 1965 MLB season. Upon returning to Japan for the winter, however, Murakami met with Hawks officials, who convinced him that he would rather play in Japan. He then signed a second contract and announced his change of plans, citing a desire to remain close to his family. A trans-Pacific showdown ensued, with the Japanese and U.S. baseball commissioners each claiming Murakami under his respective organization's reserve system.

On February 17, 1965, Ford Frick suspended MLB's relations with Japanese baseball, calling into question all future off-season exhibition trips to Japan (including one planned by the Pittsburgh Pirates for later that year), while also addressing the Murakami affair. "The Giants have proof that they legally purchased [his] contract," Frick declared. "If he fails to report and is suspended, we expect the suspension to be recognized in Japan the same as it is in the United States."[58] The two sides finally reached a compromise, allowing the Giants to retain Murakami for the 1965 season under the condition that the pitcher be free to return to the Hawks the following year, which he ultimately did. The dispute sparked further negotiations, resulting in 1967's United States–Japanese Player Contract Agreement, which spelled out terms by which the two nations' governing baseball bodies would uphold each other's contracts. Although he just pitched for parts of two seasons with San Francisco, Masanori Murakami left an impact on the baseball world that can only be described as giant.

## Major League Baseball's Domestic Expansion

As MLB officials negotiated new relationships with leagues across the baseball world in the postwar decades, they also oversaw significant territorial changes at home. Although franchise mobility had been a feature of the early decades of professional ball in the United States, MLB's basic footprint had remained unchanged since the beginning of the twentieth century. Shifting demographics, attractive offers from urban boosters, the growth of air travel, and the lure of new television markets brought about a flurry of franchise relocations and expansions in the 1950s and 1960s, beginning with the departure of the Boston Braves for Milwaukee (with its brand-new publicly financed stadium) in 1953. Like the Braves, who had been overshadowed by the Red Sox in Boston, the Browns then left St. Louis and the powerful Cardinals for Baltimore, a minor league city with a strong fan base, and the Athletics, outdrawn by the Phillies, soon moved from Philadelphia to Kansas City.[59]

The biggest change to the MLB map came in 1958, when New York's two longtime National League franchises, the Dodgers and the Giants, began play in Los Angeles and San Francisco, respectively. Both teams were lured by expanding populations and media markets, as well as by the promise of brand new stadiums. Bringing West Coast cities into Major League Baseball had been a topic of speculation for years, most notably when Pacific Coast League team owners led a failed campaign for "major" status in the years immediately after World War II.[60] In its heyday the "minor" PCL, with franchises in West Coast hubs such as Seattle and San Diego, as well as in Los Angeles and San Francisco, approached regional "major" status. One measure of the circuit's popularity is the fact that its most successful teams occasionally sold more tickets than some of the less popular AL and NL clubs.[61]

By moving franchises for the first time beyond the Northeast and Midwest, Major League Baseball's domestic expansion produced a fundamental shift in the nature of circuits like the Pacific Coast League. For a brief period following World War II, the minors experienced a historic boom, with total attendance reaching a high of 42 million in 1949. Soon, however, the combination of expanding national broadcasts of MLB games and the rise of competing forms of mass amusement made it difficult for many minor league clubs to survive. By 1957 minor league attendance had fallen to 15.5 million, and many teams that had thrived in the immediate postwar years were forced to fold.[62] Wholesale reorganization came in 1962, with a new comprehensive Player Development Plan that served to further institutionalize the minors' dependent status.[63]

The Dodgers' and Giants' simultaneous move to the West Coast was followed in short order by a series of franchise expansions throughout the 1960s. A primary catalyst came from beyond the tightly guarded circle of Major League Baseball team owners, in the form of a proposal for a third "major" circuit—the Continental League (CL)—put forward in 1959 by New York attorney William Shea, with the encouragement of New York mayor Robert F. Wagner, who was eager to secure a replacement for his city's two recently departed franchises. Branch Rickey signed on as president of the CL, attaching his substantial clout as a longtime MLB insider to the project. The roster of proposed CL franchise locations eventually included New York, Buffalo, Toronto, Minneapolis–St. Paul, Atlanta, Dallas–Fort Worth, Houston, and Denver.

Fearing the prospect of a rival circuit, National League and American League team owners worked feverishly to protect territorial control over their sport, leading CL leaders to seek congressional assistance. Tennessee senator Estes Kefauver convened hearings on MLB's antitrust status, and introduced a bill that threatened to undercut existing team owners' substantial monopoly power.[64] The bill failed in 1960, but it served to pressure team owners to pursue expansion at an accelerated clip. Over the course of the next decade, franchises were awarded to ownership groups in many of the Continental League's proposed cities. Among the most immediate results of the campaign for the CL was the 1962 debut of a new National League club in New York City, the Mets. Two years later, completion of the team's glimmering new stadium in Queens, named for William Shea, further cemented the CL's legacy.

Major League Baseball's new and relocated franchises were part of a collective reconceptualization of the industry's relationship to metropolitan space. Whereas the sport's previous building boom, which had produced structures like Philadelphia's Shibe Park (1909) and Brooklyn's Ebbets Field (1913), located the sport within the streetcar- and pedestrian-defined landscapes of modern industrial cities, the age of expansion mirrored the broader suburbanization of the United States, as new facilities, such as Los Angeles's Dodger Stadium (1962) and Houston's Astrodome (1965), were sited to maximize ease of access by car.

In light of the exploding array of leisure activities in the postwar period, team owners sought to secure a mass audience for their industry. Many baseball officials saw attracting women as especially critical to ensuring that their sport would remain a fixture of U.S. popular culture. Walter Shannon, the Cardinals' supervisor of player personnel, in a 1960 letter to local public relations executive Al Fleishman, expressed hope in the profit potential of reaching new demographics: "Television and radio have whetted the appetite of larger sections of the population, including the women, for the best in baseball performance, i.e., Major League Baseball. Therefore, our attendance and income possibilities in larger urban areas are much greater than ever before."[65] Harold E. Goodnough, the sales promotion manager for the Milwaukee Braves, urged other MLB executives in a document titled "Selling Baseball in Your Territory" to "place more emphasis on the women. They're a great group of new fans." Goodnough described the Braves' strategy, which involved making presentations and sales pitches to PTAs and sororities, as well as establishing "ladies' newcomers clubs," as the product of learning on the job during the team's first six seasons in Milwaukee (1953–1958).[66] Other MLB franchises adopted similar approaches, and within a few years the New York Mets set a new standard as the first team to employ a director of women's promotions, hiring Betty King in 1964.[67]

The emphasis on women echoed previous attempts throughout the history of baseball to recruit female spectators. As Warren Goldstein argues in his analysis of early professional baseball in the United States, teams sought out female fans for the perceived civilizing impact their presence would bring to the field of "manly" competition. Team owners' postwar recruitment efforts marked a new push to construct their sport as a respectable form of middle-class culture, engaging persistent notions of gender essentialism to confront a shifting landscape of mass entertainment.[68]

If MLB's domestic expansion was gendered, it was also deeply racialized. Like suburban development in the postwar decades as a whole, the baseball industry's flight from streetcar-centered locations like Ebbets Field to automobile-friendly sites like Dodger Stadium cultivated white consumers at the expense of communities of color. As Eric Avila details in his study of the cultural history of postwar Los Angeles, *Popular Culture in the Age of White Flight*, the opening of Dodger Stadium in 1962 marked the erasure of a working-class Latino community from Chavez Ravine. The site had been targeted a decade earlier for "slum clearance" under plans to develop public housing. The city had evicted residents of Chavez Ravine, pledging that the new housing project would welcome them back as tenants. With the 1953 election of Republican mayor Norris Poulson, however, the fate of the neighborhood changed yet again. Branding the city's public housing agenda as "creeping socialism," the city's business and political elites began to conceive of other development possibilities at Chavez Ravine. The availability of the site became critical in the campaign to attract the Dodgers. As plans for stadium construction went forward in 1959, a dramatic scene of struggle played out on television, as county sheriffs forcibly evicted the Arechiga family, longtime residents of Chavez Ravine who had stood their ground throughout the decade of changing territorial designs on their community. Though Dodger Stadium would provide a stage for one of MLB's most integrated teams, it grew out of deeply racialized inequalities of territorial power. The ballpark, like Major League Baseball itself, would remain a complex and contradictory institution, as new generations of players and fans alike made it their own.[69]

Baseball's power brokers represented and justified their industry's postwar expansion in ideological terms. In the spring of 1960, speaking before a senate subcommittee during the Continental League campaign, Branch Rickey proclaimed:

> If the history of sport in the British Empire can support the statement that Wellington got his preparation for a Waterloo from the playing fields of Eton, then America's inheritance and rivalry of British indulgence in sports afield can help us to understand what Professor William James said in effect in one of his essays, that competitive sport is the moral equivalent of war. By rapidly expanding internationally, baseball, even in this dark present hour, may conceivably become a universal peacemaker among mankind. It is a great American potential agent in that direction. Why should anybody oppose it?[70]

Rickey's comments echoed the sentiments of Vice President Richard Nixon, who had expressed his support for a third major league the previous year, suggesting that expanding the major leagues would serve the national interest as a form of cultural diplomacy. In a television interview in July 1959, Nixon called for the inclusion of Havana, Montreal, and Mexico City in MLB's expansion plans, arguing that such a development strategy would bring forth "tremendous support all over the world."[71]

Giving meaning to the proposed third league's name, the circuit's backers envisioned pushing their enterprise beyond the borders of the mainland

United States. In addition to planning a Canadian franchise, Continental League organizers considered San Juan, Puerto Rico, as a potential location.[72] In the years that followed, industry leaders continued to frame their forecasts for industry growth in broad terms. In 1966, for example, MLB commissioner William Eckert proclaimed: "I can visualize within the foreseeable future the spread of major league baseball on an international scale to include Japan, Canada, and several Latin American countries. I see major league baseball as a means of contributing to international friendship. This is a trend we should encourage, not only in the self-interest of baseball but in the interests of the Nation itself and international amity."[73] The National League's addition of the Montreal Expos in 1969 finally moved Major League Baseball beyond its old national borders. Even though MLB's relationship with Latin American and East Asian cities did not take the form of new franchises, an expansive territorial politics would remain central to the industry in subsequent decades.

For figures like Rickey, Nixon, and Eckert, the prospect of MLB's further growth resonated with broader thinking about the place of the United States in the world. In their expansionist ideologies, MLB officials and their supporters echoed the call for U.S. cultural hegemony first voiced by Time-Life publisher Henry Luce in "The American Century," his famous 1941 manifesto proclaiming a new age of U.S. power and influence on the global stage.[74] MLB's expanding power in the baseball world brought with it contradictions, conflict, and struggle, not only over the material conditions of U.S. interests' increased involvement in international leagues, but also in the realm of representation and meaning.

### Representing Baseball in the Age of Expansion

As baseball's league structures underwent significant changes in the postwar decades, so too did the sport's forms of storytelling. Daily newspapers had long been vital baseball institutions, providing key links between teams and their publics through game descriptions and box scores. In the postwar decades prominent writers like Red Smith of the *New York Herald Tribune* (and later the *New York Times*), Dick Young of the *New York Daily News,* and Jim Murray of the *Los Angeles Times* continued this tradition, playing defining roles in shaping the sport's broader cultural impact. Because newspapers were so central to baseball's daily operation, they became important sites of political struggle. Perhaps most notably, the sports pages of African American newspapers like the *Chicago Defender* and the *Baltimore Afro-*

*American* were essential to the assault on Jim Crow baseball. Writers such as Wendell Smith and Sam Lacy were influential advocates of integration on the diamond, and continued to be among the sport's most significant voices in the decades that followed the fall of the color line. Lacy's column in the *Afro-American,* for example, regularly featured sharply worded analysis and criticism of the unfair treatment that athletes of color endured in the major leagues, as well as celebrations of black ballplayers' achievements as broader victories in the movement for racial equality in the United States.

Meanwhile, the *Sporting News,* the leading national baseball publication in the United States from the late nineteenth century through the 1970s, significantly expanded its weekly coverage, featuring stories by correspondents reporting from major baseball hubs throughout the Americas. As it developed an increasingly international framework, the "Baseball Paper of the World" (as the slogan on its masthead declared) regularly trumpeted the sport as an enactment of national democratic ideals. "In baseball," Ernie Harwell wrote in "The Game for All America," a piece republished several times in the *Sporting News* from the mid-1950s through the mid-1960s, "democracy shines its clearest. Here the only race that matters is the race to the bag."[75] Despite such lofty sentiments, players of color faced unequal representation in the pages of publications like the *Sporting News.* It was common, for example, for writers to lampoon Latino athletes' efforts at speaking English, and in so doing, to present themselves as cultural gatekeepers to full citizenship in the baseball world through their construction of racial, national, and linguistic superiority.[76]

Members of the U.S. sporting press did not, however, hold a monopoly on baseball storytelling in the postwar decades. As ballplayers from Cuba, the Dominican Republic, Venezuela, and other nations became major league stars, Latin American journalists helped turn the events of games in the United States into relevant and popular topics for readers in their respective nations. Papers such as *El Caribe* and *Listín Diario* in the Dominican Republic and *El Nacional* and *El Universal* in Venezuela devoted significant space to box scores and narrative accounts, and frequently published feature articles on star players with national ties. Such papers tended to place considerably more emphasis on local players' MLB exploits (for example, *El Caribe's* coverage focused largely on the careers of Juan Marichal, Felipe Rojas Alou, and other Dominican stars) than on the wins and losses of their respective teams.

Along with game stories and player profiles, Latin American newspapers (like other publications that reached audiences of fans) featured baseball-

Gillette advertisement featuring Luis Aparicio published in the Venezuelan newspaper *El Nacional,* January 13, 1960.

themed advertising. Major League Baseball's expanding transnational influence presented advertisers with opportunities for reaching new consumer markets. The Gillette Safety Razor Company, MLB's leading corporate partner in this period, marketed its products through the endorsements of Latin American players, as well as through sponsorship of the annual All-Star Game and World Series broadcasts on radio and television.[77] In its advertising campaigns, Gillette, like other U.S. companies, not only marketed its products but also sold notions of modern masculinity. The razor blade giant's brand strategy attempted to link its promises of smooth shaves to the idealized bodies of popular baseball stars.

Baseball's increasingly interconnected world of print journalism fueled the occasional international incident. One particularly explosive instance involved Larry Bearnarth of the Mets, who signed on to pitch for the Valencia team of the Venezuelan winter league for the 1965–66 season. In November, Maury Allen of the *New York Post* published a letter from Bearnarth, featuring the pitcher's assessment of life in Venezuela, as a special interest piece. "The Venezuelans are very sensitive people," Bearnarth asserted, describing fellow bank customers' reactions to him cashing his paycheck at the front of a long line. "Later I found out there was a recent revolution and people still believe there won't be enough money left in the bank if people in the front take it all," Bearnarth explained. He also chose to weigh in on Valencia's infrastructure and pace of urban improvement: "There are no stop signs, street signs, signal lights or traffic cops here. They are always putting them in tomorrow or next year." Bearnarth paired his surface-level observations about Venezuela with expressions of homesick lament: "To tell you the truth, I would much rather be home with my family this winter than playing baseball but I want so much to be a good pitcher that I had to come here."[78] In a turn of events that surprised both Bearnarth and Allen, a Venezuelan sports writer named Eduardo Moncada, who also worked as the *Sporting News's* correspondent from the country, published a translation of Bearnarth's column in *El Nacional,* one of Venezuela's major daily newspapers. Moncada's translation appeared below a five-column headline—"Bearnarth, Pítcher del Valencia, Escribe Horrores sobre Venezuela" (Valencia Pitcher Bearnarth Writes Horrible Things about Venezuela)—and included scathing commentary interspersed between chunks of the pitcher's text.[79]

On the mound that night in Valencia, Bearnarth encountered a stadium full of enraged fans, who hurled insults and objects at him throughout the game. The situation reached a boiling point in the top of the ninth inning, when Bearnarth (who, incredibly, had yet to surrender a run) lost control of his emotions, threw the ball into the stands, striking a fan on the cheek, and was ejected from the game. Local papers reported the next day that the pitcher had been at risk of lethal assault at the hands of an angry crowd gathered outside the locker room. Bearnarth was escorted away by Valencia police and strongly encouraged to leave the country at his earliest convenience.[80] The incident was an unmistakable sign of the changing institutional configuration—and representational politics—of baseball's networks of reporting and storytelling. More and more every year, playing, watching, and writing about the sport would be transnational acts.

New genres of baseball journalism appeared in the postwar decades, as well, further expanding the sport's terrain of representation. Chief among these were the long-form pieces published in two of the period's leading weekly magazines: the *New Yorker* and *Sports Illustrated.* Roger Angell began writing for the *New Yorker* in the mid-1940s (and penned a few short items on baseball during the 1950s), but it was not until the early 1960s that he established himself as one of the sport's most influential critical voices. In his baseball pieces for the *New Yorker,* collected in multiple published volumes beginning with *The Summer Game* (1972), Angell examined baseball from the perspective of an engaged armchair fan. Along with the occasional story from other *New Yorker* contributors (John Updike's now iconic account of Ted Williams's final game with the Red Sox appeared in the magazine in 1960), Angell's articles did much to expand the production and interpretation of baseball's meaning beyond the confines of the daily sports page.[81]

At the same time, *Sports Illustrated* emerged as an especially important fixture of the new baseball journalism. Initially conceived by the Time-Life publishing empire as a vehicle that could reach a *New Yorker*–like "highbrow" audience with pieces on skiing, fishing, yachting, and other manifestations of affluent postwar leisure, *Sports Illustrated* became the preeminent home of long-form reporting on spectator sport. Beginning with its first issue in 1954 (with a cover featuring a vivid color photograph of a night game at Milwaukee's new County Stadium), the magazine set the standard for both critical commentary and high production values in mass-circulation sports journalism. Along with both new and established literary voices (William Faulkner covered the 1955 Kentucky Derby, for example), some visual artists had their work published in the early issues of *Sports Illustrated*.[82] For instance, the magazine's baseball season preview issue in 1956 included a feature on Ralph Fasanella, who depicted ballparks in several of his paintings of the everyday life of working-class New York City.[83] The magazine significantly enriched baseball journalism's symbolic texture, capturing the sense (as the magazine's publishers described their intentions in the inaugural issue) "that sport has emerged from the era of isolated contest into a new era of tremendous size, of national and international importance; again, a new phenomenon, needing and deserving its stimulating but wise chronicler."[84]

*Sports Illustrated*'s visually spectacular presentation exemplified print journalism's response to the growth of another powerful force within popular culture: television. By the mid-1960s, the medium was a vital element of the baseball industry. As with the arrival of radio in the 1920s, many MLB owners initially feared that TV would discourage fans from attending games in person, but they ultimately embraced the new medium as a valuable source of revenue. Spurred on by the success of professional football as a televised sport, baseball's owners and league officials came to view TV as essential to the future of their industry, and not simply as an auxiliary moneymaker. Its influence was clear in the franchise relocations and expansions that remade MLB's territorial identity, as teams moved into untapped media markets like San Francisco and Los Angeles. And with each league-wide television deal, teams earned increasing amounts of revenue from the sale of broadcasting rights.[85] MLB's transformative labor struggles of the 1960s and 1970s had everything to do with the small screen's large impact. When players came to see themselves as being excluded from the benefits of television revenue, they began to take the collective action that would eventually transform their sport.

Despite the growing power of television, written accounts still held pride of place in the baseball world. Few interpretations of baseball's broader cultural relevance have approached the lasting impact of Roger Kahn's 1972 best-seller *The Boys of Summer.* Combining nostalgic reverence for the great Brooklyn teams of the early 1950s with melancholy updates on the post-baseball lives of Jackie Robinson and his fellow Dodgers—Carl Furillo installing elevators in the new World Trade Center, and Robinson struggling to find common ground with the new generation of militant African American activists, to cite two examples—*The Boys of Summer* remains a powerful account of baseball's changing position in U.S. culture throughout the era bookended by World War II and the 1960s. Filled with Kahn's reflections on his own tenure as a beat reporter for the *New York Herald Tribune,* the book meditates on the passing of the baseball of an earlier age, tied to the old urban institutions of the neighborhood ballpark and the daily newspaper. In Kahn's telling, as in the work of many writers and filmmakers who followed in his wake, Jackie Robinson's Dodgers stand as an emblem for a broader story of fleeting transcendence, a brief "summer" of integrated, collective identity that, like Brooklyn's Ebbets Field, was torn down too soon and abandoned for the freeways and fractures of the 1960s.[86]

While baseball's postwar era was without question one of erasure, departure, and demolition, it was also a period of expansion and construction. As Brooklyn's Dodgers receded to the realm of memory, new teams and new locations emerged as figures of a changing culture industry. Although Kahn and others have focused historical attention on the demolished remains of Ebbets Field, we must also take into account the meanings produced and consumed in the era's new structures, like Shea Stadium. Showcasing the Mets while the World's Fair played out just beyond its walls, Shea was a marker not only of the campaign for the Continental League but also for MLB's era of expanding transnational influence. During its first season as the Mets' home field, the stadium also became a meaningful location for the return of one of New York City's recently departed National League teams, the San Francisco Giants.

On the afternoon of September 1, 1964, hours before Masanori Muraka-mi made his MLB debut against the Mets, the Giants visited the World's Fair. As the *San Francisco Chronicle* noted the next day, team members as-sembled "like any other group of tourists" in front of the U.S. Steel Uni-sphere, the twelve-story-high representation of the earth that stood (and still stands) as the 1964 exhibition's most recognizable symbol.[87] The fair, with its celebration of "Man's Achievements on a Shrinking Globe in an Expanding Universe," was an especially fitting stop on the Giants' National League itinerary. The team featured an extraordinarily integrated roster, including African American stars like Willie Mays and Willie McCovey, Puerto Rican slugger Orlando Cepeda, three standout Dominican play-ers—Juan Marichal and brothers Mateo ("Matty") and Jesús Rojas Alou—and, for the last month of the season, Masanori Murakami.

By the time they visited the World's Fair, the Giants had been through the wringer. Earlier that summer their manager, the former New York Giants star Alvin Dark, had been quoted by *Newsday* reporter Stan Isaacs offering a racist assessment of his team's failure to live up to expectations. "We have trouble because we have so many Negro and Spanish-speaking players on this team," Dark told Isaacs. "They are just not able to perform up to the white ball player when it comes to mental alertness."[88] Despite Dark's subse-quent denials and qualifications, his remarks became a major transnational story. Latin American baseball writers reported widely on Dark's comments and challenged his sentiments with facts. For example, prominent Vene-zuelan sports columnist (and eventual president of the Venezuelan win-ter league) Franklin E. Whaite responded to Dark's pronouncement with a piece in which he noted that Latino and African American players were currently at the top of most statistical categories in Major League Baseball.[89]

The 1964 Giants were an extraordinary group of athletes, whose collec-tive accomplishments left an impact on the baseball world that no man-ager's words could diminish. Even if older figures like Alvin Dark struggled to come to terms with how much the game had changed by the mid-1960s, a new generation of ballplayers, led by stars like McCovey, Cepeda, and Marichal, made Major League Baseball into an even more captivating form of popular culture than it had ever been before. Like their fellow major leaguers, Giants players enjoyed widespread fame and admiration for the work they performed on the diamond. Reporters from the countries rep-resented on the team covered their games on a daily basis, and in May the club was featured in the first live direct broadcasts of MLB games by Do-minican announcers, with Billy Berroa and Tomás Troncoso traveling to

Shea Stadium to call the Giants' series against the Mets for the Cadena Nacional Deportiva.[90] And so when the Giants stood before the Unisphere later that season, they were hardly "like any other group of tourists," as the team's hometown paper had suggested. Rather, through their exceptional labor they had come to embody the stories and struggles of an increasingly interconnected baseball world. In this sense, the glimmering ballpark at the edge of the World's Fair was the perfect place for the team's newest member, Masanori Murakami, to make his major league debut.

# 2

# A Piece of Property

## The Making and Meaning of Free Agency
## in Major League Baseball

WHILE MASANORI MURAKAMI was making history with the San Francisco Giants in the early fall of 1964, another team was rising to the top of the National League. Aided by an epic late-season collapse by the Philadelphia Phillies, the upstart St. Louis Cardinals captured the pennant and went on to defeat the defending champion New York Yankees in the World Series. The Redbirds' triumph over the Bronx Bombers in 1964 marked the coming-out party for one of the decade's most successful clubs. The Cardinals won the World Series again in 1967, defeating Carl Yastrzemski and the "Impossible Dream" Boston Red Sox, then lost a fall classic for the ages in 1968 to the Detroit Tigers. Like the San Francisco Giants, the Cardinals were one of Major League Baseball's most racially integrated teams during the 1960s, led by such stars as African American standouts Bob Gibson, Lou Brock, and Bill White, and Dominican second baseman Julián Javier.

One of the Cardinals' best players throughout their great run in the 1960s was Curt Flood, whose perennially high batting average and seven Gold Glove awards distinguished him as one of the greats of his generation. Reflecting a common opinion, in the summer of 1968 *Sports Illustrated* featured Flood on its cover under the caption "Baseball's Best Centerfielder."[1] Though he enjoyed an outstanding career on the field, Flood's most significant legacy is as the player who fought Major League Baseball's restrictive labor system all the way to the Supreme Court. Flood's challenge to his industry's power structure took center stage in the wake of the 1969 season, after St. Louis traded him to Philadelphia.[2] Having played more than a decade with the Cardinals, and having finally established himself at the top of his profession after enduring the years of bigotry familiar to other African American players of his generation, Flood was not willing to start over in a new city. With the support of his union, the Major League Baseball Players Association (MLBPA), Flood wrote to MLB commissioner Bowie Kuhn:

> After twelve years in the major leagues, I do not feel that I am a piece of property to be bought and sold irrespective of my wishes. I believe that any system which produces that result violates my basic rights as a citizen and is inconsistent with the laws of the United States and of the several States.
>
> It is my desire to play baseball in 1970, and I am capable of playing. I have received a contract offer from the Philadelphia club, but I believe I have the right to consider offers from other clubs before making any decisions. I, therefore, request that you make known to all Major League clubs my feelings in this matter, and advise them of my availability for the 1970 season.

Kuhn responded that Flood was contractually bound to accept the trade, asserting that while he agreed with the player's argument that he was not "a piece of property to be bought and sold," he failed to "see its applicability to the situation at hand."[3] Their exchange, widely circulated in the sporting press, marked the beginning of a legal confrontation that threatened to upset the balance of power in Major League Baseball. Flood ultimately lost his court challenge, but his public stand became a critical drama in one of baseball history's most significant developments: the making of free agency.

Flood's case grew out of a glaring contradiction amid Major League Baseball's great postwar expansion: that the players themselves held relatively little power over the terms and conditions of their work. Beginning in the mid-1960s, however, Flood's generation of big league ballplayers forged a remarkably strong union. By 1976 the MLBPA had overturned the major leagues' longtime labor regime and won a new system of contractual free agency for veteran players. Free agency brought significant change to the baseball industry. The ability of stars to entertain competing offers from multiple teams, coupled with the union's negotiation of steady increases in minimum salary and basic benefits, vastly improved the financial prospects of major league players. Through this period of dramatic transformation, the MLBPA itself became one of the industry's most powerful institutions, representing its members in collective bargaining with team owners as well as in a range of marketing and promotional initiatives.[4]

The players transformed their industry by asserting control over their own commodification. In the most direct sense, this meant claiming a share of Major League Baseball's rapidly expanding television revenue. Beginning in the mid-1960s, MLBPA members became increasingly militant in fighting for a stake in their teams' broadcasting proceeds, a battle that would remain one of the most galvanizing components of the union's agenda over the coming decades. The fight over television developed as part of a broader struggle over the baseball industry's forms of representation and storytelling. By the early 1970s athletes had begun to assert authority over their own public images by multiple means, from tell-all memoirs to rebellious hair and uniform styles. Players enacted what amounted to a new cultural politics of property rights, rejecting the roles that had been written for them, in both the contracts and the dominant narratives under which they worked. In so doing, Curt Flood and other athletes of his generation set the terms for the age of free agency.

## The Birth of the MLBPA

The roots of the Major League Baseball Players Association lie in the wave of union organizing and worker militancy of the immediate postwar period. In 1946, Robert Murphy, a Boston-based labor lawyer who had worked for the National Labor Relations Board, led an attempt to organize the American Baseball Guild (ABG), an effort he hoped would bring "a square deal to the players, the men who make possible big dividends and high salaries for stockholders and club executives."[5] Murphy had become interested in organizing major league players after hearing members of the Boston Braves with whom he was friendly complain about their compensation and treatment. Along with another attorney, Joseph Doherty, Murphy first contacted players in Boston and found widespread interest in taking action around their shared grievances. The ABG's goals, articulated in an early press release, included achieving "freedom of contract," as well as securing compensation for trades and a salary arbitration system. Murphy's strategy for building the guild was to proceed one team at a time, beginning with clubhouses that seemed likely to be especially receptive to the idea of unionization.[6]

The Pittsburgh Pirates, with their union-strong host city, presented an ideal first organizing target. With public backing from local labor leadership, Murphy won solid initial support among Pittsburgh's players. Team management fought back, however, and some influential Pirates—notably pitcher Truett "Rip" Sewell—made it known that Murphy's organizing efforts were not universally embraced within the team's clubhouse. Although a majority voted to go out on strike for union recognition on June 7, 1946, enough Pirates voiced opposition in a players-only meeting that plans for militant action had to be tabled. In the wake of the near-strike in Pittsburgh, which received widespread attention in the sporting press, team owners across the majors acted quickly to prevent any further inroads by the ABG, forming a player representative system (composed of delegates from each team) that served to contain dissent. Soon thereafter league officials created a new pension plan, funded by a combination of player and owner contributions.[7]

Although team owners succeeded in largely diffusing pro-union sentiment, questions emerged concerning administration of the pension plan. When veteran Pittsburgh pitcher Ernie "Tiny" Bonham died in 1949, the pension fund lacked sufficient resources to pay the mandated survivor benefits. In order to raise the sum needed to fully fund the players' pension account, commissioner Happy Chandler sold the broadcasting rights for baseball's World Series and All-Star Game for the next six seasons to the Gillette Safety Razor Company for a total of $6 million, solidifying a link between broadcasting revenue and the pension fund that players would fight to defend in future negotiations. When Gillette's partner, the Mutual Broadcasting System, resold the rights to another company, NBC, for a whopping $4 million per year, players' faith in baseball executives' fiscal acumen was further diminished. Frustrated by the owners' bungling of the retirement fund, player representatives hired attorney J. Norman Lewis to work on their behalf to reform the pension program. Team owners took the introduction of this "third party" as an affront and refused to allow him to make a presentation on player grievances and the pension plan to a meeting of their executive council. Further rebuffs inspired the players to devote new energy to advocating for their shared interests through a new organization. The Major League Baseball Players Association, a reformed version of the player representative system established in 1946, began work in 1954.[8]

That spring the owners' committee finally met with Lewis and established a formula for owners' contributions to the pension fund: 60 percent of radio and television revenue from the World Series and All-Star Game. Lewis also negotiated a few marginal improvements in other areas, including a raise in the minimum salary to $6,000 per year, though when adjusted for inflation the new figure fell below the value of the $5,000 minimum established in 1947. One of players' major grievances in the mid-1950s concerned limits placed on their ability to earn additional money playing in the off-season. At the 1954 press conference announcing the creation of the Major League Baseball Players Association, organization representatives voiced members' desire to negotiate directly with Caribbean clubs (rather than having their contracts handled through their MLB teams' front offices), and to be allowed to play an unlimited number of winter seasons. The players failed to make progress on either of these demands, even when winter league officials advocated similar positions during talks with MLB executives that resulted in a comprehensive agreement over seasonal contracts the following year.[9]

In 1959, Lewis was succeeded by Judge Robert C. Cannon of Milwaukee, under whose stewardship the players saw their minimum salary raised slightly to $7,000, yet also saw their annual work schedule increased from 154 to 162 games. The standard players' allowance for incidental expenses in spring training—known as "Murphy money" in reference to its origin in Robert Murphy's 1946 organizing drive—remained unchanged in the two decades following its institution.[10]

Despite its weaknesses, the early MLBPA nonetheless constituted a framework for future transformation into a much more powerful body. A strong impetus for reorganization developed by the mid-1960s. The pension agreement that J. Norman Lewis negotiated in 1954 was set to expire in early 1967, and association leaders had begun to hear rumors that Dodgers owner Walter O'Malley planned to lead a push for elimination of the 60 percent formula in order to increase team profits from television revenues, which were expected to rise significantly. Furthermore, no share of the revenue from broadcasts of baseball's Game of the Week, a new feature in the sport's national television package, was designated for the pension plan.[11] In light of the high stakes of the upcoming negotiations, player leaders Robin Roberts, Jim Bunning, Harvey Kuenn, and Bob Friend formed a committee to hire an executive director (both Lewis and Cannon had served in advisory roles).

The players saw filling the new position as a way of strengthening their organization, but management figures still loomed large during the search. Among the candidates the committee considered was Chub Feeney, the general manager of the Giants and soon-to-be president of the National League. In addition, MLBPA leaders consulted with league officials throughout the process, sending a list of final candidates to the owner-elected commissioner, William Eckert, and inviting management representatives to attend association deliberations on the selection.[12] The search committee ultimately offered the position to Cannon, in part because he had been able to secure $150,000 in annual funding from team owners for the MLBPA's permanent office. The deal broke down, however, when the judge balked at the players' insistence that the MLBPA office be established in New York City, requiring him to move from his home in Milwaukee. Souring on Cannon, the ballplayers turned to another candidate on their short list—Marvin J. Miller of the United Steelworkers of America (USW).[13]

## From Steelworkers to Ballplayers

Marvin Miller's appearance on the MLBPA committee's list of potential candidates points to a key transformation in U.S. labor-management relations in the two decades after Robert Murphy's attempt to organize the American Baseball Guild: the growth of industry-wide collective bargaining. As Nelson Lichtenstein has argued, it would be inaccurate to describe the postwar decades as a period of "labor-management accord," since some of the largest and most contentious strikes in United States history occurred during these years, including the four-month nationwide steel shutdown in 1959. Yet amid this tumult, unions and employers—particularly in core industries like steel production and auto manufacturing—were compelled to collaborate in developing new strategies to settle disputes through negotiation and compromise.[14] In his years with the United Steelworkers, Marvin Miller distinguished himself as an expert in collective bargaining, and he came highly recommended to the baseball players who interviewed him for their new position. Robin Roberts and his fellow members of the MLBPA's search committee contacted Miller on the recommendation of Roberts's fellow Philadelphian George W. Taylor, a professor at the University of Pennsylvania's Wharton School and a recognized leader in the field of industrial relations.[15]

Miller's career had taken him through several key institutions of the modern U.S. labor movement. After growing up in Brooklyn, graduating from NYU at age nineteen with a degree in economics, and joining the New York City Department of Welfare (where as a caseworker he was an active union member), Miller took a job as a hearing officer at the National War Labor Board during World War II.[16] This experience proved especially valuable, as the wartime body became a model for the National Labor Relations Board and the larger federal collective bargaining apparatus that emerged later in the 1940s. After the war, Miller worked for the U.S. Labor Department as a commissioner of conciliation, for the International Association of Machinists as an "organizer-researcher-negotiator," and briefly in a similar post for the United Auto Workers.[17] In 1950, with the help of Otis Brubaker, a colleague during the war years, Miller took a position as a staff economist in the research department of the United Steelworkers. Over the next fifteen years, during which he eventually became the union's chief economist and served as assistant to its president, David J. McDonald, Miller worked in the trenches on some of the era's most significant labor negotiations.[18]

In the wake of the national steel strike in 1959, industry and union officials—under increasing pressure from the federal government—sought strategies to minimize future work stoppages. The result was the Human Relations Committee (HRC), designed by USW general counsel Arthur J. Goldberg, under whom Miller served. The HRC, consisting of representatives from both the union and the nation's largest steel companies, met regularly to discuss solutions to industry challenges such as automation, absent the pressure of contract expirations and strike threats. When President John F. Kennedy tapped Goldberg to serve as secretary of labor in 1961, Miller assumed his former superior's responsibilities. In addition to his work with the HRC, Miller took the lead on a local system that carried the model even further, at the Kaiser Steel Corporation's massive mill in Fontana, California.

The Kaiser Long Range Sharing Plan grew out of a committee of union and management representatives, as well as three "neutrals," George Taylor of Wharton, John Dunlop of Harvard, and David Cole, former director of the Federal Mediation and Conciliation Service. The Kaiser committee's task was to chart a course for labor peace in the midst of massive automation. Under their plan, which earned widespread praise, union members received a share of all automation-derived profits, and the parties established a hiring pool system to ensure that workers displaced by technological change in the production process would have the opportunity to find new jobs at the mill.[19] Through his much-touted work with the Kaiser committee, Miller developed a reputation as one of the United Steelworkers' leading "technicians."[20] As a result of his efforts, in May 1963 President Kennedy appointed Miller to serve on the National Labor-Management Panel, which took as its mission advising "in the avoidance of industrial controversies."[21]

By the mid-1960s, Miller had achieved a prominent role in the labor movement and a position of stature in the field of industrial relations. Following a leadership change at the United Steelworkers, however, when I. W. Abel defeated David McDonald in a hotly contested election to become the union's next president, Miller found himself in search of other opportunities. If he had not taken the baseball job, he might very well have joined the faculty of Harvard University, where he had an invitation from John

Dunlop, chair of the economics department, to assume a visiting professor-
ship in labor relations. Instead, Miller chose to apply his expertise to a new
industry, representing ballplayers, whom he would later describe as "among
the most exploited workers in America."[22]

## Organizing Major League Players

If he was to be as successful with the MLBPA as he had been with the USW,
Miller faced the considerable challenge of advocating for workers who appeared skeptical of the very principle of trade unionism. This dynamic first
surfaced during the interview process, when Miller worked to convince the
members of the search committee that his experience with the United Steelworkers had been defined more by cooperation than by conflict. Writing
to Robin Roberts after his interview, Miller emphasized his commitment
to collaborative industrial relations. "Union-management relations in major industries have altered considerably since the early days of conflict," he
noted. "Today, the central fact of such relationships is mutual acceptance
of their interdependence and their joint attempts to work out solutions to
their complex problems."[23] While Roberts emerged as an early advocate of
Miller's candidacy, other members of the search committee needed more
convincing that someone from an industrial union would be an appropriate
choice to lead their association.

Two years before interviewing Miller, Bob Friend had been quoted ex-
tensively in a *Sporting News* piece on the idea of ballplayer unionism, a
notion that the pitcher opposed on the grounds that it would introduce
unnecessary antagonism into the sport's unique employment relationships.
"Baseball is different than the ordinary business or industry," the veteran
pitcher had argued. Friend had also addressed what he saw as a threat to
the public's view of ballplayers: "If the structure of our players' association
was changed to a union, I believe it would result in ill will for the players.
It would tend to destroy the image of the baseball star for the youngsters
because of the haggling between the players and the owners. Stan Musial
picketing a ball park would look great, wouldn't it?"[24] Given his published
remarks, it was not surprising that Friend initially opposed Miller's candidacy. Robin Roberts and the other search committee members were not
able to persuade Friend to reevaluate his position until after Robert Cannon
balked at the terms of the MLBPA's initial offer.[25]

Having finally received the search committee's endorsement, Miller then
needed to win the support of a majority of MLB players in order to be-

gin work as executive director. Given the mixed feelings toward unionism he had already encountered, a ratification vote of the full membership was no small task.[26] In his early public comments, Miller was careful to draw clear distinctions between his new role in baseball and his previous work: "This will obviously differ a lot from a trade union situation. This is unique. Baseball players are in the public eye, more an image than a million steelworkers. They have an unusual position in the land. I think it will be very important to resolve problems with the clubs' owners . . . in a private and rational manner. There will be no strikes. No strike threats. It can be done."[27] Though Miller's prediction of a strike-free future turned out to be overly optimistic, his comments articulated an astute sense of the dynamics of his new industry. In distinguishing athletes from steelworkers, Miller did more than simply speak to players' concerns about potential confrontation with team owners. Even at the very beginning of his tenure with the MLBPA, Miller was able to demonstrate an understanding of the prominent role that players' status as popular figures would play in challenging Major League Baseball's status quo.

Despite his no-strike disclaimers, Miller encountered substantial resistance as he introduced himself to each team during spring training workouts before the 1966 season. With encouragement from management, several players spoke out against Miller's candidacy, and in some cases disrupted his initial meetings. "There is no place in baseball for labor and this man has been associated with labor all his life," Angels catcher Bob Rodgers proclaimed.[28] Such sentiments made some of his introductory meetings with players rather rocky, but Miller won enough support to be elected by a decisive margin. This was due to the fact that in addition to his expertise in bargaining and dispute resolution, Miller brought the skills of an experienced organizer to his work with the MLBPA. He combated initial doubts through a simple strategy: encouraging players' active participation in their association. As Braves catcher Joe Torre later described it, rather than the "devious labor vulture" they had been led to expect, MLBPA members encountered a "soft-spoken man who mesmerized you because he kept making sense."[29] In the coming years, Miller cultivated a growing militancy among MLB players, which team owners inadvertently helped to fuel. As Curt Flood later put it, "Our anger [at the owners] drew us closer together."[30]

As he began his work at the start of the 1966 season, Miller entered an industry beset with a number of ongoing contract disputes. While isolated clashes had been common for a number of years, by 1966 "holdouts" were

Marvin Miller with Tom Seaver (*left*) and Ed Kranepool of the New York Mets, on one of many trips to visit players at spring training, March 1972. (*Associated Press*)

becoming especially widespread, with sixteen big leaguers engaged in full-blown standoffs in the spring of that year.[31] That so many individual players were engaged in such fights underscored two basic features of the politics of work in Major League Baseball in the mid-1960s: first, an enormous amount of dissent over contract issues existed among the players, and second, challenges to team owners' authority appeared almost entirely in the form of individual struggles. A fundamental challenge for Miller and the MLBPA would be to build and mobilize collective forms of militancy. Over the subsequent decades the MLBPA would achieve remarkable success both in leveraging the power of individual stars in the service of collective gains (such as minimum salary and pension increases) and in marshaling collective power to create a context in which veteran players could negotiate favorable contract terms for themselves as free agents.

The most public holdout in the spring of 1966 was that of Los Angeles Dodgers pitchers Sandy Koufax and Don Drysdale, who took the bold step of demanding that their team negotiate with them together. During their holdout the pair signed a contract with Paramount Pictures to perform together in a film (*Warning Shot,* in which Drysdale was to play a TV reporter and Koufax a detective), and according to published reports briefly joined the Screen Actors Guild in preparation for their new careers.[32] The pitchers also pursued the possibility of a tour of Japan, where promoters purportedly anticipated that each could earn "six-figure" compensation.[33] Foreshadowing the holdout, Drysdale had caused a stir the previous fall when he announced that he was considering a lucrative offer to pitch in Japan, bringing a swift response from Ford Frick. The MLB commissioner, only months removed from his prominent role in the Masanori Murakami contract dispute, threatened to ban any player "jumping" to Nippon Professional Baseball.[34]

In emphasizing their opportunities beyond Major League Baseball, Drysdale and Koufax made an effective public display of how their industry's system of contracts constrained their star power. The players' actions and comments brought new focus, in particular, to athletes' frustration with their lack of control over the terms of their own commodification. As Koufax asserted: "I have a product to sell. It happens to be myself. Unfortunately I can only sell it to one person. If he doesn't buy, that's it."[35] Elaborating on the larger meaning of the standoff, Koufax voiced a critique of baseball's labor regime that Curt Flood would make even more forcefully four years later: "You might say Don and I are fighting for an antiprinciple—that ballplayers aren't slaves, that we have a right to negotiate."[36] Many observers took note of the joint holdout as a harbinger of future upheaval, particularly when Koufax and Drysdale won substantial raises.[37]

Although the two Dodgers stars succeeded in demonstrating the power of collective action, their joint holdout was hardly a viable model for industry-wide bargaining in baseball—only players of Koufax's and Drysdale's stature could achieve even marginal success through such isolated actions. Marvin Miller had been hired primarily to oversee pension negotiations, but he immediately understood his job as building the MLBPA into an organization that could advocate for players' interests more broadly. His first step in laying the groundwork was to secure a viable organizational funding structure. The owners had previously consented to set aside $150,000 annually in All-Star Game revenue to fund the association. When it became apparent, however, that Miller would be in charge of those resources instead of an unimposing figure like Judge Cannon, the owners balked.

In addition, the initial funding scheme raised legal concerns, since U.S. labor law prohibited management's financing of a union.[38] Miller proposed a new model—a dues check-off system in which players would voluntarily fund the MLBPA with the equivalent of what they had previously contributed to their pension plan. After heated negotiations, the owners agreed to a noncontributory pension model, meaning that they would now be solely responsible for funding players' retirement benefits. Players' near-universal approval of the check-off system signaled a new collective consciousness, catching the owners—who Miller later speculated must have calculated that their employees would never voluntarily finance the MLBPA— by surprise.[39]

The reorganized pension plan marked the first step in the players' march toward increasing measures of bargaining power through the late 1960s and 1970s.[40] In 1968, MLBPA leaders and MLB team owners, negotiating through their own recently established Player Relations Committee, agreed to the industry's first comprehensive collective bargaining agreement. Miller would later describe the 1968 Basic Agreement as "the building block for major gains to come."[41] In addition to securing an increase in the minimum salary (to $10,000), the MLBPA succeeded in incorporating the Uniform Player's Contract into the text of the Basic Agreement. This made it impossible for owners to implement unilateral changes to the standardized language that appeared in all individual player contracts, as had been the practice in the past. Perhaps most significantly, the agreement established a grievance procedure. Though the owner-elected commissioner was the final arbiter of grievances, this limited mechanism constituted the foundation for future changes, and in subsequent Basic Agreements the association would continue to erode owners' power.

In the 1970 collective bargaining agreement the players secured an impartial grievance procedure, which provided the framework for a successful challenge to the reserve clause in 1975, opening the door for veteran players to become free agents and entertain competing offers from MLB clubs. In addition, a salary arbitration provision that the union negotiated in the 1973 agreement created a mechanism for established players to petition for increased wages without resorting to the old tactic of the contract holdout. The cumulative effect of players' increased bargaining power, measured in individual earnings, would prove staggering: from 1967 to 1976 the average major league player's annual salary grew from $19,000 to over $52,000. By 1980 the figure would stand at $143,000.[42] The impact of the players' movement, however, cannot be measured in dollar figures alone.

## The Politics of Representation

Through the late 1960s and early 1970s, the MLBPA was at its most militant when fighting for a greater share of the baseball industry's expanding television revenues. While negotiations over the 1968, 1970, and 1973 Basic

Agreements were certainly heated, periodic negotiations over the pension plan led to some of the period's most dramatic confrontations between players and team owners. The intensity of these fights grew out of players' long-held understanding that a portion of industry receipts from broadcasting would be designated to fund their retirement benefits. In a key early policy statement issued in July 1967, outlining principles in advance of negotiations for the first Basic Agreement, the union noted that teams' $23 million annual revenue from radio and television (on top of earnings from the All-Star Game and World Series) "more than doubles the entire payroll for all major league players, coaches, managers and trainers." Given the fact that as recently as 1950 clubs' broadcasting revenue totaled less than half of payroll expenditures, the document continued, "it is difficult to be modest in making proposals." Along with calling for a greater share of their industry's growing profits, the MLBPA further argued that players were "entitled to representation" in the teams' negotiations of television contracts.[43]

In presenting their analysis of the industry, players thus articulated a collective property claim, asserting a shared stake in the televised images of their work. In short order, players demonstrated their willingness to take collective action in support of their position. When pension negotiations stalled during the 1968 season (the plan was set to expire at the end of the year), the MLBPA threatened a mass holdout. Frustrated with continued lack of progress in pension talks, hundreds of players refused to sign their contracts in the lead-up to spring training in 1969, forcing the owners to increase their offer substantially. The two sides reached a deal in time for spring training to open as scheduled after newly appointed commissioner Bowie Kuhn, not wanting to preside over a work stoppage in his first weeks on the job, pressured the owners to compromise. Curt Flood later described the 1969 collective contract holdout as a galvanizing experience for the players: "We had finally showed our guts. It was a great feeling."[44]

Players' militant stand for a fairer share of television profits was closely tied to daily grievances over uncompensated requirements to serve as the public faces of their employers. For decades every player's individual contract had included a standardized "Pictures and Public Appearances" clause:

> The Player agrees that his picture may be taken for still photographs, motion pictures or television at such times as the Club may designate and agrees that all rights in such pictures shall belong to the Club and may be used by the Club for publicity purposes in any manner it desires. The Player further agrees that during the playing season he will not make public appearances,

participate in radio or television programs or permit his picture to be taken
or write or sponsor newspaper or magazine articles or sponsor commercial
products without the written consent of the Club, which shall not be withheld
except in the reasonable interests of the Club or professional baseball.[45]

During spring training in 1966, members of the St. Louis Cardinals banded
together to push for modest compensation for radio and television appearances. The *Sporting News* quoted an anonymous Cardinal who noted that
the "shows have paying sponsors, and we don't like the idea that we're being
used." Nevertheless, the players found that they ultimately had very little
leverage, given the terms of their individual contracts. Negotiating a "truce"
during a meeting with player representatives Tim McCarver and Bob Pur-
key, Cardinals management officials "pointed out the fine print" that required players to participate in "promotional activities."[46] Even though athletes remained bound to represent their teams in public appearances, they
would find increasing amounts of collective power through their union by
organizing for shared stakes in television proceeds.

In 1970, as the owners prepared to begin negotiating a new TV deal with
NBC, Miller again registered the MLBPA's rejection of owners' "contention that the Clubs have ownership of the players' property rights for the
purpose of commercially televising Major League games."[47] Following negotiations in 1971 for a new $70 million TV package, commissioner Kuhn
suggested that if the players had grievances regarding lack of participation
in the talks "they will have to take them up with John Gaherin [chair of the
owners' Players Relations Committee] and they will be handled as a basic
bargaining problem at the appropriate time."[48] Reporting on the new deal,
the *New York Times* noted the players' collective claim to a financial stake in
television revenue, forecasting that the matter would form the "backdrop"
for upcoming negotiations between players and owners.[49] And indeed,
when the players' benefit plan was set to expire again in 1972, the union
demanded an increase in retirement benefits equal to the 17 percent rise in
the cost of living over the previous three years. When the owners refused,
on April 1 the players walked out on strike for the first time in the history
of their union, an action that lasted nine days into the regular season before
the two sides reached a settlement. As in the 1969 holdout, the union won
a decisive victory.[50] In addition to representing an important struggle over
television revenue and retirement benefits, many players saw the 1972 strike
as a fight for the very survival of the MLBPA. As Gary Peters, player representative for the Red Sox, put it: "We were forced into doing what we did. If

we had gone any other way, it would have ruined our association. We would like to think that the owners will believe that we are serious now."[51]

As baseball's establishment came to the reluctant realization that the MLBPA was indeed "serious," team owners turned to the press, airing their grievances against the very notion of a union of professional athletes. Criticism of the union, and its introduction of a new approach to labor-management relations, centered on the figure of Marvin Miller. His critics framed him as an outsider, and a threat to baseball's special identity. Bob Howsam, general manager of the Cincinnati Reds, expressed sentiments shared by many of his colleagues in a press release issued during the 1972 strike: "[Miller] has not had time to get to know our game. Baseball is not the steel industry, and he can't use the tactics of a steel negotiator."[52] A number of influential sportswriters treated Miller with equal disdain, even as some recognized his considerable skill as an organizer and negotiator. Atlanta sports columnist Furman Bisher, one of the most vocal antiunion voices in the baseball press, wrote: "Marvin Miller is a dangerous man. He could pick your pocket and never use a hand. . . . If the Commies had him, we'd be in deep trouble. Thank God he isn't pushing dope."[53] The vehemence of writers' antagonism toward Miller proved to be an index of the MLBPA's growing power in the industry.

In order to build the union's strength, Miller sought new sources of operational funding. Among the most significant early innovations under Miller's leadership was the MLBPA's entry into the business of group licensing, which proved a valuable revenue pool for the organization beginning in the mid-1960s. Following the 1966 season, Miller negotiated a two-year contract with Coca-Cola worth $120,000 over the next two years, allowing the soft drink company to use players' images on the underside of bottle caps. In order to make this deal, he first had to gain permission from each of the roughly five hundred individual players. Securing their signatures, along with dues-deduction authorizations, brought Miller to every team during the fall of 1966, and in this way became an excellent opportunity for players to engage with and ask questions of their new executive director. The licensing deal with Coca-Cola was the first step in what became a central component of the MLBPA's operations. In 1968 the union negotiated an agreement with the Topps Company, holder of the monopoly on the baseball card business, which for years had been paying paltry sums for the rights to reproduce players' images on cards sold in bubble gum packs. The new deal earned players double their previous annual rate, and the MLBPA banked a percentage of card sales, which helped fund the union's operation to the tune of $320,000 in the first year.[54]

At the same time, the players' employers were also beginning to explore new licensing strategies. In the late 1960s team owners joined together in efforts to enhance baseball's popularity in response to a growing perception that the sport had fallen out of step with the rapid social and cultural changes of the period. *Newsweek's* Pete Axthelm seemed to speak for many observers when he suggested in his coverage of the 1968 World Series that the sport had "become an anachronistic bore."[55] Attempting to combat such sentiments, which coincided with the growing popularity of professional football, industry executives mounted a concerted campaign to promote MLB as a cultural brand. Their strategy took the form of a shared venture: the Major League Baseball Promotion Corporation, launched in 1968. Teams' joint licensing and marketing efforts, packaged with a new corporate logo (featuring a batter's silhouette against a red and white background), signaled the arrival of a new era in the business of Major League Baseball.[56]

It was a sign of players' growing power and autonomy in the industry that their own licensing program developed simultaneously with that of team owners. In the first ten years of efforts in this area, the union brought in nearly $5 million. By the late 1970s the program was banking more than $1 million each year, and players had collectively received more in individual income from union licensing agreements than they had paid in dues.[57] The MLBPA's innovative deployment of players' marketable identities signaled more than simply the realization of a new revenue stream. As in the ongoing battle with the owners over broadcasting revenue, players embraced licensing as a defining mission of their union. In both cases the athletes asserted collective power over the terms of their own commodification—the extraction of profit from images of themselves and their work. Indeed, the politics of property rights formed the heart of the players' movement in the 1960s and 1970s.

## Curt Flood's Challenge to the Reserve System

Thanks to renewed attention in recent years—beginning with his prominent position in Ken Burns's influential 1994 documentary film *Baseball*, and extending through the 2005 publication of Brad Snyder's excellent biography—Curt Flood has begun to receive the recognition he deserves for his significant role in baseball's labor history.[58] By refusing to consent to be traded, and by bringing a landmark legal case against Major League

Baseball, Flood played a central part in major league players' collective fight to overturn their sport's long-standing labor regime.

Flood's challenge to the reserve clause came out of an analysis of the industry gained through years of experience. He grew up in Oakland, California (a city with some of the best youth baseball in the United States, as evidenced by the many MLB players with roots there), and after graduating from high school signed a professional contract with the Cincinnati Reds in 1956.[59] His career began in the segregated city of Tampa, Florida, where the Reds conducted spring training. Upon arriving from Oakland at the Floridian Hotel, which had been featured in the brochure he received in the mail from the Cincinnati front office, Flood was ushered out a side door by an African American porter and soon found himself joining other black players in residence at a boardinghouse five miles away from the rest of their teammates.

Segregated spring training housing was but one of the many forms of racism that Flood faced in his first years of pro ball, playing for Reds affiliates in the Carolina and South Atlantic leagues. In spite of vile epithets from the stands, segregated dining and locker room facilities, and exclusionary treatment by white teammates, Flood excelled in the minor leagues. "Pride was my resource," he later wrote. "I solved my problem by playing my guts out."[60] Prior to the 1958 season he was traded to St. Louis, where he soon made the major league roster, but he endured two and a half seasons under manager Solly Hemus, who failed to see Flood and other black players—including future Hall of Famer Bob Gibson—as worthy of much more than bench duty.[61]

After Johnny Keane replaced Hemus as manager in 1961, Flood got more opportunities on the field and soon established himself as a top player and team leader. The Cardinals of the 1960s forged a new model of integrated baseball, distinguished not only from other clubs but also from the recent history of their own franchise.[62] The Cardinals' identity as an integrated team was on special display in their World Series appearances in 1964, 1967, and 1968 against the Yankees, Red Sox, and Tigers, respectively, three of the era's whitest clubs.[63] When the Redbirds lost to the Tigers in the 1968 Series, a scuffle broke out at Detroit's Wayne State University. The *South End,* Wayne State's student newspaper, reported that the fight erupted over objections "to the way in which white students were celebrating the defeat of the St. Louis Cardinals, a great black team."[64]

Throughout Flood's years in the National League, the playing field itself remained home to simmering racial tension. Athletes of color were hit by

Curt Flood's 1964 baseball card. (*Courtesy Topps Company*)

pitched balls much more often than their white teammates. In mid-June 1965 the *Baltimore Afro-American* reported that over two-thirds of the batters who had been struck by pitches so far that year were black. In a period when fewer than a quarter of major league players were African American, this startling statistic suggests just one of the ways in which racial division and antagonism defined athletes' daily working lives.[65] Later in the decade, Flood's closest friend on the Cardinals, pitcher Bob Gibson, recast the politics of pitching inside when he equated his own style to the forms of urban rebellion exploding across the country: "If you're getting pushed around, if they're knocking you all around the lot, you're going to protect yourself. You're going to brush him back from the plate. You're going to riot and get him to think a little. Blowing up places and rioting are, in my opinion, just like a brushback pitch."[66] Flood was similarly outspoken on matters of racial justice, both within and outside the baseball industry. For example, he appeared with Jackie Robinson and the boxers Floyd Patterson and Archie Moore at a rally during the NAACP's convention in Jackson, Mississippi, in February 1962, helping to draw four thousand people, more than had ever turned out before at an NAACP rally in that city.[67]

Like other players of his generation, Flood began to challenge the notion that his employer could dictate his identity as a public figure. In addition to his stands for racial equality, Flood departed from the norms of the baseball business by pursuing a side career as a portrait artist. Having studied and practiced drawing and painting from an early age, Flood eventually opened a small studio in St. Louis. At first the press characterized it as a colorful personality trait, and highlighted the fact that he had painted a portrait of Cardinals owner and beer magnate August "Gussie" Busch Jr.[68] Later, however, his painting came to be flagged as evidence of his lack of commitment to his most important job—playing center field for the Cardinals. When Flood refused to accept his trade to the Philadelphia Phillies following the 1969 season and cited his business as an important tie to St. Louis, many members of the baseball establishment scoffed. Former Cardinals general manager Frank Lane sarcastically predicted that Flood would have to relent "unless he's better than Rembrandt."[69]

Not until 2005 did Brad Snyder's biography, *A Well-Paid Slave: Curt Flood's Fight for Free Agency in Professional Sports,* reveal that Flood did not actually paint the works he sold as his own. "Instead," Snyder writes, "he sent photographs of his subjects to a Burbank-based portrait artist who enlarged the photographs and painted over them. Flood simply signed his name to the finished products."[70] The discovery that Flood's work as a painter was fabricated, while a stunning revelation, does not diminish the fact that he made an occupation outside baseball an important part of his public image. This dimension of Flood's identity echoed other players' claims to professional lives beyond the diamond, which for some athletes became key strategic elements in contract negotiations. In addition to Sandy Koufax and Don Drysdale, whose 1966 threats to launch film careers rather than accept less than they were due from the Dodgers received widespread attention, in 1972 pitcher Vida Blue announced that he was considering a position with Dura Steel Products during his own contract standoff with Oakland A's owner Charlie Finley. Blue's negotiating tactic prompted *Sports*

*Illustrated* to place his image on the cover with the sarcastic caption "Vida Blue: Plumbing Executive."[71]

Of all the team owners, the Cardinals' Gussie Busch was perhaps the most indignant in the face of the rise in player power that began in the mid-1960s. He greeted each successive round of negotiation and confrontation with increasingly flamboyant exhortations to his fellow owners to hold the line against Miller and the union. In the wake of the MLBPA-organized collective contract holdout in early 1969, Busch took the rare step of calling a team meeting in the presence of reporters, effectively berating the Cardinals in front of a mass audience.[72] Claiming that fans had been "saying our players are getting fat" and "only think of money," Busch predicted a dire future for the game if such trends continued. "Fans are telling us now that if we intend to raise prices to pay for the high salaries and so on and on, they will stop coming to the games, they will not watch and will not listen. They say they can do other things with their time and with their money. It doesn't take a crystal ball, gentlemen, to realize that with so many fans being so aware of the big payrolls in baseball, they will become even more critical of all of us." Busch ordered 100,000 copies of the diatribe printed in an elegant pamphlet and made them available to Anheuser-Busch's stockholders and employees, as well as to other corporate executives.[73] Commissioner Bowie Kuhn lauded Busch's approach—which other teams' officials moved to replicate with their own players—as a model for upholding Major League Baseball's responsibility to its fans.[74]

To Flood, Busch's speech was an outrage. He would later identify the clubhouse meeting as a turning point for the team, as players lost motivation to play well for the benefit of Busch's organization. (The Cardinals slumped to a disappointing fourth-place finish in 1969.)[75] Flood had reason to feel personally attacked, having been identified as one of the more militant participants in the collective contract holdout, as rumors circulated that he had threatened to quit if his salary demands were not met.[76] Flood and other Cardinals' distaste only increased when the team traded clubhouse leader Orlando Cepeda away to the Atlanta Braves soon after Busch's tirade.[77]

After receiving notification of his own trade after the dismal 1969 season, Flood sought advice from Marvin Miller, and upon further deliberation declared his intention to bring legal action. Flood presented his case to a meeting of MLBPA player representatives, which ended with the union leadership agreeing wholeheartedly to lend support. Miller used his United

Steelworkers connections to secure the services of Arthur Goldberg, who was now in private practice after having served as an associate justice of the Supreme Court and ambassador to the United Nations. For Miller and the MLBPA, the Flood case represented an opportunity to challenge the team owners on the most critical element of MLB's player contracts since the turn of the twentieth century: the reserve clause.[78]

Even as players had gained a substantial measure of collective bargaining power, they continued to work under their sport's restrictive labor regime, anchored by the combination of contractual language and ingrained tradition that granted teams exclusive rights to their players' services in perpetuity. The reserve clause itself was a small section of the Uniform Player's Contract, granting the team the right to renew the terms of the agreement for another season in the event that the two parties could not settle on a new pact. In practice, baseball players labored under an entire "reserve system" that prevented them from ever soliciting competing contract offers, thus severely constraining their negotiating power and earning potential. Marvin Miller would later note that when he began his work with the MLBPA, considering himself already versed in the reserve clause from his decades as a fan, he was stunned to read the relevant contract language, which seemed to him to only specify a simple one-year extension option for the club. But for decades the clause had been understood—by owners and players alike—as perpetually renewable.[79] As Flood's case highlighted, the reserve system had sweeping implications for players' professional lives: in addition to setting contract terms, team executives could easily sell or trade their players as well.

Most within the baseball industry viewed the reserve system as fundamental to the sport's integrity, arguing that players who were free to offer their services to the highest bidder could not be trusted to play honestly against a team that might soon be their own.[80] Legal justification lay in two U.S. Supreme Court decisions: *Federal Baseball Club v. National League* (1922) and *Toolson v. New York Yankees* (1953). The Court's 1922 ruling (with a majority opinion penned by Justice Oliver Wendell Holmes Jr.) held that Major League Baseball did not constitute interstate commerce and was thus not subject to federal antitrust law. The 1953 decision, involving a minor league player, George Toolson, who believed he was good enough to play for an MLB club but was denied an opportunity to do so since the Yankees owned his services, left the industry's antitrust exemption intact. The Court's ruling in *Toolson* took note of the fact that Congress had not

deemed it necessary to address baseball's anomalous legal status. Club owners, then, had a legal justification for their rhetorical claims that the sport
was a special institution, outside the normal rules of industry.[81]

In 1965 teams tightened their control even further by instituting an annual amateur draft. Under the rules of the draft, teams would select U.S.
high school and college prospects in a series of rounds, obtaining exclusive
rights to negotiate with their drafted prospects. The system brought an end
to what had become popularly known as the "bonus baby" phenomenon,
whereby top prospects had been able entertain competing bids for their
services, thus forcing signing payments to new heights. In 1964, the final
year before the draft, the Los Angeles Angels paid a $205,000 bonus to Uni-
versity of Wisconsin outfielder Rick Reichardt. The top choice in 1965's inaugural amateur draft, Arizona State University star Rick Monday, signed
with the Kansas City Athletics for $104,000, just over half Reichardt's figure
from the previous year.[82]

Marvin Miller and the members of the MLBPA discovered the depth
of owners' and league officials' commitment to the reserve system during
their periodic negotiations of the basic collective bargaining agreement.
Teams' defense of the system sometimes reached the level of the absurd,
as when Yankees pitcher Jim Bouton joked at a meeting with the owners'
representatives that the reserve clause should expire when a player turned
sixty-five, and National League attorney Lou Carroll responded—apparently in total seriousness—that such modification would only encourage
further assaults on the game's integrity.[83] The first Basic Agreement, negotiated in 1968, bound the two parties to participate in a "joint study" of the
reserve clause. The effort went nowhere, as owners only feigned interest in
the subject, seeing no positive benefit in engaging with the players over the
fate of what both sides knew to be the most fundamental mechanism in the
existing labor regime. Miller recognized that it would be difficult to reform
the reserve system through collective bargaining alone, with the owners
firmly opposed to the slightest change, not to mention the lack of consensus
among the players themselves, who were not nearly as united in their opposition to the reserve clause as they were in their indignation at owners'
refusal to share broadcasting revenue. Indeed, several prominent players
defended the status quo, arguing that the integrity of the game depended on
the existing reserve system.[84]

The heart of Flood's case concerned baseball's special legal status. Flood
and the union argued that Major League Baseball constituted interstate
commerce, noting in particular the recent growth of national television

revenue. They maintained that baseball constituted an illegal monopoly engaged in the restraint of trade, and furthermore stood in violation of the Thirteenth Amendment, outlawing involuntary servitude. Kuhn and the owners (all named as defendants in the suit) argued that the sport's exemption from antitrust law was established legal precedent, and that Congress had repeatedly declined to address it. The teams also maintained that their unchecked ability to control players' contracts, in the form of the reserve system, was fundamental to the game's integrity and economic viability. Their further argument that the contract language in question should be a matter for collective bargaining, not for the courts, struck some as especially disingenuous.[85]

The case was heard in U.S. District Court in the spring of 1970, where Judge Irving Ben Cooper ruled against Flood. After the Second Circuit refused Flood's appeal, the case landed in the U.S. Supreme Court in early 1972. On June 18, in a five–three decision, the high court sided with the owners, leaving baseball's reserve system intact.[86] The majority agreed with Flood that baseball constituted interstate commerce but held that Congress—not the Court—should be charged with addressing MLB's antitrust exemption. Justice Harry Blackmun's majority opinion was steeped in romantic rhetoric: one long paragraph consisted of a list of ballplayers, "celebrated for one reason or another, that have sparked the diamond and its environs and that have provided tinder for recaptured thrills, for reminiscence and comparisons, and for conversation and anticipation in-season and off-season." Justice Byron White excluded himself from section I of the opinion simply to avoid being associated with what many agreed was an irrelevant jaunt through baseball history.[87]

Although MLB's owners managed to persuade five justices to leave the reserve system alone for the time being, they were considerably less successful in the court of public opinion. A number of influential observers registered objections to the owners' arguments. Red Smith, one of the most widely read and respected sports columnists of his day, accused the Supreme Court of "averting its gaze from a system in American business that gives the employer outright ownership of his employees" and setting "greater store by property rights than by human rights."[88] Both the *New York Times* and the *Wall Street Journal* published editorials calling for modifications to the reserve system.[89] This represented a significant shift: when the Court upheld the reserve system in 1953, the *Times* had hailed the decision.[90]

In the next Basic Agreement (1973), MLB owners consented to the so-called ten–five rule, giving players with ten years' experience in the major leagues and five years with the same team, as had been the case for Curt Flood, the right to veto any trade.[91] As Brad Snyder has argued, the owners' position during the trial that the reserve system was best left to collective bargaining strengthened the MLBPA's hand. "Before the Flood case," Snyder writes, "the owners had refused to entertain any modifications in the reserve clause. Now the pressure was on the owners to negotiate in good faith."[92] In bringing his case Flood also performed significant symbolic work, helping Miller and the MLBPA develop a consensus among players that the reserve system needed modification. Flood's former teammate Jim "Mudcat" Grant emphasized his own stake in the matter, speaking to a reporter in the spring of 1970: "Look at me last year. I was transferred three times. I had to move my family three times. I would get settled in one place, get some things going for me, then I'd have to pack up and go elsewhere." Summing up the feelings of many fellow players, Grant concluded, "We're just like puppets, high priced puppets, but puppets, nevertheless."[93]

Through his reserve clause fight, Flood's identity as a public figure took on new dimensions. His autobiography (written with Richard Carter), published in 1971 while his case was winding its way through the courts, stands as a powerful document of the legal fight's larger symbolic stakes. *The Way It Is* narrates the lifetime of hard work and struggle that brought him from Oakland's sandlots to center field at Busch Stadium and beyond. One of the most political memoirs ever written by an athlete, the book frames Flood's challenge within the larger contexts of the African American freedom struggle and the other social upheavals of the 1960s. The opening chapter concludes with Flood's meditation on a piece of racist hate mail:

> I assembled a martini, *very* dry. I probably had spoiled the animal's breakfast. I might even have ruined his day. No doubt it had started splendidly, with a front page full of grand news about undesirable elements being bombed, shot, incinerated, beaten, arrested, suspended, expelled, drafted and otherwise coped with here and abroad. Then he must have turned to the sporting page, where horror confronted him. Curt Flood had sued baseball on constitutional grounds. If the newspaper was typical, it lied that a victory for Flood would mean the collapse of our national pastime. God profaned! Flag desecrated! Motherhood defiled! Apple pie blasphemed! The animal was furious. Them niggers is never satisfied.
>
> I am pleased that God made my skin black but I wish He had made it thicker.[94]

Here, while placing his reserve clause challenge in a wider frame, Flood invites readers to reexamine the daily sports page itself as a fundamental site of the relations of power under which ballplayers labor. This passage is reflective of the book as a whole, which served to cast Flood's lawsuit as part of a larger case against baseball's dominant politics of representation. In his narrative, as in his legal challenge, Flood refused to allow Major League Baseball's entrenched interests to determine the limits of his agency.

## Jim Bouton, Antimythologist

Flood's memoir was not the only one of its era to expose the inner workings of the baseball industry. In June 1970, *Look* magazine published the first of two excerpts from Jim Bouton's *Ball Four.* A diary-style treatment of the pitcher's 1969 season with the Seattle Pilots and Houston Astros, *Ball Four* offered a frank account of life in the big leagues. Bouton's narrative was a bombshell, shocking readers with discussions of such controversial subjects as players' widespread amphetamine use (taking "greenies"), voyeurism ("beaver shooting"), and infidelity. The book's significance, however, lay not just in salacious anecdotes about individual athletes.

Bouton also laid bare his own personal struggles, punctuating the text with discussions of past contract holdouts, fears of trades and demotions, and reflections on the fractured racial dynamics of major league clubhouses. By describing revered baseball heroes as flawed human beings, and by presenting his own experience of pro ball as anxiety-ridden and full of conflict with his boss, Bouton's exposé made a significant departure from baseball's accepted modes of representation. *New York Times* columnist Robert Lipsyte applauded Bouton for breathing "new life into a game choked by pontificating statisticians, image-conscious officials and scared ballplayers."[95]

Bouton's book broke through the pervasive sense of baseball as a tradition-bound cultural form. As *Newsweek* columnist Pete Axthelm's condemnation of the sport as an "anachronistic bore" suggested, by the late 1960s many observers had come to see the "American pastime" as simply past its time in an era when the made-for-television violence of football seemed to do a better job of capturing the collective imagination. If some saw baseball as outmoded, however, others saw it as a refuge from the social upheavals of the day. The 1968 World Series, the subject of Axthelm's piece, became a flashpoint for competing claims to baseball's cultural meaning. Before the start of the fifth game, held on October 7 at Tiger Stadium in Detroit, José Feliciano performed a version of the "Star-Spangled Banner" that departed from traditional renditions. Feliciano's contemplative vocal with acoustic

guitar accompaniment took liberties with the anthem's melody and ca-
dence, stunning many listeners and viewers who expected to hear a more
orthodox version. Some saw Feliciano himself, a young Puerto Rican per-
former whose cover of the Doors' hit "Light My Fire" had soared up the
pop charts that summer, as a figure of the counterculture. Television and
radio stations carrying the game received angry phone calls, and several
newspapers published stern rebukes in editorials and letters to the editor.[96]

As David W. Zang suggests in his valuable study *SportsWars: Athletes in
the Age of Aquarius,* by the late 1960s sports and rock music could be seen
as "nations unto themselves, with different constitutions, dress codes, and
values . . . [and] in the antipathy between them one could feel the tensions running through American society."[97] Though some players may have
identified with the new cultural currents of the 1960s, their sport tended to
be framed—by many fans, writers, and team owners alike—in opposition
to the changes under way outside stadium walls. This representational dynamic appeared in especially vivid form in *Newsweek*'s coverage of a tragic
incident in 1970—the Greenwich Village townhouse explosion in which
members of the Weather Underground died while assembling bombs. In a
biographical sketch of Ted Gold, who was among those killed in the explosion, the magazine noted that the young radical had been a lifelong baseball
fan and had recently told a friend, "Sometimes I think I'll have to wait for
Willie Mays to retire before I become a good Communist."[98]

Jim Bouton was far from a revolutionary, but his book brought to the
surface simmering tensions over baseball's identity. The future author of
*Ball Four* had arrived on the national scene as "Bulldog" Bouton, a fireball-
ing young right-hander on the great Yankees teams of the early 1960s, the
last World Series clubs in New York's long mid-century American League
dynasty. Throughout his career, Bouton had been one of the most outspoken of ballplayers. He repeatedly staged contract holdouts, going head-to-
head both at the bargaining table and in the press with Yankees brass, and
became an active member of the MLBPA.[99]

Bouton was also among the most overtly political ballplayers of his generation. In 1968 he joined the successful campaign to uphold a ban on the
all-white South African Olympic team. At the conclusion of that summer's
baseball season Bouton traveled to Mexico City to join longtime anti-
apartheid organizer Dennis Brutus and other members of the South African Non-Racial Olympic Committee. As part of his visit, Bouton met with
representatives of his own nation's athletic leadership, who lashed out at the
pitcher. Responding to Bouton's antiracist stand, Douglas Roby, president

of the United States Olympic Committee, asked: "Did the Russians pay your way here? Are you mixed up with the Commies?" One of Roby's colleagues, press officer Robert Paul, told Bouton, "I won't talk to you, you're the un-American ballplayer I've heard about."[100]

For most of the baseball establishment, Bouton's writing represented a far more serious transgression than his political activism. Immediately following publication of the initial excerpts from *Ball Four*, commissioner Bowie Kuhn called Bouton in for a very public dressing-down, accusing the pitcher-turned-author of doing the game a "grave disservice."[101] *Ball Four*'s portrait of the day-to-day working lives of ballplayers violated one of the sport's long-standing informal codes of conduct, which Bouton addressed explicitly in the book: "In the Milwaukee clubhouse there's a sign that reads: 'What you say here, what you see here, what you do here and what you hear here, let it stay here.' The same sign hangs in the clubhouse in Minneapolis. Also, I suppose, in the CIA offices in Washington. If I were a CIA man, could I write a book?"[102] Reviewing *Ball Four* in *Harper's*, David Halberstam applauded the book's challenge to baseball's norms and power structure, suggesting that "a comparable insider's book about, say, the Congress of the United States, the Ford Motor Company, or the Joint Chiefs of Staff would be equally welcome."[103]

In his enthusiastic review, Halberstam counted Bouton among those whom he termed the "antimythologists," noting that the book had elicited especially strong reactions from defenders of baseball's traditional myths and meanings. Indeed, Dick Young, columnist for the *New York Daily News* and the *Sporting News* and one of the era's most prominent commentators, called Bouton and his editor Leonard Shecter "social lepers" after the book's publication. As far as Young was concerned, Bouton had joined Curt Flood (whose challenge to the reserve clause he sarcastically labeled the "Dred Flood" case) and other malcontents in defacing the game.[104] "Bouton's action reflects the deplorable disregard among some of our young people for the meaning of the word honor," Young wrote. "He was trusted by his teammates, in the clubhouse, in their private moments, and he dishonored the trust. It is the same as if a newsman, told something off the record, writes it. Bouton knew he had a tacit 'This is off the record.'"[105] To Bouton's mind, the angry responses from Young and other sportswriters stemmed from their being scooped by a ballplayer. "I was not a social leper when Dick Young needed quotes," recalls Bouton. "No, I became a social leper when I infringed on Dick Young's territory. I mean, here was a guy writing a column called 'Clubhouse Confidential.'"[106]

Dick Young's outraged response to *Ball Four* came amid a period of larger uncertainty and change for newspaper writers, who had served as baseball's most influential public voices since the nineteenth century. As television cameras provided fans new levels of access, writers saw challenges to their own professional roles. On at least one occasion the simmering conflict between newspaper reporters and television broadcasters bubbled over into official protest. Controversy erupted at Fenway Park on May 15, 1971, when NBC caused a delay while preparing a live shot from the bullpen, prompting the Boston chapter of the Baseball Writers' Association of America to file a protest with Joe Cronin, president of the American League. Bill Liston, a baseball writer for the *Boston Herald-American*, who was serving as official scorer for the game between the Red Sox and Orioles, recorded the writers' protest in the formal account he filed with the league. Liston's box score noted the difference between the game's "elapsed" and "official" times, highlighting the four minutes it took for NBC announcer Tony Kubek and his camera crew to move their equipment into the bullpen during the fifth inning. The incident led to a meeting between Kuhn and a special committee of the Baseball Writers' Association, in which the scribes demanded greater access to players before and after games.[107] The uproar highlighted the fact that players were not the only workers in their industry with a stake in baseball's political economy of representation.[108]

One of the defining themes in baseball journalism in the era of emerging player militancy was disdain for the ways in which unionism was transforming the meaning of the sport. During the 1972 strike, *Los Angeles Times* columnist Jim Murray offered a biting revision of "The Game for All America," Ernie Harwell's romantic tribute to baseball's enduring meaning as the national pastime, published each year in the *Sporting News*. Calling Harwell's piece a "faded valentine," Murray presented a damning assessment of baseball's vacant symbolic landscape in the age of collective bargaining and work stoppages: "Baseball is the $120,000-a-year player walking out of camp because he's insulted to be offered that little money for six months which will largely be spent standing still in left field and occasionally having to run as far as 270 feet at a clip. . . . Baseball is yesterday. It will be gone like the Kansas picnic, the county fair, the Fourth of July fireworks and the rest of Americana."[109] In stark contrast to David Halberstam, who welcomed the interventions of "antimythologists" like Jim Bouton, Murray found nothing praiseworthy in baseball's new politics of work and representation. For Murray, as for many other influential observers in the late 1960s and early 1970s, industrial conflict between players and owners seemed to cut at the core of baseball's identity. Similar sentiments about the detrimental impact of unionism and the specter of the "overpaid ballplayer" would remain common features of sports pages for decades to come.

Even as a new generation of MLB players created shockwaves by rejecting the sport's old labor regime and modes of representation, they also helped to construct ideologies of power and exclusion. Both Curt Flood and Jim Bouton devoted significant space in their memoirs to elaborate discussions of ballplayers' sexual exploits. For all of the political rebellion embodied in these two texts, they gave voice to an aggressively masculine view of the baseball world. In the midst of intense battles between players and owners over the distribution of power, leading figures from both sides seemed to agree wholeheartedly that women's only possible roles in the sport were passive—either as fans or as sexual objects. In 1977, Bowie Kuhn barred *Sports Illustrated* reporter Melissa Ludtke from conducting locker room interviews during the World Series. Ludtke brought a successful suit against Kuhn, opening new opportunities for female journalists in one of the most important—and understudied—legal struggles in the history of modern sport. The fact that it took a federal judge's intervention to allow equal access, however, made it clear that players and league officials alike were invested in keeping the production of baseball's meaning the exclusive province of men, well into the age of free agency.[110]

If overt misogyny formed one key feature of baseball's new politics of style and representation, another central legacy would be that of a liberated individualism. Though Flood and a number of other athletes of color brought broader social claims to bear on their industry, players' militancy around issues of racial justice rarely took the form of collective mobilization.[111] And Bouton's narrative did not voice a sense of shared purpose or united political consciousness among ballplayers, even if it described experiences and perspectives that other athletes could recognize as their own. Rather, the memoir functioned as an act of solitary rebellion, and actually angered many fellow players. Members of the San Diego Padres burned a copy of *Ball Four*, leaving the charred remains for its author to find in the visitors' clubhouse of Dodger Stadium.[112] Joe Morgan, Bouton's teammate on the Astros, said: "I always thought he was a teammate, not an author. I told him some things I would never tell a sportswriter."[113] Bob Gibson put it more bluntly, saying of Bouton, "He stabbed his friends in the back for money."[114]

The politics of individualism were, of course, at the heart of the most important contractual accomplishment of ballplayer militancy—the opportunity to sell one's own labor as a free agent on the open market. Asserting new control over the terms of their own commodification, baseball players found power within what scholars have come to recognize as one of the distinctive historical transformations of the 1970s and 1980s: the political redefinition of freedom as that of the free marketplace. If a fundamental element of the history of neoliberalism is the collapse of collective claims to liberation and social justice into a politics of free-market individualism, ballplayers' labor struggles stand as central acts in the cultural history of the second half of the twentieth century.[115]

## The Politics of Style and the Rise of Star Power

By the early 1970s, more and more players were displaying a new rebellious-ness, both on and off the playing field. This sometimes took the form of direct challenges to team authorities. Cardinals manager Red Schoendienst later wrote: "The biggest change I noticed was a change in attitude among the players. It probably was caused by all of those societal developments as well as the coming of free agency, but it made a manager's job much harder. When you asked a player to do something, there were guys who wanted to know why, and you didn't have the automatic power and authority that a manager was used to having."[116]

In addition to explicitly questioning managers' power, players asserted autonomy in more subtle ways, including through their personal appear-ance. Particularly for African American athletes, hair styles became mean-ingful modes of baseball's cultural politics. In the midst of the upheavals of the late 1960s, team officials attempted to prevent athletes from cultivating rebellious looks, adopting rules against mustaches, goatees, and sideburns at a general managers' meeting in late 1968.[117] Many players simply refused to obey such restrictions, and by the early 1970s a number of observers of the sport had come to identify the new styles as signs of fracture within the industry.

The historian Matthew Frye Jacobson offers an example of this dynamic in his analysis of media representations of African American slugger Dick Allen. One of Allen's many claims to fame was as the star player the Car-dinals received in the Curt Flood trade. Allen staged a brief holdout at the beginning of his tenure in St. Louis before agreeing to terms during training camp in 1970. That spring, amid the first stages of Flood's legal challenge, *Sports Illustrated*'s editors chose to feature a cover photograph of Allen, with his prominent sideburns and afro, next to the headline "Baseball in Turmoil." The image of Allen, who had long been the subject of racialized antagonism by members of the Philadelphia sporting press, apparently worked better to signify the emergence of black rebellion in the national pastime than would a photo of Flood, who did not wear such a recognizably rebellious hair style. As Jacobson suggests, "it was Allen who more looked the part."[118]

In addition to asserting independence by crafting their own public images, some ballplayers in the 1970s took the further step of actually marketing themselves. No player embodied this new brand of stardom more than Reggie Jackson, the Oakland Athletics' electrifying right fielder. An outspoken leader of the MLBPA, a brilliant self-promoter, and a full-fledged superstar, Jackson loomed large in the early 1970s, as his team won three straight World Series titles. Writing his own *Ball Four*–like diary-style account of the 1974 season, Jackson presented himself as a cocky moneymaking machine: "I have attorneys. I have managers. . . . They get me deals and manage me as much as I let anyone manage me."[119]

Jackson figured prominently in an instructive episode in the cultural politics of individual style. When he arrived in spring training camp in 1972 with a mustache, team owner Charlie Finley urged manager Dick Williams to force Jackson to shave. Jackson refused to alter his appearance. As Bruce Markusen reports in his informative history of the A's of the early 1970s, Finley then encouraged other members of the Athletics to grow mustaches, in an attempt to make his star right fielder feel less invested in his facial hair as a marker of individual style. As Finley watched the players sprout whiskers, however, he came to embrace his team's emerging mustachioed identity as a marketing opportunity. The owner then offered players financial incentives to cultivate their facial hair, and scheduled a "Mustache Day" promotion for Fathers' Day at the Oakland Coliseum, offering free admission to all whiskered fans.

Finley's "Mustache Gang" marked the latest in a series of the idiosyncratic owner's innovative strategies to attract fan interest, such as installing a mechanical rabbit named Harvey to deliver baseballs to the home plate umpire, and introducing the gaudy green and gold uniforms that set the A's apart from MLB's significantly less colorful status quo.[120] The dynamics of commodification at work on the 1972 Athletics, as Charlie Finley figured out a way to reframe players' expressions of individualism and star power into a brand image for his team, resonated throughout the baseball industry

Reggie Jackson showing his power, hitting a game-winning home run against the Texas Rangers at the Oakland Coliseum, April 14, 1974. (*Associated Press*)

over the rest of the decade. A new generation of owners, led by Ted Turner of the Atlanta Braves and George Steinbrenner of the New York Yankees, would come to value high-profile players nearly as much for the marketing potential they embodied as for their anticipated productivity on the field.

Through their collective mobilization of star power, MLB players brought about the new contractual system of free agency itself, finally instituted in 1976 after a decade of MLBPA organizing and militancy. The impartial arbitration process that the union established through collective bargaining provided the players with a viable institutional channel for winning free agency. Oakland's Jim "Catfish" Hunter became a free agent in December

1974, when the arbitrator, Peter Seitz, found Charlie Finley in breach of contract for failing to pay for an insurance annuity that the pitcher had negotiated as part of his compensation package. A bidding war immediately ensued, with the star pitcher eventually signing with the New York Yankees.[121] As he moved from Finley's A's to Steinbrenner's Yankees, Hunter's liberated contractual status became part of his public identity, as captured in Bob Dylan's 1975 song "Catfish," written with Jacques Levy: "Used to work on Mr. Finley's farm / But the old man wouldn't pay / So he packed his glove and took his arm / An' one day he just ran away."[122] The year after the bidding war for Catfish Hunter's services became a cultural phenomenon, two other major league pitchers brought a successful challenge to the reserve system.

During the 1975 season Andy Messersmith and Dave McNally prepared to test the legitimacy of Major League Baseball's labor system by going the entire campaign without signing their contracts, which had been renewed from the previous year under the terms of the reserve clause. At the end of the season their cases were heard via the impartial arbitration procedure established in the 1970 Basic Agreement. In December, arbitrator Seitz ruled in the pitchers' favor, declaring them to be free agents.[123] Seitz's ruling set off a contentious period of bargaining between team owners and union leaders. Finally, in midsummer 1976, the two sides agreed to a new system of free agency for veteran players, the fundamental terms of which would remain largely unchanged over the coming decades. Players with six years of big league experience now had the opportunity to entertain contract offers from any interested MLB club.

Free agency, however, meant much more than simply a new system of contracts. Increased power at the bargaining table was one manifestation of a larger shift. Rejecting baseball's old ways of being, players—particularly stars—fashioned new public identities and claimed new forms of power over the terms of their own commodification. Though much of the baseball establishment initially greeted free agency with trepidation, many team owners quickly came to understand the marketing value of making a splash on the free agent market. Reggie Jackson, who was among the first class of free agents, embodied his sport's new directions in the mid-1970s. After being traded to the Baltimore Orioles before the 1976 season (having made it clear that he intended to test the free agent market at the end of the year), Jackson was credited with substantially increasing attendance for his new team. As Ron Fimrite of *Sports Illustrated* wrote: "Of all the liberated players, he has the greatest star quality. . . . He is . . . a colorful and engaging personality who has demonstrated this year that he can put people in the stands. He is a big reason why the Orioles have drawn 67,900 more fans this season than last, while the A's have attracted 300,000 fewer."[124]

Team owners took special note of the ability of stars like Jackson to "put people in the stands." George Steinbrenner, his team fresh off a disappointing World Series sweep at the hands of the Cincinnati Reds, saw Jackson as the key to what he hoped would be a new Yankees dynasty, and signed the player to a five-year contract worth nearly $3 million. By 1976 Jackson had earned a reputation for having a strong feel for the power of his own brand, exemplified in a comment to the press the previous fall: "If I played [in New York] they'd name a candy bar after me."[125] Jackson's style rubbed some people the wrong way, including prominent players on the Yankees like team captain Thurman Munson, the white catcher with a celebrated "blue-collar" public image, who famously feuded with his new teammate throughout the late 1970s.[126] Jackson, however, more than lived up to his words, leading the Yankees in spectacular fashion to their World Series victory in 1977, highlighted by his three booming home runs in the decisive sixth game. In a sign of the enormous star power he now embodied, before leaving for spring training the next year Jackson joined representatives from Standard Brands at a press conference to announce that the company's latest product, the Reggie Bar, would be available for purchase within the first month of the 1978 baseball season.[127]

# 3

# Two Strikes

## Star Power and Solidarity
## in the United States and Mexico

R EGGIE JACKSON played his final games as a member of the New York
Yankees during the 1981 World Series. He suffered an injury during the
American League playoffs and watched the first three Series games against
the Los Angeles Dodgers from the bench. Though the slugger went three
for three with a home run in Game 4, his return to the lineup wasn't enough
to overcome the surging Dodgers, who captured L.A.'s first title since 1965.
The 1981 World Series defeat ushered in a period of decline for the Yankees.
While Jackson left New York as a Big Apple–sized celebrity, signed a new
free agent contract with the California Angels, and returned to the playoffs
twice over the next five seasons, his former club struggled to put a winning
team on the field and did not qualify for postseason play again until 1995.

If the 1981 World Series signaled the end of one of the first great cou-
plings of star power and geography in the age of free agency, it also celebrated the emergence of a new one. The Dodgers' winning pitcher in Game
3 was Fernando Valenzuela, whose gutsy complete-game victory was the
final triumph of a remarkable debut season. Over the course of the 1981
campaign Valenzuela had captivated the baseball world. Just twenty years
old, the rookie from Mexico seemed almost overnight to become the sport's
most talked-about southpaw since Sandy Koufax, the legendary pitcher
who had led Los Angeles to its last World Series victory in 1965. In fact,
Valenzuela was unlike any previous baseball hero, his stardom taking a different shape from that of earlier legends like Koufax and even Jackson. "Fernandomania," as the crazed fan response to the pitcher came to be known,

75

heralded the arrival of baseball's first transnational sensation in the age of free agency.[1]

Just two years before his historic 1981 season, Valenzuela was an unproven prospect in the Liga Mexicana. On the strength of evaluations provided by their unusually extensive scouting operation in that country, the Dodgers identified Valenzuela's enormous potential and purchased his contract in the summer of 1979 for $120,000 from Jaime Pérez Avella, the owner of the Puebla Ángeles.[2] For a relatively untested pitcher, $120,000 represented a significant expenditure, even by one of MLB's richest teams. The franchise's investment in talent development beyond the borders of the United States dated to the era of Branch Rickey, whose commitment to international scouting had helped the Brooklyn Dodgers become one of Major League Baseball's best teams in the postwar period. Now, in the age of free agency, the Los Angeles Dodgers were emerging as trendsetters in new Latin American recruiting strategies. In addition to investing resources in Mexico, the team built one of MLB's top scouting operations in the Caribbean, the centerpiece of which was a state-of-the-art baseball academy in the Dominican Republic, which opened in 1987.

Although no one in L.A.'s front office could have imagined the bonanza that Fernandomania would become, marketing concerns were certainly a significant reason for team executives' interest in Mexican players. Dodgers officials had made previous efforts to find players who might draw new fans from the city's large Mexican American community, but had met with decidedly mixed results. Soon after moving to Los Angeles from Brooklyn, the Dodgers signed Phil Ortega, a highly touted pitching prospect, with plans to attract new fans by building a marketing strategy around the young phenom's identity. In a telling case of institutional obliviousness, team executives presented Ortega as Mexican American, despite the fact that he identified as Yaqui. Given that the team was preparing to move into its new stadium at Chavez Ravine, a site from which a working-class Mexican American community had been forcibly removed, the organization's ignorant marketing of the young pitcher's ethnicity only further soured many Angelenos toward Walter O'Malley's baseball team.[3]

While team executives continued to view L.A.'s Latino community as an attractive if untapped market, influential local media institutions like the newspaper *La Opinión* called on the Dodgers to do a better job of representing the whole city by featuring a more diverse lineup. Although Dominican standout Manny Mota was a popular player with the team during the 1970s, through the Dodgers' first two decades in L.A. the club did not feature a single star of Mexican ancestry, a fact not lost on the city's Mexican American community. The most notable attempt to do so in the years immediately prior to Valenzuela's debut was the team's signing of Los Angeles native Bobby Castillo, who joined the Dodgers in 1977. Castillo, however, never became the star or the marketing success that team executives hoped he would be; he ultimately achieved his greatest acclaim in the organization as Fernando Valenzuela's instructor in the art of the screwball, after being assigned to work with the pitcher in the winter of 1979.[4]

Castillo's instruction was especially valuable for the young prospect, as the screwball is one of baseball's most challenging pitches. Designed to break in the opposite direction from the more traditional curve and slider (so screwballs thrown by left-handers like Valenzuela break away from right-handed hitters), the pitch creates enormous stress on the elbow and is very difficult to repeat with consistent results. Relatively few MLB pitchers have featured the screwball in their repertoires, but some who have—including Carl Hubbell, Warren Spahn, and Juan Marichal—rank among the sport's most successful hurlers. Mastering the new pitch with astounding speed, Valenzuela moved quickly through the minor leagues and debuted with the Dodgers in September 1980, pitching nearly flawlessly in relief in the last month of a close pennant race against the Houston Astros. Given a chance to begin the 1981 season in the starting rotation because of injuries to key veterans, Valenzuela ran off an incredible string of eight consecutive victories and went on to win the National League's Rookie of the Year and Cy Young Awards (the latter given to the league's best pitcher), leading the Dodgers to their victory in the World Series against the Yankees.

The young pitcher's great performances on the mound helped boost his team's attendance figures substantially. Not only did Valenzuela's games at Dodger Stadium invariably sell out, but his appearances drew large crowds at other parks as well. When the Dodgers traveled to New York to play the lowly Mets, the home team promoted the phenom as a reason for New Yorkers to come out to Shea Stadium. Nearly forty thousand of them showed up, thirteen thousand more than at any previous Mets game that year.[5] Over the course of the season, the Dodgers' road attendance increased by an average of nine thousand fans per game when Valenzuela pitched.[6]

Even more than a box office draw, the southpaw was a media sensation. With their close-up camera angles and slow-motion replays, television broadcasts captured his distinctive twisting windup, in which he would gaze skyward while holding his hands high above his head before swiveling to deliver the ball to home plate. Millions of radio listeners tuned in not only to hear Vin Scully, the Dodgers' longtime play-by-play announcer, but also to hear Jaime Jarrín's Spanish-language broadcasts. Jarrín's accounts of Dodgers games had been carried on Los Angeles radio station KWKW for years, and, thanks to Valenzuela's popularity, they were now picked up by a growing transnational network. Mexico's television giant, Televisa, soon began broadcasting each of the games "El Toro" pitched, as well.[7] To handle the explosion of attention surrounding the overnight sensation, the Dodgers scheduled special press conferences for Valenzuela in each city the team visited. By early May, his picture and story seemed to be everywhere—not just in sports publications but on the cover of *Time* and *Newsweek*, as well. Bantam Books even rushed a bilingual biography to press by June.[8]

In their depictions of Valenzuela, many sportswriters appealed to a combination of baseball myth and ethnic stereotype. As Steve Wulf of *Sports Illustrated* put it: "The Natural is supposed to be a blue-eyed boy who teethed on a 36-ounce Louisville Slugger. He should run like the wind and throw boysenberries through brick. He should come from California. The Dodgers have one this year, only he's *El Natural*. His name is Fernando Valenzuela, and with apologies to the 150 citizens of Etchohuaquila, Mexico, he comes from nowhere. His ancestry is Mayan Indian, and he speaks just enough English to order a beer."[9] Journalists were not the only public figures to employ racialized language in their analysis of Valenzuela. Dodgers manager Tommy Lasorda told the *Washington Post,* "He's an old Aztec chieftain sent down from heaven by Mr. O'Malley because he knew I needed him."[10] After facing the star pitcher in a nationally televised game in Cincinnati, Reds catcher Johnny Bench compared himself to one of the Texan soldiers at the Alamo: "You feel like Jim Bowie waiting for Santa Anna to crush you."[11] As these comments suggest, many within baseball made a fetish of the ethnic and national difference they saw in Valenzuela. Some fans of the teams that Valenzuela defeated got into the act, as well. Among the hand-stenciled signs on display at the Shea Stadium game in early May (and featured in *Newsday*'s coverage the following morning) was one that read, "Deport Valenzuela."[12]

Although expressions of national and racial chauvinism appeared throughout portrayals of Valenzuela in the English-language press, such representations were not the only cultural content of Fernandomania. On the contrary, one of the phenomenon's most defining features was a new collective presence within MLB's fan culture. Whenever Valenzuela pitched, the stands at Dodger Stadium, still identified with the racialized

Fernando Valenzuela on the mound at Dodger Stadium at the
height of Fernandomania, May, 1981. (*Bettmann/CORBIS*)

urban renewal campaign that had brought the facility into being, blos-
somed with Mexican flags and homemade banners carrying slogans spelled
out in Spanish. If the white press could package Valenzuela in stereotypes,
formerly marginalized Chicano fans could claim the superstar as a symbol
of national and ethnic pride.

In the euphoric aftermath of the team's World Series victory, the pitcher
touched off a minor controversy by failing to appear at the parade marking
his team's triumphant return from Yankee Stadium. His teammates heard
chants of "We want Fernando!" as they made their way through the streets
of downtown Los Angeles to a rally at City Hall. Even more revealing was

the itinerary of festivities that Valenzuela *did* attend in the month after the World Series, including appearances in Guadalajara, Puerto Vallarta, Mexico City, and Acapulco, as well as a stint as grand marshal of the East L.A. Christmas parade, whose 250,000 attendees more than tripled the estimated size of the crowd at the Dodgers' victory celebration.[13]

Team and league officials were of course delighted at the potential revenue represented by the new communities of fans who now identified with Valenzuela and the Dodgers. With Major League Baseball's profits from ticket sales, broadcasting, advertising, and merchandising dependent on fans' identification with individual star players, the appearance of this new transnational icon held out the promise of new markets and marketing strategies for the industry. At the same time, Valenzuela himself moved to take advantage of the mass cultural phenomenon surrounding his performance on the field. In May of his breakout rookie season he signed the first of multiple merchandising agreements, a $50,000 contract with a poster company. In announcing the deal, Valenzuela's agent Antonio DeMarco said that he and his client would be pursuing legal action against the producers of unlicensed Fernando bumper stickers, T-shirts, and other items that had flooded the market over the season's first two months.[14] After the poster deal, others followed—a juice endorsement, a commemorative coin, and an exclusive promotional contract with Televisa.[15] Each of these contracts registered Valenzuela's currency as a popular sensation and marketable commodity.

Star power has its limits, however, especially for players with only one full season of big league experience. After earning a salary of $42,500 during his rookie campaign, Valenzuela attempted to negotiate a raise for 1982 that would reflect his considerable worth to the team. His initial proposal was $1 million. When the Dodgers countered with a $350,000 offer at the beginning of spring training, the pitcher refused to report to camp, initiating a standoff that lasted nearly until opening day. As a second-year player Valenzuela had little leverage, and he was eventually compelled to agree to terms close to the Dodgers' original offer.[16]

The holdout inspired a significant amount of animosity toward Valenzuela from many quarters, much of which was reported and amplified by the sporting press. At the height of the controversy, the Dodgers suggested that if Valenzuela refused to sign his contract, he would face deportation, prompting the League of United Latin American Citizens (LULAC) to send a telegram of protest to U.S. Labor Secretary Raymond Donovan and Immigration and Naturalization Services commissioner Alan Nelson.[17] Weighing in on these events, Jim Murray of the *Los Angeles Times* attempted to place Valenzuela's contract dispute in the larger context of the economic recession that had gripped the country:

> Unemployment is rising. Auto plants are going belly up. Stocks are taking nose dives. Financial institutions are failing. Welfare is being cut back. America is in big trouble. And a kid from Etchohuaquila, Mexico, with little or no formal education, a non-citizen who cannot speak the language, wants $1.4 million a year for a job where he works only every fourth day and then for no more than an hour and a half. And he usually requires a backup to come in and finish the job for him. He doesn't contribute a jot to the gross national product, will not alleviate suffering, bring goods to market or revolutionize medicine. And he doesn't do windows. . . . Fernando will doubtless sign. But even if it's for half what he asks, in a year when Ford loses a billion dollars, the man on the street thinks he should get on his knees and thank Our Lady of Guadalupe he's got a job.[18]

Coming just months after Valenzuela had helped bring a World Series title to Los Angeles, the column seemed designed to serve notice that despite his great rookie season, at the end of the day Valenzuela couldn't claim full citizenship in Murray's vision of the national pastime. Murray's turn to the language of ethnic and national superiority was a familiar rhetorical move by 1982, echoing the ways in which earlier generations of Latino athletes had been treated by members of the sport's media establishment. But there was also a new dimension to Murray's criticism, juxtaposing the escalation in player salaries with the increasingly precarious position of other U.S. workers. By constructing Valenzuela as an ungrateful interloper, Murray placed the pitcher in a position familiar to many immigrant workers in the early 1980s: a scapegoat for white anxieties over deindustrialization, job loss, and economic decline.

Murray's racialized anger typifies one response to a fundamental question: What relationship do athletes have to the larger story of work in hard times? How should we understand the labor history of baseball's age of free agency in its larger context: the erosion of the social compacts of the mid-twentieth century and the emergence of an increasingly globalized and deregulated organization of work and daily life? For the small elite of professional baseball players who were able to reap the rewards of the market mobility won through major league free agency, the period was defined by extraordinary gains in wealth and opportunity. The vast majority of professional ballplayers, however, never appeared in a Major League Baseball game, let alone enjoyed the benefits of free agency. Instead, athletes encountered employers increasingly adept at nimble manipulations of near-monopoly power. Even as MLB stars became exemplars of individual success and entrepreneurship in the new economy—as in business writer Daniel Pink's book *Free Agent Nation,* for example—most professional ballplayers faced an uphill battle just to make a living.[19]

The baseball industry experienced significant labor upheaval in the early 1980s. Fernando Valenzuela began his career during a period of significant player militancy, marked by strikes in both the Liga Mexicana (1980) and MLB (1981). The two strikes of 1980–81 were flashpoints in the reconfiguration of work, territory, and power in the age of free agency. The Major League Baseball strike was a struggle over the limits of star power, provoked by team owners' attempt to constrain players' hard-won gains. MLBPA members won a decisive victory and preserved their own power to sell themselves as marketable commodities in the new cable TV–driven free agent market. The strike in the Liga Mexicana was a different kind of struggle. Mexican athletes fought for basic improvements in wages and working conditions, as well as measures of professional autonomy and mobility. Members of the Asociación Nacional de Beisbolistas (ANABE), faced with intransigent team owners, eventually formed their own league—a circuit designed to serve the interests of players and their communities, rather than those of the Liga Mexicana's elite power brokers.

Through their labor struggles members of both the MLBPA and the ANABE played critical roles in the contested development of free agency in their industry. While the members of the MLBPA achieved exceptional market power as individual stars, the organizers of ANABE erected—for a short time—an alternative, collective model of professional baseball. The two instances of ballplayer militancy played out against the backdrop of broader struggles, marked by new assaults in the United States on the right to strike and new constraints on Mexican workers' labor and consumer power during their country's neoliberal transformation. Like other workers, baseball players in this period found forms of autonomy, agency, and mobility distributed unequally throughout the transnational networks that structured their industry. Emerging from the period of militant unionism in the early 1980s was a baseball world defined at once by the expanding labor power of major league stars and by team owners' continual drive to develop and control sources of cheap young talent.

The phenomenon of Fernandomania serves as a vivid example of the stakes involved in each of the baseball strikes of the early 1980s. For both Mexican and U.S. observers, Valenzuela's remarkable rookie season highlighted emerging new possibilities for transnational star power. For other Mexican players, Valenzuela embodied their own potential, given the opportunity to play at the game's highest level, while for Mexican team owners, Fernandomania held out the hope of future lucrative player sales to eager MLB teams. For his fellow major leaguers, Valenzuela's success as a marketable commodity and his struggles at the bargaining table spoke to their ongoing campaign to win a greater share of the industry's profits, while many team owners saw the pitcher as evidence of the great untapped resources accessible through Latin American scouting. And for audiences throughout the Americas, Fernandomania represented a captivating new chapter in baseball history, one that—especially for fans of the Los Angeles Dodgers—seemed to hold a world of possibility.

### Strike One: The Irreplaceable Power of MLB Stars

Arbitrator Peter Seitz's ruling in late December 1975 that holdout pitchers Andy Messersmith and Dave McNally were free agents brought a period of tense negotiations over the terms of a new collective bargaining agreement. Many among the owners were not willing to concede to the reality of a more limited reserve system and a more powerful MLBPA. With talks stalled, in late February 1976 the teams declared that spring training camps would remain closed past the scheduled start of workouts on March 1. After a seventeen-day lockout, in a move that forever irked some hard-line owners, commissioner Bowie Kuhn ordered the camps opened. Talks continued through the spring and early summer, and the parties finally reached an agreement during the annual All-Star break in July. The midsummer accord established the basic terms for free agency: upon completion of six years in the majors, a player would be allowed to sign with any interested club. A team losing one of its members through free agency would receive compensation from that player's new club in the form of a first- or second-round selection in the next amateur draft.[20]

The negotiations over the collective bargaining agreement had brought acrimony and uncertainty to the first half of the 1976 season. Creating further drama, dozens of players declined to ink new contracts, hoping to follow the path blazed by Messersmith and McNally and seek free agency as soon as possible. In mid-March, against the backdrop of stalled negotiations between the owners and the union, nearly one-third of MLB players (193 of approximately 600) remained unsigned. When the season began most had come to terms with their teams, but in mid-May a remarkable fifty-five players continued to play without new deals, and in late July the number stood at forty-one. Under the terms of the collective bargaining agreement reached at the All-Star break, anyone who "played out their option" in either 1976 or 1977 would be allowed to entertain offers from any team. Twenty-four players remained unsigned at the end of the 1976 season and became the sport's first class of free agents.[21]

A disproportionate number of those playing out their options in 1976 were members of Charlie Finley's Oakland A's. In an attempt to recoup value from players he was sure to lose to free agency at the end of the season, Finley sold Joe Rudi and Rollie Fingers for the unprecedented price of $1 million each to the Boston Red Sox, and Vida Blue for $1.5 million to the New York Yankees. Bowie Kuhn voided the sales, using his power as commissioner to act in "the best interests of baseball." In appealing to principle in order to stand in the way of Finley's eye-popping player sales, Kuhn claimed powers with their origins in the aftermath of the 1919 "Black Sox" scandal, when team owners created the office of the commissioner in an effort to restore the game's public image. Kuhn invoked the "best interests" clause repeatedly during his career in MLB's top office. As Daniel Okrent puts it: "Kuhn's interpretation of the authority granted him under the clause was like a conservative's view of the Warren Court's interpretation of the Fourteenth Amendment of the Constitution: it enabled him to do whatever he pleased."[22] The Finley-Kuhn affair was only the latest in a series of high-stakes showdowns occasioned by players' growing power. *Newsweek's* Pete Axthelm declared the episode "the most dramatic sign yet of the money madness that has gripped sports."[23]

A striking byproduct of baseball's chaotic battles over the terms of free agency was a growing sense of the sport's renewed cultural relevance. Axthelm himself had proclaimed baseball to be "an anachronistic bore" amid the social tumult of the late 1960s; but by the "money madness" years of the mid-1970s a number of commentators were heralding a new renaissance. *Sports Illustrated* proclaimed the arrival of "The Baseball Boom" with a cover story in the summer of 1975, and *Time* greeted the opening of the 1976 season with the words "Baseball Springs Eternal" accenting a cover image of hordes of rabid fans running into a remodeled Yankee Stadium under a smiling cartoon figure of Babe Ruth.[24] As baseball's stars transformed their industry, they seemed to possess more drawing power than ever before.

Major League Baseball's boom in the early years of free agency only raised the stakes for the next round of collective bargaining between players and team owners. The 1976 agreement expired in 1980, and an eleventh-hour truce delayed an inevitable confrontation until the 1981 season. In advance of bargaining, the owners hired a new chief negotiator, C. Raymond Grebey, a senior labor relations official at General Electric. Grebey joined a negotiating team—the Player Relations Committee (PRC)—dominated by hard-line management leaders set on rolling back free agency, such as Reds general manager Bob Howsam and Cardinals owner Gussie Busch.

The PRC leaders pushed for agreement on a new "compensation" system, in which a team signing a free agent would be required to send the player's former team a major leaguer in return. This plan was untenable to the MLBPA, as it threatened to curtail teams' interest in signing free agents, thus substantially weakening individual players' bargaining power. Marvin Miller and player leaders came to the determination, however, that the owners were not prepared to budge on their compensation position. In addition to the lack of progress in talks by the spring of 1981, the fact that team owners had secured a $50 million strike insurance policy from Lloyds of London the previous fall seemed a clear signal of their determination to roll back free agency, even if it meant a long suspension of games.[25]

In their negotiations with the MLBPA, as well as in their comments to the press, team owners and league officials repeatedly claimed that the continued financial stability of Major League Baseball depended on the PRC's proposed free agent compensation package. To the players, these claims lacked credibility, particularly since teams had been unwilling to share their internal financial records with union negotiators as part of the collective bargaining relationship. In a last-ditch negotiating ploy, the union filed a formal complaint with the National Labor Relations Board, alleging that since the owners had made an issue of their financial well-being, their refusal to "open the books" constituted a failure to bargain. The labor board issued a request for a temporary injunction against the owners, but the union's strategy for holding off a strike fell through when a federal judge, Henry F. Werker, denied the NLRB petition. With the owners dug in and other options exhausted, the players walked out on June 12. The strike brought a wave of criticism from writers and fans. Although some influential journalists and publications framed the dispute in terms favorable to the union, as exemplified by the June *Sports Illustrated* cover that labeled the strike "The Walkout the Owners Provoked," many commentators criticized the players and the teams alike. An editorial in the *Chicago Tribune* titled "Let the Fans Strike" captured a common sentiment: "Throw the bums out—both of them."[26]

With public scorn steadily mounting, the sides finally reached an agreement to resume the season with the annual All-Star Game in early August, ending the strike after fifty-one days. The compensation issue, the major sticking point in negotiations over the previous year, was settled with a new system in which teams losing elite free agents (classified as such through a negotiated formula) would be able to select from a list of players left unprotected by their clubs. Teams that did not sign free agents could protect twenty-six players, while those that made acquisitions via free agency could protect only twenty-four. Since each major league roster included twenty-five players, the "compensation pool" consisted mainly of unproven prospects. Although the team owners were able to claim a limited victory on the compensation issue, the pool system did not come close to the curb on free agency that the PRC had initially sought. The strike's settlement represented a clear win for the MLBPA, not only in further cementing the modern free agency system but also in increasing the minimum salary.[27]

The outcome of the 1981 MLB strike was a product of division among team owners and unity among major league players. The most dramatic divide among the owners fell between those determined to roll back free agency and those willing to deal within the new system. Edward Bennett Williams, the owner of the Baltimore Orioles, who emerged as the most vocal dissenter from the PRC's hard-line position, ultimately rallied enough support among other owners to force a settlement with the MLBPA. One of the most politically connected trial lawyers in Washington, D.C., Williams had taken on millions of dollars in debt to purchase the Orioles in 1979. While sustaining a loss of baseball revenue may not have been a devastating prospect for many of the most hawkish owners (the Anheuser-Busch beer fortune, for example, was not about to dry up), Williams was not prepared to fight the MLBPA to the end. Other owners soon joined him: Jerry Reinsdorf and Eddie Einhorn of the White Sox, Eddie Chiles of the Texas Rangers, and George Steinbrenner of the New York Yankees. The emergence of the Williams-led bloc forced a softening of the PRC's hard-line position, and ultimately helped bring the strike to a conclusion.[28]

The walkout also brought to the surface simmering divides among the players. A significant objection came from Latino union members. "We don't have a voice in this thing," said Chicago Cubs infielder Ivan DeJesús. "We have a lot of good, experienced players . . . and none of them are player representatives."[29] DeJesús's critique pointed to a core challenge for a union with an increasingly diverse membership. Early on in his work with the MLBPA, Marvin Miller had valued his relationship with Puerto Rican superstar Roberto Clemente, and had seen Clemente's participation in union affairs during the late 1960s and early 1970s (including being the first Latino player representative) as critical to building an effective, unified organization. Miller had also worked to ensure that MLBPA documents were available in Spanish.[30] As increasing numbers of Latino athletes joined MLB teams in the 1980s and 1990s, union leadership would place a greater emphasis on representing their interests. One especially important figure in this history was the Puerto Rican former major leaguer Tony Bernazard, who served as a special assistant with the MLBPA following the end of his playing career. But in 1981 a key cohort of players did not see themselves and their experiences represented in the leadership of their union.[31]

Despite internal struggles and organizational challenges, major league players remained unified in their opposition to team owners' efforts to roll back their hard-fought gains at the bargaining table. For veterans and rookies alike, the explosion in player salaries over the course of the previous five years made the economic benefits of sticking with the union clear. Miller's years of organizing, combined with the collective stands that players took throughout the late 1960s and 1970s, created a remarkably strong organization. One of the most striking features of the MLBPA was its identity—relatively unique among unions—as a collective body fiercely devoted to free market individualism. As John Helyar recounts in his excellent blow-by-blow history of the MLBPA in this period, a number of the union's most committed player leaders, such as Doug DeCinces and Phil Garner, were dedicated champions of the free market. DeCinces, for example, would not refer to the organization as a union, carrying on a practice that predated Marvin Miller, in which players chose not to identify their own need for a collective voice with the models utilized by other workers.[32]

Some outside observers, however, did see ballplayer unionism as connected to labor struggles more broadly. In the lead-up to the strike, the *New York Times* printed a column by Lee Ballinger, an Ohio steelworker and author of a recently published book critical of the U.S. sports industry. "Those who trouble to peer behind the iron curtain of scare headlines," Ballinger wrote in the *Times*, "will see that ballplayers are not an exclusive club of millionaires on a par with their employers but in fact have more in common with steelworkers." Drawing comparisons between the brief careers of professional athletes and the uncertain futures of his own colleagues in an era of plant closings, Ballinger insisted that the MLBPA's fight was meaningful for the larger U.S. labor movement.[33]

Another Ohioan, Youngstown-based writer and publisher Jim Villani, interpreted the size and behavior of the crowd at the season-resuming

All-Star Game as evidence of widespread solidarity with the striking ball-players. "Baseball fans are workers," Villani argued. "And when Commissioner Bowie Kuhn, N.L. President Charles Feeney, and A.L. President Lee McPhail were introduced at the All-Star classic, 74,000 fans roundly booed them, and I say ROUNDLY BOOED them in a rousing toast of sympathy for the baseball workers of America."[34] Though some saw resonances between major league diamonds and other workplaces, for most observers the distance between the ballplayers' union and the mainstream of the U.S. labor movement, in ideological orientation as well as in terms of relative power, was unmistakable.

This distinction came into sharp relief during the summer of 1981. In the week between the resolution of the MLB walkout and the resumption of play, President Ronald Reagan fired the nation's striking air traffic controllers and hired replacements to fill their posts. Reagan's ruthless treatment of members of the Professional Air Traffic Controllers Organization (PATCO) marked the start of a new era of attacks on workers' rights in the United States. PATCO was just the tip of the iceberg. As the 1980s unfolded, the use of permanent replacement workers became standard strikebreaking procedure in both the public and private sectors. Beginning with a bitter struggle at Phelps Dodge in 1983, a range of companies—from Greyhound Bus and Continental Airlines in 1983 to International Paper in 1987 and the *New York Daily News* in 1991—used the strategy. The Supreme Court's 1983 decision in *Belknap, Inc. v. Hale,* which affirmed employers' power to hire permanent replacement workers, undercut a fundamental element of modern industrial democracy: the right to strike.[35]

What distinguished the MLBPA strike from the PATCO struggle, more than even the considerable differences between the jobs, labor histories, and public perceptions of ballplayers and air traffic controllers, was the issue of replaceability. Not once during the summer of 1981 was there a credible possibility that replacement players would take over for the striking major leaguers.[36] On the contrary, much of the conflict revolved around the *irreplaceable* value of star players, as evidenced by the intensity of negotiations over free agent compensation.

Within a few years of the 1981 baseball strike, replacement players would become critical to labor-management relations in other professional sports, as National Football League owners proved in breaking a 1987 strike. In the wake of that action, MLBPA executive director Donald Fehr suggested that using replacements was more feasible in a sport populated by masked gladiators. "If they've proven one thing, they've proven football looks the same on television no matter who the players are," Fehr said, "even the skill-position players." Moreover, Fehr argued, the members of the National Football League Players Association had not remained unified. When stars crossed the picket lines to play with and against replacements, the NFLPA strike was effectively neutralized.[37]

The closest that replacement players ever came to appearing in MLB games was in the spring of 1995, in the final stages of the long strike that had begun the previous summer. Following the cancellation of the 1994 playoffs and World Series, and with negotiations over a new collective bargaining agreement stalled, owners were prepared to open the season with replacements ranging from never-heard-of young prospects to former MLB players like Pedro Borbón and Dennis "Oil Can" Boyd. A last-minute deal allowed the season to open (albeit a few weeks late) with teams' regular rosters.[38]

While the ability of major leaguers to withstand their employers' moves against their union during the 1981 walkout seemed to separate professional ballplayers from other workers facing threats to their bargaining power and basic workplace rights, there were important resonances between the baseball strike and other labor conflicts of the period. In particular, the MLBPA's fight to claim a share of cable television revenue echoed similar struggles by entertainment workers in 1980 and 1981. Pay television had been a factor in MLB since the beginning of the expansion era. The owners of the Giants and Dodgers intended to take advantage of the promise of pay television on the West Coast when they moved their franchises from New York after the 1957 season, but a series of legislative and infrastructural roadblocks prevented the new medium from coming online. A small number of Dodgers and Giants games finally appeared on pay TV in the summer of 1964, but California voters approved a ballot measure that November restricting the medium on the grounds that it violated the public trust. By the time the state Supreme Court struck down the measure two years later, the company that had televised the games in 1964 had gone out of business.[39]

Although pay television did not impact the fortunes of the Dodgers and Giants as quickly as team owners Walter O'Malley and Horace Stoneham had hoped, by the mid-1970s the medium was an emerging factor in the business of Major League Baseball. The Cleveland Indians televised selected games via the subscription cable service Home Box Office (HBO) in 1973, and the New York Yankees sold a similar package of games on HBO the following year.[40] In 1977 the U.S. Appeals Court for the District of Columbia struck down Federal Communications Commission "anti-siphoning" regulations that had restricted cable outlets' ability to feature programming—including sports events—that had previously been available on over-the-air channels.[41] This ruling enabled teams to make local pay TV deals more easily, and by the early 1980s several had done so. The industry's television and radio profits continued to rise—they were up 12 percent in 1981 over the previous season—with the majority of the annual gain reflecting revenue from local television agreements negotiated by individual teams.[42]

The growth of pay television did not win universal approval among baseball's owners and officials. Even as increasing numbers of teams looked to pay TV as a way to build more local revenue, some, including commissioner Bowie Kuhn, expressed concern over the detrimental impact the medium might have on the industry. At the start of the cable age, many team owners were concerned that overexposure would limit other revenue streams, echoing the fears that earlier generations of owners had expressed at the rise of radio and then broadcast television. Although by the mid-1970s a consensus was well established that some exposure helped build a team's fan base, and MLB's national TV deals were now the lifeblood of the industry, teams still refrained from televising their entire schedule. For example, at the start of the 1981 season the Dodgers announced a local television slate that included fewer than 60 percent of the team's games. During the height of Fernando-mania, L.A. papers printed angry letters from fans frustrated that they could not watch every pitch thrown by their local star.[43] As the cable industry expanded in the 1980s and 1990s, some teams situated in larger media markets began televising their entire schedules, while others continued to have more limited exposure on—and revenue from—the small screen.[44]

The prospect of pay television in the baseball industry raised concerns in some quarters about the medium's potential impact on MLB's national broadcast package. Throughout the 1970s, as the FCC gradually loosened its regulatory approach to cable, MLB commissioner Bowie Kuhn consistently held that baseball would never move its flagship events—the playoffs, World Series, and All-Star Game—from free television. Since these games were the crown jewels of baseball's national network deal, moving them to cable would significantly reduce the value of the overall package and, as Kuhn put it, "jeopardize our relationships with our broadcast friends."[45] MLB officials did eventually negotiate supplementary agreements to show a limited number of games during the regular season on national cable networks, starting with the USA Network from 1981 to 1983, and later with ESPN.[46]

Looming especially large over the territorial politics of televised baseball in the late 1970s and early 1980s were the so-called superstations. Pioneered by Ted Turner, who purchased the Atlanta Braves to provide content for his own WTCG (later renamed WTBS), superstations were locally operated channels beamed via satellite to cable systems around the country, and were usually included in basic subscription packages. The majority of MLB owners saw superstations as threats to the balance of baseball's national television map, which for years had been structured around collectively agreed-upon territories. Thanks to Turner, by the late 1970s cable subscribers in many MLB markets could watch the Braves more regularly on television than they could their hometown team, jeopardizing the old divisions of broadcasting areas.[47] In 1985, after years of negotiations among the owners, Peter Ueberroth (Kuhn's successor as MLB commissioner) secured agreements from Turner and other owners who televised games via superstations, requiring them to pay extra fees into MLB's general fund.[48]

From the very beginning of baseball's age of free agency Turner harnessed his ambitions for building a cable television empire to his players' star power. In one of several notorious episodes in shameless marketing looked upon disapprovingly by other team owners and league officials, Turner gave Andy Messersmith—whom he had signed to the Braves following the pitcher's successful challenge of baseball's reserve system—number 17, which also happened to be the location of WTCG (and later WTBS) on the television dial. "Super 17, that's Andy," Turner told the press.[49] In early May the team unveiled a new uniform design that featured each player's nickname—rather than their last name—in the space above the number on the back of their jersey. Messersmith wore "Channel" as his nickname, completing his transformation into a human billboard for his boss's television network. The episode brought a quick rebuke from National League president Chub Feeney, and the Braves soon abandoned their nickname jerseys.[50]

Although Turner's decision to link his new free agent star so explicitly with his fledgling superstation amounted to little more than a short-lived spectacle, it demonstrated the essential connection that many team owners saw between individual players and media markets. Even as Turner remained something of an outcast among MLB owners for what they perceived as uncouth behavior, his counterparts followed his lead toward a business model based on pay television. Local and national cable TV arrangements would continue to reflect divergent and at times competing economic interests among MLB executives, but by the 1980s more and more of the owners were beginning to look like television producers.

For their part, leaders of the Major League Baseball Players Association also saw cable as a potentially revolutionary force in the industry, opening up new revenue streams for the owners. The union's reaction to the emergence of cable TV recalled the players' militancy over the expansion of broadcast television revenue in the late 1960s and early 1970s. A decade later, future television revenues remained an important subject of discussion at MLBPA executive board meetings.[51] As team owners profited handsomely from the latest national television deal, signed in 1979, and seemed poised to cash in on the expansion of pay TV in the immediate future, the MLBPA continued to assert the players' collective property rights in televised broadcasts of MLB games. While the issue of free agent compensation was the major point of contention in the 1981 strike, the matter of future television revenues was never far below the surface. In late May, just before the strike deadline, the MLBPA's executive board voted to authorize legal action regarding the unsanctioned broadcasting of players' images.[52] Two weeks after the strike's conclusion, the *New York Times* published paired opinion pieces by Miller and PRC chairman C. Raymond Grebey. Miller emphasized the association's continuing concerns over the growth of cable revenue, signaling that TV would remain a battleground in the immediate future. "Although the Basic Agreement in baseball does not terminate until Dec. 31, 1984," Miller wrote, "the parties to the agreement will face tests of their ability to mutually resolve problems long before then. Dealing with the matter of the separate television rights of owners and players may well be one of such tests. How well that test is met could be a harbinger of the future."[53]

When attempts to engage in new discussions with team owners over television rights proved fruitless, in May 1982 the MLBPA sent letters to several stations advising them that they were televising games without the players' consent. This prompted the owners to file a lawsuit against the MLBPA, to which the union responded with a countersuit. The case wound its way to the U.S. Supreme Court, which upheld a lower court's ruling in favor of the owners in March 1987.[54] Other professional players' associations supported the MLBPA's legal case, reflecting a unified approach to the issue of pay TV. The National Basketball Players Association had filed a similar suit in 1979, effectively using the legal case as negotiating leverage before withdrawing it the following year as part of a collective bargaining agreement with team owners. In 1983 the basketball players signed a pact that secured a 53 percent share of the NBA's gross revenues, including television proceeds. This agreement came less than a year after the National Football League Players Association had failed to win their own demand for a 55 percent share of NFL television revenue.[55] Clearly, baseball players were not the only professional athletes in the United States to see cable television as a central battleground during the 1980s.

In staking claims to emerging sources of media revenue, the athletes were part of an even larger trend among unions of entertainment workers. In 1980, film and television performers, represented by the Screen Actors Guild and the American Federation of Television and Radio Artists, shut down the film and television studios of southern California, striking for a greater share of industry revenue from so-called residuals, which in this period included rebroadcasts of films on TV and sales of home video cassettes. The actors, who won a 4.5 percent share of residuals, were joined on strike by members of the American Federation of Musicians, who made similar demands. Unlike the actors, the musicians failed to win substantial gains in compensation from residuals when they finally settled in January 1981, their strike having been weakened by the fact that the actors had settled and returned to work without them. But the Hollywood strike wave continued later that year, as the Writers Guild of America walked out over residuals, and was nearly joined by the Directors Guild of America, which only avoided escalating the showdown by signing an eleventh-hour agreement.[56] The MLBPA's 1981 strike was thus part of a larger moment of labor upheaval over pay TV's impact on the mass entertainment industries, revealing key similarities between athletes and other culture workers.

Beyond the issue of pay TV, just like the MLBPA, the Hollywood unions drew their strength in large part from star power, the irreplaceability of their marquee performers. In this way, the labor politics of the entertainment industry echoed the broader workplace struggles that would come to define the Reagan era. The president himself saw this connection. On September 3, 1981, Reagan addressed the convention of the United Brotherhood of Carpenters and Joiners in Chicago, offering his administration's most substantive statement on labor policy since the previous month's PATCO firings. Reagan devoted much of the speech to a defense of his actions, arguing that public employees could not be allowed to strike "against the public safety." In a key rhetorical ploy early on in remarks trumpeting his long-standing "relationship with organized labor," Reagan highlighted his own tenure as a member and onetime president of the Screen Actors Guild, and went on to reflect on the place of star power in collective bargaining:

> Now I know that there are some who read of the pay scale for top stars and wonder why a bunch of actors need a union. Well, it's true a handful of superstars have an individual bargaining power based on their box-office rating, but the fact is that taken as a whole the membership of the Screen Actors Guild averages about the same income level as members of the craft unions. As for those in the high brackets let it be understood they used their star status and individual bargaining power to help their lower-paid fellow actors in S.A.G. to achieve gains at the collective bargaining table.[57]

Although Reagan didn't mention baseball players in his speech, by presenting an analysis of star power in one breath while justifying the use of permanent replacement workers to break strikes in the next, the president highlighted the core issues framing the MLBPA's position within the broader politics of work in the early 1980s. In winning and defending the system of free agency over the previous fifteen years, Major League Baseball players had managed to place themselves and their union on the winning side of a replaceability divide that was impacting more and more workplaces and industries. If Reagan's brazen move against PATCO stands as a signal action in the consolidation of neoliberalism, the MLBPA's success in that same moment can be seen as an instance of elite culture workers positioning themselves as free market winners, drawing power from their status as stars.

The 1981 strike marked one of the most critical moments in the history of the Major League Baseball Players Association. The settlement of the strike ensured that the union and the system of free agency it had created would remain fixtures of the industry. Though the owners would continue trying to recapture lost power through collective bargaining and other means (most notably by colluding to refrain from free agent bidding later in the decade), the MLBPA had become one of the strongest organizations in professional sports, and would only increase its influence within the industry in the decades that followed.[58] The 1981 MLB strike, however, formed just one part of the labor upheaval that marked the early years of baseball's age of free agency.

## Strike Two: Power and Autonomy in Mexican Baseball

Fernando Valenzuela grew up dreaming of a career playing professional baseball in Mexico. Like many other young fans he followed the career of Héctor Espino, the great power-hitting first baseman who dominated Mexican professional baseball from the 1960s through the early 1980s.[59] Unlike the top Dominican and Venezuelan players of his generation who became famous MLB players, Espino spent nearly his entire career in his home country. A fiercely independent figure, Espino performed on his own terms, conducting several contract holdouts and twice turning down the opportunity to play in the United States. When asked why, he claimed that as a star in Mexico he commanded a salary that was twice what he could earn as a relative unknown in the United States.[60] As one of the best players in the history of the Liga Mexicana, Espino came to enjoy relative prosperity and autonomy throughout much of his career, but he was a rare exception. Liga Mexicana owners ran their enterprise with a collective iron fist.

In the years after the Liga Mexicana's 1955 accord with Major League Baseball, Mexico City Tigres owner Alejo Peralta emerged as the dominant figure in the business of Mexican baseball.[61] Over the course of his life Peralta became one of Mexico's most powerful executives, enjoying close ties with the Partido Revolucionario Institucional (the nation's long-governing political party) while building the massive Industrias Unidas Sociedad Anónima conglomerate, which at his death in 1997 included over one hundred companies and employed seventeen thousand workers. Peralta started out in electrical parts, and by 1989 his holdings included Iusacell, a major telecommunications company. The centerpiece of the Peralta empire was the sprawling manufacturing zone he created in Pastejé, outside Mexico City. At the time of his death, his family fortune was estimated at $2.5 billion. Along the way he also earned a reputation as a ruthless authoritarian. While serving as the director of the Instituto Politécnico Nacional in the mid-1950s, Peralta called in troops to dispel a student strike. He advised Mexican president Gustavo Díaz Ordaz during the government's murderous response to student protests in October 1968 and continued to justify the massacre in hindsight: "At the moment that these things happen, you feel bitterness; you feel bad that there were so many victims, but over time you understand that this was necessary."[62]

Peralta exerted considerable influence over the direction of Mexican professional baseball. Thanks to the Liga Mexicana's semiautonomous position in the baseball world, Peralta and his fellow team owners were able to do much more to shape the circuit's development than most of their counterparts in other MLB-affiliated minor leagues. Of special significance was the fact that Liga Mexicana team owners retained contractual rights to all Mexican prospects, an autonomy secured in the circuit's 1955 accord with Major League Baseball. Led by Peralta, the owners placed a special focus on developing native talent. As part of this effort, in 1959 he spearheaded an early effort to create a winter "baseball school" in Mexico City in which to train local recruits.[63] While emphasizing a baseball version of "import sub-stitution" by featuring more Mexican players, Peralta and other team own-ers profited by selling players' contracts, both to other Liga Mexicana teams and to foreign clubs. Some even managed to earn extra income by selling the contracts of Cuban players signed in the wake of that country's revolu-tion, as when Peralta shipped pitcher Luis Tiant to the Cleveland Indians in 1961 for $35,000.[64] The business model pushed by Peralta and his colleagues was lucrative, as evidenced by the fact that the league underwent a series of expansions, reaching a peak of twenty teams by the end of the 1970s.[65]

Through the postwar decades Liga Mexicana players mounted periodic attempts to gain more power within their tightly controlled, expanding in-dustry. In the early 1950s Tampico Alijadores player Jesús Valenzuela led an attempt to form a players' association, but owners' threats of reprisals quashed the movement. In 1961 a group of players formed the Mutualidad de Peloteros Profesionales Mexicanos, which met a similar fate.[66] But in April 1980, players' long-held grievances reached a breaking point when league officials fined members of the Puebla Ángeles and suspended the team's manager, Jorge Fitch, after a violent postgame incident in Veracruz. Angered by the manner in which Puebla players had expressed their dis-pleasure for an umpire's ruling, a Veracruz team official had compelled the local police to arrest the entire visiting team. In the midst of the arrest, mul-tiple Puebla players suffered beatings at the hands of the police. Outraged at Liga Mexicana officials' decision to bring sanctions against him and his teammates, Puebla's star infielder Alfonso "Houston" Jiménez joined with other prominent Mexican ballplayers to organize the Asociación Nacional de Beisbolistas (ANABE).[67]

Devoting themselves to mutual protection against the kind of unchecked employer power experienced by the Puebla team, the group moved quickly to formulate collective demands, calling for a health and pension plan, ad-equate meal money for road games, occasional days off (it was not uncom-mon to play eight games each week), and improved working conditions. Additionally, one of the players' chief grievances concerned team owners' ability to trade or sell them without consultation or compensation. Mexi-can labor law had been amended in 1970, prodded by a movement of soc-cer players, to provide some basic rights and protections for professional athletes, including that they be consulted and receive a percentage of the transaction price when their contracts were sold to another team.[68] But Liga Mexicana executives rarely obeyed the poorly enforced law. Although Fernando Valenzuela did receive a reported $20,000 of the $120,000 that his former team earned from the sale of his contract (still less than the 25 percent called for by law), few players were so fortunate.[69]

Within weeks, ANABE's ranks had swelled to such an alarming level that league officials moved to take action against the organization. When Alejo Peralta fired player leader and Mexico City Tigres catcher Vicente Peralta for his union activity on June 30, ANABE members responded by walking out on strike the next day. With dozens of players—including many of the league's top stars—now refusing to play until a fair settlement could be reached, team owners fired all strikers, consolidated the twenty-team league into six clubs made up largely of imported players, and finished the season. Mexican president José López Portillo, under pressure from the country's labor movement, agreed to intervene and brokered a settlement between ANABE and Liga Mexicana owners. In the mid-August accord the owners agreed to many of the players' demands, including recognition of their rights under the 1970 law. Nevertheless, the agreement did not include formal recognition of ANABE as a union, nor did it require teams to bargain collectively with the players. These shortfalls set the stage for further confrontation between ANABE and Liga Mexicana owners in the months ahead.[70]

ANABE also reached an agreement with team owners in the winter Liga Mexicana del Pacífico, and many members, or "Anabistas," participated in the league's 1980–81 season. The culmination of the winter season brought a new struggle, as ANABE joined with players' associations from Venezuela, Puerto Rico, and the Dominican Republic in demanding improved compensation for appearing in the Serie del Caribe, the annual tournament featuring the champions from the top Latin American circuits. Acting jointly through their umbrella organization, the Confederación de Peloteros Profesionales del Caribe (CONPEPROCA), the players also called on teams to reduce their reliance on imported players, and to share a larger percentage of broadcasting revenue.[71] Unwilling to do so, despite attempts by Venezuelan president Luis Herrera Campíns to broker a deal, tournament organizers took the drastic step of calling off the games.[72] In the aftermath of the cancellation, CONPEPROCA issued a statement, signed by representatives of the players' associations from the participating leagues, including ANABE officials, outlining the reasons for their insistence on fairer compensation. Given that the annual tournament was demonstrably profitable, the player leaders argued, they had been justified in fighting to "raise the standard of living of professional ballplayers, who are the show."[73]

As attention shifted to the upcoming summer season, it became clear that the Liga Mexicana's owners were committed to driving ANABE out of existence. Counting three hundred members, the organization pushed for implementation of the previous summer's agreement, plus signing bonuses for all players and an end to the league's ongoing practice of blacklisting. For their part, Peralta and the other owners refused to bargain with ANABE, and pressured individual players to abandon the organization. In late February, with negotiations nonexistent and their members in need of employment, ANABE leaders took a dramatic next step: they announced the establishment of their own league, the Liga Nacional.[74] They issued the "February Declaration," condemning the team owners for their "intransigence" and "willful blindness," and their denial of the notion that "work demands respect for the dignity of those who carry it out." The statement went on to outline the players' vision for the new league—an alternative model of Mexican professional baseball. As they described plans for the Liga Nacional, ANABE leaders noted that they had begun thinking about the possibility of a players' circuit from the very beginning of their movement, even as they held out hope that Liga Mexicana owners would respond fairly to their demands. In comments to the press the players highlighted the fact that they were not conceiving of their circuit as a source of great profit, but rather as a way of serving the larger social good by providing jobs to the athletes and other workers who would bring the Liga Nacional to life.[75]

Over the coming months, ANABE leaders succeeded in building a league of eight teams—a remarkable achievement in light of the long-standing power and influence of figures like Peralta. With many native players joining the new league in the summer of 1981, Liga Mexicana owners were forced to hire more players from other countries, leading ANABE supporters to dub the circuit the "Liga Extranjera" (Foreign League).[76] As they worked to build the Liga Nacional into a viable enterprise, ANABE leaders looked to the broader Mexican labor movement as a critical source of support. For example, during the inaugural 1981 season, two key ANABE leaders and members of the Liga Nacional's Mexico City–based Metropolitanos Rojos, Ramón "Abulon" Hernández and René Chávez, solicited "solidarity contributions" from unions. Their fellow Anabistas in Veracruz secured support from unions in the building and metal trades, as well as from a local public university.[77]

In its early stages the Liga Nacional enjoyed consistent, enthusiastic coverage in leftwing publications like *Unomásuno* and *Proceso*. From the beginning of the ANABE strike and throughout the history of the Liga Nacional, the sporting press constituted a central front in the players' campaign for an increased voice in their industry. Just as a number of influential sportswriters in the United States had sided with the owners during the formation of the MLBPA, many of their Mexican counterparts voiced support for the Liga Mexicana and either criticized or simply ignored the Liga Nacional. The latter response was perhaps the most damaging, as lack of coverage threatened to cut the players and their nascent league off from essential sources of revenue: fans and advertisers. Seeing media as critical to their league's success, ANABE members started their own magazine, titled *El Caballo* (The Horse), a term used in the baseball vernacular to mean an exemplary player. As ANABE's public relations director Candelario Pérez put it, "There aren't any sports publications that really say how athletes live."[78]

The Liga Nacional's first season unfolded alongside other dramatic storylines in the baseball world during the summer of 1981, coinciding with Fernandomania and the long strike in Major League Baseball. For Valenzuela, the strike's interruption of his rookie MLB season provided an opportunity to travel to Mexico for a series of events and publicity opportunities. On June 26 he visited with José López Portillo in Mexico City, presenting the Mexican president with an autographed baseball and mitt.[79] The next day, Valenzuela made a public appearance at the city's Estadio Seguro Social, the home field of the Liga Mexicana's Diablos Rojos. Wearing his Dodgers uniform, he thanked the crowd before showing off his signature windup from the pitcher's mound with a few ceremonial tosses. For ANABE's supporters in the progressive press, such as *Unomásuno*'s Jaime Bravo, the event represented the lowest of publicity stunts by Liga Mexicana team owners, using Valenzuela's star power to draw fans who were otherwise shunning the circuit in favor of the Liga Nacional. Bravo's account of the event, under the headline "Valenzuela, Flor en la Tumba del Beisbol" (Valenzuela, Flower in Baseball's Tomb), reported that the stands were two-thirds empty, and that most of the fans who did show up departed after the Dodger star's brief appearance, choosing not to stick around to see the Diablos Rojos in action.[80] Also commenting on Valenzuela's Mexico City appearances, *Proceso* columnist Francisco Ponce suggested that the pitcher risked being used by Liga Mexicana owners in their battle against the "dissidents" of the Liga Nacional.[81] Other reporters also observed that Valenzuela appeared vulnerable to manipulation during his visit to Mexico City, commenting in particular on the fact that his agent, Antonio DeMarco, seemed to be controlling the pitcher's comments during his brief media appearances.[82]

Even as some came to see Valenzuela as being manipulated to serve others' interests, it was impossible to ignore his status as a national icon. On the day after his controversial appearance at the Estadio Seguro Social, Valenzuela was honored with a festival at Mexico City's Palacio de los Deportes, where he received the keys to the city and the cheers of thirty thousand fans. The free event, aimed in particular at children, featured the requisite appearances by local politicians, as well as a parade of youth baseball teams and star turns by several figures from Mexican popular culture, including soap opera luminaries Angélica María and Christian Bach. The composer Armando Manzanero made an appearance, while Tito Guízar and Valente Pastor performed "El Torito Valenzuela" in the pitcher's honor. The famous actor and comedian Adalberto Martínez, known as "Resortes," performed at the event as well. Referring to one of Martínez's most successful films, *El Beisbolista Fenómeno* (The Phenomenal Baseball Player, 1952), *Unomásuno's* Benito Terrazas noted, "One of them portrayed a phenomenal baseball player and the other is one."[83]

Having risen to the level of pop star, Valenzuela represented a world of possibility unbounded by the power of Liga Mexicana team owners. If the upstart Liga Nacional constituted an alternative, collective model of national professional baseball, Valenzuela embodied transnational star power. Both the new league and the young star held out to Mexican ballplayers the possibility—however uncertain—of a brighter future. Francisco Ponce had captured the resonances between the Liga Nacional and Fernandomania in *Proceso* six weeks earlier, devoting half of his column to each of the year's remarkable baseball stories under the simple headline "Esperanzas" (Hopes).[84]

Liga Nacional leaders and supporters did their best to sustain their portion of Ponce's "hopes" through a vibrant media presence, but they faced an uphill battle. The government-owned IMEVISION television network aired weekend Liga Nacional games in 1982 but soon stopped under pressure from Alejo Peralta.[85] Liga Mexicana owners' influence on the Mexican print and broadcast media, as well as their control over access to major ballparks, particularly in Mexico City, eventually made it impossible for the Liga Nacional to survive. David LaFrance, the author of the most comprehensive English-language study of the Mexican players' movement of the 1980s, has persuasively argued that ANABE and the Liga Nacional were ultimately "casualties of free-market reform."[86] Mexico's debt crisis and structural adjustment of the early 1980s led to a decline in state support, which combined with the erosion of the economic power of the Liga Nacional's supporters and fans to render the league unsustainable.[87]

Though ANABE and the Liga Nacional ultimately failed to last beyond the mid-1980s, for some members the struggle against the Liga Mexicana opened up new opportunities in Major League Baseball. Having been black-listed from participation in the Liga Mexicana, three top Anabistas used what they interpreted as de facto free agency to secure opportunities in the United States. During the winter after the ANABE strike, Ángel Moreno signed a contract to play in 1981 for the Houston Astros' minor league affili-ate in Tucson. By February of that year fellow pitcher Eleno Cuen was work-ing out with the Detroit Tigers, and shortstop Alfonso "Houston" Jiménez was in camp with the Minnesota Twins. Before the season began, however, the players received word from their respective MLB teams that they were ineligible, owing to their lack of status with the Liga Mexicana. Thanks to the agreements between MLB and Liga Mexicana officials over the mutual respect of contracts and territory dating back to the 1950s, the players found themselves faced with a challenging route to free agency.[88]

Cuen, Moreno, and Jiménez, like many other of Mexico's top professional baseball players, had grown accustomed to trying out for U.S. teams only to have their career ambitions blocked by Liga Mexicana owners, who in-variably demanded high prices for the top talent under their contractual control. Returning to Mexico City after being shut out of Twins camp, Ji-ménez told *Unomásuno* that this was his fifth such experience: "Ever since I became a professional I have belonged to the Ángeles de Puebla. Always at the end of the season they send me to major league spring training and every time I have had the opportunity to be signed. And every time [Ánge-les owner] Jaime Pérez Avella intervenes and I have to return to Mexico."[89] The same team owner who had sold Fernando Valenzuela to the Dodgers for $120,000 had repeatedly prevented Jiménez from being able to pursue a career in Major League Baseball.

Empowered by the union movement they had helped to build, the three players joined together to file grievances through official government chan-nels, bringing their cases to the Procuraduría Federal de la Defensa del Tra-bajo (Federal Labor Legal Defense Office).[90] On March 30, 1981, the players were declared free agents and thus allowed to entertain contract offers from MLB clubs. Using his new free agent status, Eleno Cuen signed a minor league contract with the Pittsburgh Pirates organization. Although Cuen never made it to MLB (returning to Mexico to pitch in the Liga Nacional in 1983), both Ángel Moreno and Houston Jiménez did.[91] Each attracted immediate interest from the Chicago White Sox, but they balked at team official David Dombrowski's offer of tryouts in the United States without guaranteed contracts.

Alfonso "Houston" Jiménez as a member of the Ángeles de
Puebla of the Liga Mexicana in 1980, soon before the ANABE
strike began. (*Courtesy Salón de la Fama del Béisbol Profesional
de México*)

Rejecting the White Sox offer, the two players sought help landing with
MLB organizations from Richie Lee, who was the agent for Detroit Tigers
reliever Aurelio López. As they awaited offers from MLB clubs, Moreno and
Jiménez joined teams in the Liga Nacional for its first season, attempting
to help build the league into a successful alternative to Peralta's Liga Mexi-
cana.[92] In mid-July, California Angels representative Preston Gomez signed
Moreno, proclaiming that he had the potential to be the next Fernando
Valenzuela.[93] According to Gomez, California had competition—the White

Sox had apparently sent manager Tony LaRussa and general manager Roland Hemond to Mexico to further evaluate the pitcher, taking advantage of the layoff during the MLB strike.[94] Moreno pitched well in the minor leagues and earned a promotion to the majors by mid-August. ANABE's supporters saw his call-up as an important development for the cause of ballplayers on both sides of the border. "In Ángel Moreno," the sports editors of *Unomásuno* wrote, "the U.S. unionists will have a faithful representative from the most honorable workers' organization in Mexico: ANABE."[95]

Houston Jiménez suffered an injury in the first half of the 1981 Liga Nacional season, a development that may have prevented his attracting as much MLB interest as Ángel Moreno. He worked out with the Twins again in 1982, but Liga Mexicana officials intervened once more, despite the previous spring's ruling.[96] He returned in 1983 and at long last made his MLB debut on June 13 of that year. Jiménez played parts of four seasons in the majors: with the Twins in 1983 and 1984, and briefly with the Pirates in 1987 and the Indians in 1988. His best season was 1984, when he played in 108 games with a Minnesota team that gave the Kansas City Royals a run for their money chasing the American League's Western Division championship.

After being released from Major League Baseball during spring training in 1989, Jiménez faced the challenge of continuing his career while being blacklisted from the Liga Mexicana for his role with ANABE. He played one season of professional ball in Italy before returning to Mexico. There Jiménez played in a semi-pro league until he decided to seek a reconciliation with Liga Mexicana owners through a meeting with Roberto Mansur, the owner of the Mexico City Diablos Rojos. As a result of the meeting, in which both sides agreed not to rehash the events of the 1980s in public, Jiménez was invited back into the Liga Mexicana, where he played for three more years. After his playing career ended, he went on to manage and coach in both Mexico and the United States.

When asked in 2007 about whether it had been difficult to make a commitment not to discuss his years with ANABE and the Liga Nacional, Jiménez quickly replied: "No. Not really. Because I love the game . . . and I'm still in the game because of my passion [for it]." His story demonstrates more than a single player's love for the game, however. It also highlights the fact that limits to players' mobility are fundamental elements of the baseball industry in the age of free agency. For Jiménez, persevering in the face of such limits became one of the great accomplishments of an extraordinary twenty-six year professional career: "I made it to the big leagues the hard way. The very hard way."[97]

Although the Major League Baseball Players Association secured a winning combination of free agency for veteran players and excellent minimum compensation levels for its entire membership, these benefits did not
extend to the overwhelming majority of the world's professional ballplayers. On the contrary, as the economic stakes of professional baseball were
raised in the wake of MLB free agency, team owners everywhere moved
to ratchet up their control over the thousands of players who did not enjoy the protection of collective bargaining and union membership. Figures
like Jiménez and Moreno, who in the early 1980s managed to fight their
way to measures of professional autonomy and mobility, were exceptions to
the baseball world's emerging labor regime. Their career trajectories were
made possible by a remarkable history of collective struggle and shared
sacrifice. The stories of these players and of the thousands of others who
have struggled to make a living under the decidedly constricting terms of
employment created and enforced by powerful team owners are as central
to the history of free agency as are those of stars like Reggie Jackson and
Fernando Valenzuela.

## Mexican Baseball after ANABE

Between the challenge from a rival league and the concurrent national economic crisis, the Liga Mexicana struggled throughout the 1980s and beyond. The circuit would never again reach its size of the late 1970s, con-
tracting to sixteen teams in the wake of the strike while also reducing its
once extensive minor league structure. In place of a traditional system of
developmental leagues, Alejo Peralta revived and retooled one of his earlier
institutional innovations and established a new school—this time labeled a
"baseball academy"—as a talent factory for young prospects, located adjacent to his other manufacturing plants outside Mexico City.[98] The formation of the academy was widely understood as a response to the ANABE
movement: if players were cultivated more carefully, they would be less
likely to rebel. Following the devaluation of the peso in 1982, Peralta came
to see the academy as essential to sustaining national professional baseball.
In 1983 he portrayed his academy as key to once again "Mexicanizing" the
sport, providing enough trained professional ballplayers to field competitive teams when the nation's currency crisis made it exceedingly difficult to
hire foreign athletes. Along with furnishing a cost-effective means of training new generations of ballplayers for the Liga Mexicana, the academy had

another ambition: to develop young prospects who could be sold directly to MLB teams.[99]

The baseball academy became one of the sport's most important institutional forms in the age of free agency. At the same time that Peralta was developing his academy, MLB teams were beginning to finance their own camps elsewhere. With Liga Mexicana owners continuing to retain contractual control over all native talent, MLB teams scouted much more heavily in the Dominican Republic and Venezuela, where they could sign many young players for the cost of a single highly touted Mexican prospect.[100] While the 1980s and 1990s saw a significant increase in the number of Mexican players on major league rosters, including a growing number of full-fledged stars such as Colorado Rockies slugger Vinny Castilla, far more players came from Latin American countries in which MLB teams could dictate contractual terms.[101]

At the same time, MLB broadcasting, marketing, and merchandising figured more prominently in Mexico than ever before. The first signs of this shift were visible in the early days of Fernandomania, as the popularity of broadcasts of Valenzuela's Dodgers eroded live attendance at both Liga Mexicana and Liga Nacional games.[102] The early 1990s saw MLB establish new partnerships with Mexican corporate sponsors. In 1992, Fomento Económico Mexicano, Mexico's largest beverage company, sponsored an exhibition game between the Minnesota Twins and the Atlanta Braves.[103] Four years later the San Diego Padres and New York Mets played the first official MLB contest in Mexico, with Fernando Valenzuela, nearing the end of his major league career, earning the victory for San Diego. In 1999 Mexico hosted the official season opener, as Vinny Castilla and his Colorado Rockies took on the Padres in front of a massive global television audience. Significantly, all three of these games took place in the northern city of Monterrey. A welcoming home to transnational corporations seeking territory in Mexico, Monterrey formed the central site for MLB's marketing efforts in the country. In the first years of the new century there was even brief speculation that an MLB team might move to the city.[104] In another significant development in the reconfiguration of Mexican baseball, the Liga Mexicana established a new academy in El Carmen, on Monterrey's outskirts, replacing Alejo Peralta's original facility. The academy hosted regular visits from MLB scouts, underscoring the growing importance of export-oriented talent development to the league's business model at the end of the twentieth century.[105]

Although the late-century developments in Monterrey signaled MLB's expanding role as a transnational corporate actor and the city's own emergence as a key location in post-NAFTA neoliberal globalization, the implications for the fate of Mexican baseball were more complicated. While Monterrey had for decades been a prominent baseball city (as home to both the country's Hall of Fame—the Salón de la Fama del Béisbol Profesional de México—and Héctor Espino's longtime team, the Sultanes), it had long been part of a larger national constellation that also included the nation's capital. But while Monterrey was emerging as an increasingly important transnational baseball venue, the sport was becoming less and less of a presence in Mexico City. As league attendance fell off significantly through the 1980s and 1990s, Peralta's Mexico City Tigres moved to Puebla, more than sixty miles from the capital. The shifting geography of franchises, combined with the sport's lack of consistent media coverage, signaled an uncertain future for the Liga Mexicana, and for baseball's long-term popularity nationwide.[106] Although the Liga Mexicana del Pacífico remains a top winter circuit, sending its annual champion to the Serie del Caribe to compete against representatives from Puerto Rico, Venezuela, and the Dominican Republic, the league is very much a regional enterprise, with its teams representing only eight cities in the northern states of Sonora, Sinaloa, and Baja California.

While much of Mexican professional baseball has become more precariously situated within the MLB-dominated baseball world of the early twenty-first century, one figure has remained constant: Fernando Valenzuela. Though "El Toro" retired from Major League Baseball in 1997, he continued to pitch professionally in Mexico for another decade, starring in the Liga Mexicana del Pacífico in the months when he wasn't working as a color commentator on the Dodgers' Spanish-language radio broadcasts alongside Jaime Jarrín. His statue stands outside the Salón de la Fama in Monterrey, alongside memorials to Héctor Espino and Beto (better known in the States as Bobby) Ávila, and across a small brick patio from tributes to Cy Young, Babe Ruth, and Ty Cobb. Valenzuela's status as a national athletic hero in Mexico reflects the enduring impact of his explosion onto center stage in 1981 as a player who embodied his sport's most captivating promises of mobility and acclaim. The subsequent history of Major League Baseball in the age of free agency, with its labor economy of transnational star power, would continue to build on the model of Fernandomania. Like his statue in Monterrey, however, Valenzuela's career stands apart from the experience of most professional ballplayers in the age of free agency.

# 4

# On the Borders of Free Agency

## Dominican Baseball and the Rise of the Academies

O NE MARKER OF Fernando Valenzuela's considerable cultural impact
is the symbolic position he occupies in one of Hollywood's most celebrated baseball films—*Bull Durham* (1988). In a pivotal scene, Annie Savoy (played by Susan Sarandon) refers to Valenzuela's unmistakable windup
while offering pitching advice to Ebby Calvin "Nuke" LaLoosh (played by
Tim Robbins), a minor league prospect with "a million-dollar arm and a
five-cent head," whose unfortunate tendency to think too much has led to
a losing record.

*Savoy:* Now, I want you to breathe through your eyelids.

*LaLoosh:* My eyelids?

*Savoy:* Yeah—like the lava lizards of the Galapagos Islands. You see,
there are some lizards there that have a parietal eye behind their heads
so they can see backwards. Haven't you ever noticed how Fernando
Valenzuela—he just doesn't even look when he pitches? He's a Mayan
Indian. Or an Aztec. I forget which one—I get 'em confused.

*LaLoosh:* So do I.

These memorable words of wisdom (along with Savoy's further suggestion that LaLoosh rechannel his boundless sexual energy into his pitching)
prove so helpful to the young fireballer that by the end of the film he earns a
call-up to the big leagues.[1] In this pivotal if fleeting reference, *Bull Durham*
frames Fernando Valenzuela's remarkable success during the 1980s as a case

of mystical, innate power of body over mind. The characters' expressions of ethnic ignorance are especially significant: the specifics of Valenzuela's identity are dismissed as irrelevant to the more central rhetorical concern of establishing him as an exotic foil for LaLoosh.

Figuring Valenzuela as a magical other with uncanny athletic powers, *Bull Durham* joined a long tradition of representation stretching back to baseball's emergence within the cultural logics of nineteenth-century nationalism and imperialism. The 1980s, however, saw an explosion of racialized portrayals of Latino ballplayers, such as Pedro Cerrano, the caricatured Cuban slugger in the comedy *Major League* (1989), who prepares for games by performing such stock "voodoo" rituals as pouring ceremonial shots of rum at an altar in his locker.[2] The proliferation of this brand of popular representation coincided with a steady increase in the number of MLB players from Latin American countries. And while cohorts of Mexican, Venezuelan, and Cuban athletes certainly figured prominently during this period, the transnational transformation of Major League Baseball in the 1980s was defined more than anything else by the growing numbers of players from one small Caribbean nation: the Dominican Republic.

Seeking cheaper and more flexible models of talent development, MLB teams increasingly turned to the Dominican Republic, and to the system of "baseball academies" that had begun to take shape there by the early 1980s. The Dominican academies, where teams could train young players in facilities they controlled and monitored, rather than relying on school- or corporate-sponsored amateur leagues, represented one of the distinctive territorial developments of the baseball world in the final decades of the twentieth century.

Local scouts began to lay the groundwork for the trend in the 1970s, seeking competitive advantage over their contemporaries in finding top prospects. By the 1990s several MLB teams were running full-scale Dominican operations, often including dorms, dining areas, and classrooms in addition to fields, batting cages, and other basic baseball training facilities. The low cost of signing Dominican recruits easily justified the expenditure of capital on such facilities. For example, the Texas Rangers signed Sammy Sosa in 1986 for $3,500. By contrast, that same year the team's first pick in the annual amateur draft—pitcher Kevin Brown, who had been a star at Georgia Tech—secured a bonus of $174,500.[3] Both players went on to have very successful MLB careers (though, unfortunately for Texas fans, they enjoyed their most productive seasons in other uniforms). The fact that the Rangers could acquire Sosa for 2 percent of what top draft picks like Brown commanded is evidence of the powerful incentives MLB teams had to expand their Dominican operations.

Academies have by no means been exclusive to the Dominican Republic, as the history of the Liga Mexicana's facilities in recent decades demonstrates. The Dominican academy system, however, became unique in its size and impact. By the turn of the twenty-first century nearly every MLB team owned or contracted with a Dominican academy, and all had employed players developed within the system. Whereas Liga Mexicana team owners retained contractual rights to all prospects, scouts operating in the Dominican Republic faced no barrier to offering contracts to eligible prospects other than competition from representatives of other teams. This free rein for scouts, combined with baseball's strong infrastructure in the country (thanks to a history of organized play there dating back to the nineteenth century), created the conditions for the academy system's rapid development.

The growing cohort of Dominican major leaguers became a subject of widespread interest throughout the baseball world by the early 1980s, as the Caribbean nation achieved popular acclaim as a bottomless source of talented young ballplayers. The commissioner of Major League Baseball found occasion to comment on the Dominican Republic's expanding influence within the sport in 1983, in remarks at the Hall of Fame ceremony honoring Juan Marichal, one of the stars of the first generation of Dominican major leaguers. "I doubt that any country in the world has produced as many ballplayers per capita," Bowie Kuhn commented to the crowd assembled in Cooperstown to honor the great right-hander, the first player from his country to receive MLB's highest honor.[4] Commissioner Kuhn had not needed to look far to find evidence for his assessment: thirty-seven Dominican athletes appeared in major league games that summer, more than from any country other than the United States. That figure more than tripled the number of Dominican players in Major League Baseball twenty years earlier, when Marichal was approaching the prime of his career. And by 1983 a clear trend was developing, as increasing numbers of Dominican players appeared in MLB games every year. Major league rosters in 1989 featured over fifty Dominicans, and by the turn of the twenty-first century, the annual figure was over one hundred and growing.[5] As popular depictions—from daily sports pages to works of fiction—made clear, however, Dominican major leaguers remained marked as "others."

W. P. Kinsella's 1984 short story "The Battery," inspired in part by newspaper coverage of Marichal's entry into Cooperstown, exemplifies the symbolic "othering" of Dominican athletes during the age of free agency.[6] "The Battery" centers on a uniquely gifted pair of twins, Esteban and Julio Cortizar, who emerge from their mother's womb equipped with baseball mitts and endowed with supernatural talents as a pitcher-and-catcher duo. Esteban becomes a star MLB pitcher and Dominican national hero, honored as Great Knight Commander (among other titles) on the occasion of his induction into the Hall of Fame. The story culminates in the moment of the Cooperstown ceremony, which is marked by the simultaneous birth on the outskirts of Santo Domingo of the pitcher's four children (by four different women), prophesied to constitute "the greatest infield in all the history of baseball."[7]

Beginning with the success of his 1982 novel *Shoeless Joe*, Kinsella had come to occupy a privileged position among baseball's storytellers. For many readers and critics, the Canadian writer's tales of long-dead ballplayers who come back to life, romantic fans who replace artificial grass with the real thing during MLB work stoppages, and games that manage to pause time and stretch on forever served to liberate the magic and beauty suppressed in baseball's modern corporate form. Kinsella's place as one of the sport's major voices was cemented with the success of the 1989 film *Field of Dreams*, which brought the author's blend of mystical nostalgia to an even wider audience.[8] Based on *Shoeless Joe*, the film stars Kevin Costner as Ray Kinsella, a onetime hippie turned Iowa corn farmer who plows under several acres of crop to create a magical baseball diamond, where "Shoeless" Joe Jackson and his fellow "Black Sox" of 1919, along with the protagonist's deceased estranged father, come back to life to play the game they all once loved. Thanks to *Shoeless Joe* and its adaptation in *Field of Dreams*, Kinsella's writing became most closely associated with the midwestern United States (especially Iowa), but a significant portion of his baseball fiction is set in the Caribbean, beginning with "The Battery."[9]

Like *Bull Durham* and *Major League*, "The Battery" portrays Latin American ballplayers as absurdly magical figures, possessing powers and identities fundamentally different from athletes who convene on other, more iconic fields of dreams. It is especially worth noting the ways in which the story's magic and exoticism center on reproduction and birth, from the image of the Cortizar brothers springing from the womb with baseball gloves in hand to the simultaneous arrival of Esteban's multiple baseball-playing children. Reflecting an era in which fans of Major League Baseball encountered the Dominican Republic as the "land of shortstops," Kinsella's story trades in stereotyped territorial notions of boundless, natural talent.[10] Kinsella would later describe "The Battery" as his most intentional evocation of the "magical realism" style associated with the likes of Colombian novelist Gabriel García Márquez, thus suggesting a certain symmetry between his own mining of Latin American culture and the scouting practices of the sport figured in his fiction.[11] Whether seen as an appropriation of Latin American literary form or as an example of what Frances Aparicio and Susana Chávez-Silverman have called "tropicalization," Kinsella's story serves to construct the Dominican Republic as a site of innate difference, and to place the nation's ballplayers within a separate symbolic space from that of the teammates and competitors they encounter in Major League Baseball.[12]

Kinsella's narrative thus resonates with the larger story of the Dominican Republic's place in Major League Baseball's organization of work and territory. The history of the academy system is defined by the categorical differentiation of Dominican athletes from their contemporaries. That is, teams created the academies in order to scout and train young prospects under terms and conditions distinct from those at work in player development practices in the United States. Team executives' ability to fashion advantageous conditions of labor recruitment by exploiting transnational markets reveals a key point of contact between the history of free agency and the larger history of neoliberalism. The academies developed in the context of the Dominican Republic's neoliberal transformation, marked by the rise of a new export-based economy, centered in particular in tourist enclaves and free trade zones.[13] As the academy system incorporated and transformed older institutions of Dominican baseball, it came to look more and more like MLB's version of neoliberal export processing.

In order to place the developments of the academy era in their proper context and gauge their impact, it is important to examine the power struggles that shaped Dominican professional baseball in the preceding decades. From the founding of the Liga Dominicana de Béisbol Profesional (LIDOM) in 1951 through the 1970s, Dominican players worked hard to establish and defend national baseball institutions, efforts that sometimes brought tense confrontations with MLB interests. Investment in the academy system transformed the political economy of Dominican baseball. By the 1980s new forms of territorial power (marked by MLB teams' expansive operations) and resulting redefinitions of local agency (encountered and enacted by those who trained there) had begun to redefine Dominican baseball and its place in the sport's larger transnational configuration. The history of the Dominican academy system, one of the industry's principle developments in the wake of MLB free agency, demonstrates that the modern baseball world has been defined as much by the practices of enclosure as by the promises of mobility.

## Constructing Dominican Professional Baseball

For much of the twentieth century, amateur and semipro leagues represented the best of Dominican baseball. Throughout this history the nation's sugar refineries, or *ingenios,* were among the most important institutions in Dominican sport. Company teams, such as those in the cane-rich areas around the sugar industry's major port city, San Pedro de Macorís, featured many of the nation's elite ballplayers, and attracted large crowds to their games. Although many players on *ingenio*-sponsored teams were drawn from the refinery's regular workforce, some top players were specially recruited for their skills on the diamond.

Along with the sugar refineries, other businesses sponsored teams, including the Manzanillo-based Grenada Company, the Dominican arm of United Fruit. Juan Marichal, who grew up in nearby Laguna Verde, was recruited to play for Grenada in 1956, earning a weekly salary of $18. "They put me and other players on the payroll just to play baseball," Marichal recalls. "They paid us pretty well, but we made more money when they had a shipment of bananas going out of a port city and the company sent us over there. . . . We were the inspectors, which was the easy work, and we didn't know anything about bananas. . . . They did it because they liked us as baseball players and wanted to keep us happy and playing for the team."[14]

As with every element of life under the dictatorship of Rafael Leonidas Trujillo, the state was deeply involved in the operation of Dominican baseball. The nation's top amateur team was sponsored by the air force, commanded by Ramfis Trujillo, the dictator's son. Aviación, as the team was called, played against the best Dominican clubs and also participated in elite international competitions. Top players like Juan Marichal were recruited after establishing themselves with other teams. As Marichal recalled years later, starring in international amateur competition had been his greatest athletic ambition from an early age: "I used to tell my mother, 'I want to be a baseball player to represent my country.' She'd say, 'You don't make a living playing baseball.' This is what she used to tell me. And I'd say, 'Well, you are going to be really proud when you hear my name on the radio, playing for the Dominican team.'"[15] Marichal's dream came true in 1956, though it arrived in the form of a military induction notice. One day after pitching the Granada club to victory over Aviación, he received a visit from an air force lieutenant, bringing what the eighteen-year-old pitcher understood as an "order from God."[16] Called up to the armed forces for his brilliant athletic talent, Marichal pitched as a member of Aviación for fourteen months, traveling throughout the Caribbean.

In the years when Marichal was growing up, a movement emerged within Dominican baseball circles to create a national professional league. An earlier pro circuit had collapsed in bankruptcy after the legendary 1937 season, when the nation's dictator himself signed international stars such as the African American greats Satchel Paige and Josh Gibson to play for his Ciudad Trujillo Dragones.[17] For many players and observers, the lack of a national professional league was a major impediment to a robust baseball culture, especially in light of the success of pro circuits elsewhere in the region.[18] One of the most important institutions in the push to establish a professional league was a new national ballplayers' association, the Federación Dominicana de Peloteros Profesionales (FENAPEPRO). Founded in December 1950 by Enrique Lantigua, Horacio Martínez, and other top athletes, FENAPEPRO helped rally support for what would eventually become one of the baseball world's best professional circuits. Central to FENAPEPRO's early mission, and to the revival of national professional baseball, was organizing the return of Dominicans who had been playing for pay elsewhere in the Caribbean. Many of these players embraced the chance to return to their home country to join the Liga Dominicana de Béisbol Profesional.[19]

LIDOM's 1955 affiliation with MLB marked a turning point in Dominican baseball. Moving to a winter schedule, LIDOM became a key circuit in the new configuration of Caribbean professional ball in the era of expansion and integration. Through "working agreement" relationships, Dominican teams began to share scouting resources and access to top local players with MLB clubs. For example, a working agreement with LIDOM's Escogido Leones allowed the New York (soon to be San Francisco) Giants to sign Juan Marichal in 1957, after the pitcher had turned heads with Aviación. FENAPEPRO founder Horacio Martínez, now working as a coach with Escogido, evaluated a number of Dominican players in this period— including Marichal—as a "bird dog" for Giants scout Alejandro "Alex" Pompez.[20] Dominican players of Marichal's generation often performed nearly every month out of the year, fulfilling professional obligations to both winter and summer circuits that distinguished them from most of their MLB contemporaries.

The pressure that stars like Marichal felt to suit up for their LIDOM teams during the MLB off-season was one of the ways in which informal nationalisms came to define Dominican professional baseball in the late 1950s and 1960s. Formal expressions of nationalism, through the symbolic presence and material intervention of the Dominican state, also played a prominent role in this period. Throughout the first decade of the new league, the circuit was closely linked to the figure of Rafael Trujillo. Although his son Ramfis was much more closely involved in the sport, the dictator himself would regularly appear—either in person or in name—at ceremonial occasions such as opening day.[21] These events paralleled similar practices in Nicaragua, where the Somoza regime was an ever-present force in national professional baseball.

To the extent that authoritarian regimes supported stable arrangements, MLB executives—like U.S. government officials—were generally quite willing to have them as their partners. But as a tide of revolutionary and antiauthoritarian politics took shape, baseball officials in the United States viewed their relationships with Latin American leagues with increasing concern. By 1960, MLB teams had begun to see the instability of the Trujillo regime as a threat to their partnership with Dominican baseball interests. In the wake of the Cuban Revolution, and with the Organization of American States imposing sanctions against the Trujillo regime, MLB officials expressed apprehension about the safety of "imported" players. As Clifford Kachline reported in the *Sporting News* (in a piece subsequently translated and reprinted in the Dominican daily *El Caribe*), National Association president George Trautman requested "a guarantee that loop officials would take full responsibility for the well-being of U.S. players while in the Dominican" during the 1960–61 winter season.[22] LIDOM president Hipólito Herrera Billini responded by announcing plans to operate the league without imported players, in a spirit of "dignity, patriotism and loyalty to . . . Generalísimo Trujillo."[23]

Billini's comments reflected the nature of public culture under the dictatorship. In what the historian Lauren Derby has termed "a political economy of discourse," praising Trujillo became essential to securing legitimacy in the eyes of the Dominican state.[24] The nationalist symbolism that surrounded Dominican baseball in the final stages of the Trujillo regime took shape alongside other expressions of national pride. In an interview in November 1960 with sports columnist Arturo Industrioso, Horacio Martínez, who had helped create LIDOM a decade earlier as a founding member of FENAPEPRO, proclaimed that the all-native season was "of great im-

Dominican winter baseball at Estadio Trujillo (later renamed Estadio Quisqueya), December 1959. (*Hank Walker/Time & Life Pictures/Getty Images*)

portance for Dominican baseball," representing a valuable opportunity to showcase the depth of the nation's baseball talent.[25] The idea that the focus of the nation's signature professional league should be to feature native stars would continue to motivate many within Dominican baseball circles over the coming decades.

After Trujillo's assassination in May 1961, the prospects for professional baseball's survival in the Dominican Republic became uncertain. The 1961–62 winter season was forced to end prematurely, and the following season was canceled entirely as a result of the ongoing political turmoil. Without LIDOM in operation, many Dominican athletes sought opportunities in other Caribbean winter leagues.[26] In addition, a number of top players participated in local exhibition games, placing those with MLB affiliations in conflict with the commissioner's office for violating contractual rules regarding unsanctioned, "outlaw" competition. In November 1962 the Dominican government sponsored three exhibitions, pitting a team of local players against a Cuban club. Felipe Rojas Alou, one of the Dominican stars recruited to participate, explains in his autobiography: "Because of the political unrest in my land, the government felt that it had to try something to calm down the people." According to Alou, when MLB commissioner Ford Frick got word of the planned games, he made it known that any MLB players found participating would be fined. Dominican president Rafael Filiberto Bonnelly intervened, proclaiming to concerned players (as Alou describes it), "I am the president . . . and I say that it is all right to play." The games went forward as planned, drawing large crowds.[27]

In the wake of the exhibitions, commissioner Frick followed through on his threat, issuing fines to Alou, Marichal, and other MLB-affiliated participants. A standoff ensued, with the athletes refusing on principle to accept punishment for performing in such an important national cultural event. According to Alou, who became the most outspoken player in the dispute with the commissioner, Frick "had no concept of the political consequences of the three-game series, nor did he have any idea that once the games had been set up there was no way the Dominican people would have permitted big leaguers from their country not to compete."[28] Faced with a challenge to his authority, Frick further escalated the confrontation, threatening banishment. "If Alou doesn't care to pay the fine," the commissioner announced, "he will not play ball in this country."[29]

Members of the U.S. sporting press lined up in support of Frick's position, with some invoking racialized stereotypes in their reporting. Dismissively characterizing the protest as a "rhumba," Joe King of the *Sporting News* described Alou as having "his Latin blood fired" over the matter.[30] The *Sporting News* also published an editorial in support of the commissioner's actions, suggesting that the Dominican exhibitions represented a self-serving distraction from the primary obligations of a big league ballplayer:

> Ford Frick's crackdown on wildcat Latin-American exhibitions is a warning to players that major league baseball is their primary business, with a paramount interest in their services. . . . No other business anywhere would allow its employees the freedom to disperse their efforts so widely. At times there is no dignity whatever, but only a seeming cynicism, in the rat-race by some big leaguers for an extra buck. . . . The Players' Association would do well to support Frick by setting up a standard of ethics to guide its membership in enterprises that are not connected with the business of playing baseball, but which could reflect on it.[31]

The editorial's invocation of the MLBPA was telling. In 1963 the association lacked much power or autonomy, and the players' adviser, Judge Robert C. Cannon, did not get involved in the dispute.[32] Without the support of the

MLBPA, and facing a threat to his livelihood, Alou ultimately paid the fine and moved on. The larger dynamic on display in the confrontation, however, remained, with Alou and other players working to sustain Dominican national baseball despite U.S. baseball interests' frequent refusal to recognize the legitimacy of such labors.[33]

LIDOM resumed play in the winter of 1963, but larger events continued to threaten the league's survival. In the wake of the U.S. invasion of the Dominican Republic in 1965, FENAPEPRO leaders organized a makeshift three-team winter season. A number of players pursued opportunities elsewhere, prompting Marichal, Alou, and their fellow leaders of FENAPEPRO to voice protest about other Caribbean circuits' poaching of fellow Dominican players.[34] Upon the completion of the other winter leagues' seasons, FENAPEPRO officials could not agree whether or not to permit returning athletes to perform in what was left of their own ad hoc schedule. When FENAPEPRO's leadership elected to allow their fellow Dominican players to join them for the remaining games, Alou registered his dissent by sitting out for the rest of the season.[35] Even with these bitter internal conflicts, the 1965–66 player-organized league demonstrated the commitment that leading Dominican athletes shared in the project of sustaining national professional baseball in the midst of significant uncertainty about the future of the country itself.

With their unparalleled star power and their enduring association with Dominican pride, ballplayers represented key national symbols in the chaotic post-Trujillo period. Politicians aspiring to their own measures of adoration and loyalty did not miss the chance to invoke Dominican major leaguers in campaign speeches and advertisements. Joaquín Balaguer, the former Trujillo protégé who wielded considerable power of his own during three separate stints as president (1960–1962, 1966–1978, 1986–1996), brazenly referred to himself as "the Marichal of the Palace" on political posters in early 1966, hoping to claim as his own the pitcher's level of national support. "A group of his people came to see me in San Francisco when he was running for president," Marichal recalls. "They wanted me to say something like, 'Let's vote for a revolution with no blood and death.' They were saying we should have a peaceful revolution. I did speak for him and he used my name." After his playing career was over, Marichal agreed to serve in a district-level post for Balaguer's ruling political party.[36]

Politicians' attempts to appropriate ballplayers' star power for their own gain represented just one element of the collective construction of athletes as figures for the Dominican nation. In the late 1960s, as the battle for free agency was heating up, Dominican stars, like other top major leaguers, engaged in increasingly bold salary standoffs with their employers. For Dominican writers and fans, these occasional, individual labor disputes often took on larger meanings, tied to the broader political economy of the region. "People from the United States don't always have the last word," Ramón A. Reyes proclaimed in the weekly newsmagazine ¡Ahora! in the spring of 1967, describing Marichal's success in winning a substantial raise through a recent contract holdout. "Traditionally the United States has treated Latin American countries as sources of raw materials. They set the prices for their purchase of sugar, coffee, cocoa, tobacco, cotton, copper, and other products that Latin Americans produce. . . . With Marichal, on the contrary, our neighbors have had to sit at the bargaining table because Juan said NO to what they offered, telling them what his 'merchandise' costs."[37] Reyes's appeal to the language of commodification resonates with other interpretations of Major League Baseball's labor relations in the late 1960s. While Curt Flood would later frame his own struggle within the larger context of racialized exploitation within the United States, commentators like Reyes saw Dominican athletes' transnational performances—both on the field and at the bargaining table—as confronting a deeper hemispheric history of resource extraction and market manipulation.

Contestation over LIDOM's status and identity was a defining feature of the circuit, like other MLB-affiliated winter leagues. What local interests treated as a national "major" league was, in the eyes of MLB executives, a "minor" developmental enterprise. Top Dominican athletes were often caught in the middle of this struggle, torn between the competing claims of LIDOM fans, who wanted to see local heroes perform, and MLB teams, who wanted to minimize the risk of off-season injury to valuable established players. By the early 1970s, some Dominican major leaguers faced accusations in the Dominican press of waning commitments to national baseball.

More than anyone else, Juan Marichal became subject to such criticism, so much so that in a tribute article on the occasion of the pitcher's 1975 retirement from Major League Baseball, sportswriter Roosevelt Comarazamy felt compelled to defend the pitcher's choice to rest during previous winters and to debunk the related rumor that Marichal had planned to renounce his national identity to become a U.S. citizen.[38] The controversies over Marichal's perceived abandonment of LIDOM and its Dominican fans were microcosms of the larger cultural politics that structured the winter league's position in the baseball world. Like Marichal himself, who had helped nur-

Dominican star Juan Marichal at work with the San Francisco Giants at Candlestick Park in 1960, his first season in Major League Baseball. (*Diamond Images/Getty Images*)

ture the institutions of Dominican professional baseball throughout his rise to athletic fame, critics of stars' winter playing schedules were deeply invested in baseball's endurance as a national sport.

Even as they struggled to negotiate the grueling schedule that their dual citizenship in the baseball world demanded, Dominican athletes continued to fight for a collective vision of national professional baseball. In 1970 FENAPEPRO members took militant action to insist that LIDOM serve the interests of Dominican players, beginning with a symbolic fifteen-minute strike on the first day of the season.[39] In addition to calling for increases in minimum salary and players' share of league revenue, they objected to the number of non-Dominican athletes participating in the league. The fact that the percentage of imports on LIDOM rosters had remained constant since 1955, a fifteen-year period in which the number of Dominican players in MLB-affiliated ball had grown considerably, was of particular concern.[40] LIDOM owners reluctantly met with FENAPEPRO leaders and eventually agreed to compromise on some of the association's demands, including a reduction in the number of imported players allowed on league rosters.[41]

The association's criticism was not reserved for LIDOM officials. FENA-PEPRO also called on Major League Baseball's liaison to the winter leagues, Bobby Maduro, to reconsider his announced interest in placing new limits on native stars' winter league participation, a possibility he had raised after Rico Carty of the Atlanta Braves suffered a serious knee injury in a LIDOM game. In a press statement, the organization asserted that decisions about whether Dominican players would rest or work during the winter should be their own.[42] FENAPEPRO leaders saw connections between their own issues and the labor struggles of other players. In an interview in late 1970, association leader Winston Llenas noted that Curt Flood's legal fight over MLB's reserve clause had great relevance for players in LIDOM because "[the league] has been organized in the image of the U.S. system."[43]

Dominican players' organizing during the 1970–71 season led to a historic conference of Caribbean players' associations at the Serie del Caribe, held in February 1971 in San Juan. A five-hour meeting between representatives of FENAPEPRO and their counterparts from the Puerto Rican and Venezuelan players' associations produced a new entity—the Confederación de Peloteros Profesionales del Caribe (CONPEPROCA). Víctor Pellot (known to baseball fans in the United States as Vic Power) spoke at the meeting on behalf of his fellow Puerto Rican athletes, and Dionisio Acosta represented Venezuelan players. Enrique Lantigua, one of the founders of FENAPEP-RO, was appointed along with fellow Dominican Rafael Valdez to lead an effort to foster Mexican participation in the new body.[44]

Even before CONPEPROCA finally included organized representation from Mexican athletes in the aftermath of the ANABE strike in 1980, it acted as a key collective advocate for the interests of native players throughout the Caribbean winter leagues. Lantigua would continue to serve in a leadership role for the organization, and was elected to a two-year term as president by the Dominican, Venezuelan, and Puerto Rican representatives who assembled at CONPEPROCA's fifth annual assembly in Santo Domingo in 1975. A quarter century after he and his fellow Dominican ballplayers had created their nation's modern professional league, Lantigua carried their association's legacy of leadership forward to a new generation of Caribbean athletes.[45]

Dominican players were also instrumental in creating two new summer leagues, which got under way in 1975. Former St. Louis Cardinals player Julián Javier was among the founders of the Liga de Verano del Cibao, which operated in the northern region of the country, while Felipe Rojas Alou served as both league president and star player of the Liga Profesional de Verano de la República Dominicana, which operated in the south. Although the southern circuit lasted only a few seasons, the Liga de Verano del Cibao survived into the 1980s, featuring teams in La Vega, San Francisco de Macorís, Santiago, and Puerto Plata.

A number of former MLB players performed in the summer leagues. After being released in spring training 1976 by the New York Mets, Jesús Rojas Alou had two successful years in the Liga de Verano del Cibao before returning to the majors with the Houston Astros in 1978. Zoilo Versalles, the star shortstop from Cuba who won the American League's Most Valuable Player award with the Minnesota Twins in 1965, also spent two seasons in the league.[46] The two summer circuits born in 1975 were not conceived as "outlaw" leagues; they did not compete directly with MLB affiliates for players or territory. Rather, they existed as alternatives to an MLB-dominated summer professional league system that was failing to provide sufficient playing opportunities for Dominican professionals.

The fate of the Liga de Verano del Cibao in the 1980s stands as a meaningful marker of the emergence of the new configuration of Dominican professional baseball ushered in with the rise of the academy system. The league faced a series of financial problems and was forced to reduce player salaries on multiple occasions.[47] While it drew some revenue from sponsoring companies and ticket sales, the circuit also relied heavily on government support, which fell short during the lean years of the early 1980s. In 1985, attempting to establish a more secure footing, circuit officials negotiated a new affiliation with Major League Baseball.[48] For its first affiliated season the league continued to receive government funding and local sponsorship, but ongoing financial woes forced it to cease operations in 1986. That same summer a new academy-fed circuit began play in and around San Pedro de Macorís. In 1987 the academy-based initiative expanded into a two-division national summer league, incorporating the old Liga de Verano del Cibao territories, as well as sites in the southern region of the country. Though

Dominican sportswriters still referred to the summer circuit as the Liga de
Verano del Cibao, it was now an entirely different enterprise from what it
was before 1985.[49]

In 1988 league founder Julián Javier spoke out against the academy system's impact on Dominican professional summer ball. The Liga de Verano
del Cibao, he said, had been founded as a source of employment for veteran
ballplayers. With league rosters now filled with young academy recruits,
according to Javier, there were "more than one hundred" unemployed Dominican professionals "sitting at home because they were out of the [league]
for no good reason." Javier also noted that the old league featuring established Dominican veterans was much more popular with fans than the new
MLB-dominated, academy-based model.[50] Despite Javier's protest, a new
era was well under way, in the form of the Dominican Summer League, run
by the MLB academies. Most accounts of the circuit, which as Rob Ruck
notes "became baseball's largest professional league," make no mention of
its relationship to the two institutions of player-organized ball founded in
the mid-1970s.[51] Not until 2009 did a movement materialize to resurrect the
original model. With the participation of a new generation of Dominican
professionals, led by former MLB pitcher Julián Tavárez, the revived Liga
de Verano del Cibao began play that summer, twenty-four years after the
original circuit had been swallowed up by the MLB academy system.[52]

Some individuals who had played important roles in the original league
also became leaders in the construction of the academy system. One such
figure was longtime scout Epifanio "Epy" Guerrero, who managed a club
in the Liga de Verano del Cibao (the Indios del Valle) while also working
in partnership with the Toronto Blue Jays to create an academy that would
soon be the envy of other MLB teams.[53] Guerrero's contemporary and
counterpart Rafael "Ralph" Ávila, who built the Dodgers' state-of-the art
academy, voiced concerns about the implications of the old league's transformation during the summer of 1985, its first year of MLB affiliation. "The
caliber of play . . . has dropped," Ávila told the *Sporting News*. "The fans are
losing interest, and so are the sponsors. And who can blame the companies? Who wants to have their name associated with a horse-manure product?"[54] MLB teams' investment in Dominican academies, beginning with
the partnerships forged by the Blue Jays and Dodgers with Guerrero and
Ávila, replaced a model of summer baseball conceived as a local "product"
marketed to Dominican fans with a new system, devoted to the production
of young prospects for export. The enclosure of the old Liga de Verano del
Cibao within the new Dominican Summer League stands as an unmistak-

able sign, not only of MLB's expanding territorial power in the academy era, but of a distinct shift in the forms of agency at work in Dominican baseball.

## Power and Agency in the Academy Era

Like many scouts, Epy Guerrero began his professional life in baseball as a player. He signed with the Milwaukee Braves in 1960 and played two seasons before being released from the organization's Class A minor league affiliate in Cedar Rapids, Iowa. After returning home to the Dominican Republic, Guerrero transitioned to a new career in talent development, taking a position evaluating local amateur players under the supervision of Houston Astros scout Tony Pacheco. While working for Pacheco and the Astros, Guerrero met Pat Gillick, Houston's eastern regional scouting director. Successfully working together to sign César Cedeño, who went on to become a star player for the Astros, Guerrero and Gillick embarked on a professional partnership that would last over twenty years.

The Gillick-Guerrero player development team moved from the Astros to the New York Yankees in September 1974, then on to the Toronto Blue Jays in August 1976, in advance of the expansion franchise's first season in the American League. As a new team in need of an economical player development strategy, the Toronto club saw the Dominican Republic as an especially attractive source of potential big league talent. Within a year of starting his relationship with the Blue Jays, Guerrero began construction on a training facility. Borrowing money on his own while also receiving some financial assistance from Toronto, Guerrero developed what became a trend-setting baseball academy. In addition to playing fields, the Epy Guerrero Sports Complex in Villa Mella, approximately twelve miles north of Santo Domingo, included housing and dining facilities for Guerrero's recruits.[55]

While Guerrero was working on his facility in Villa Mella, Dodgers scout Rafael Ávila was engaged in a parallel effort. Ávila grew up in Cuba, and played an active role in his nation's revolution before later breaking with Fidel Castro and participating in the failed Bay of Pigs invasion. After settling in Miami, he began scouting for Dodgers general manager Al Campanis, covering territory that included the Dominican Republic, which soon became his main focus.[56] Beginning in 1974, Ávila operated the Academia Nacional de Béisbol, training young players exclusively for the Tigres del Licey of LIDOM. Since Licey had a working agreement with the Dodgers, Ávila's academy trained a number of L.A.'s prospects during this period. In 1981

Ávila changed his approach: rather than operating an academy for Licey, he began running his own training facility, to which Licey sent a smaller number of young players (most of whom had been signed by the Dodgers).[57] Perhaps most significantly, Ávila now concentrated his energy on training younger, unsigned amateur players rather than developing prospects already under contract to MLB clubs. "We started with twelve ballplayers," he later recalled, "and we started to hire unsigned amateurs to the academy: work with them, develop their skills."[58]

Over the next six years, with increasing amounts of financial support from the Dodgers, Ávila ran a scouting and training program, using a series of sites in and around San Pedro de Macorís, including baseball diamonds owned by the Santa Fe and Porvenir sugar mills. Although this approach yielded positive results, Ávila's ultimate goal was a self-contained state-of-the art facility. The culmination of his work was the Dodgers' Campo Las Palmas facility in Guerra (approximately twenty-five miles east of Santo Domingo), which established the industry standard for academies when it opened in 1987.[59] Demonstrating the MLB club's strong commitment to the project, Dodgers officials Peter O'Malley, Fred Claire, and Al Campanis attended the opening ceremony in March of that year.[60] The new facility, even more extensive than Guerrero's, included beds for 120 players, two kitchens and dining rooms (one set for the players, another for employees and staff), four baseball diamonds (two full-sized fields and two half-sized practice fields), three batting cages, six bullpens, and two running tracks. In addition, Campo Las Palmas featured a water purification system, an independent power supply consisting of four generators, a large garden for growing fruits and vegetables, and livestock. Satellite dishes were installed, allowing prospects to study televised broadcasts of MLB games.[61]

Guerrero's and Ávila's academies—and the great players the Blue Jays and Dodgers trained there—served as inspirations for other teams. From Tony Fernández and George Bell, whose brilliant play in the 1980s helped put the previously ignored Blue Jays on the map, to Pedro Martínez, whom the Dodgers traded away only to watch him become the sport's most electric pitcher of the late 1990s, Dominican players' success in Major League Baseball from the 1980s on gave irrefutable evidence of an academy's potential impact on a team's fortunes. Early investment in the academy model brought acclaim for figures like Pat Gillick, who as general manager of the Blue Jays from the late 1970s through the team's two consecutive World Series titles in the early 1990s provided other MLB clubs with ample evidence of the rewards of Dominican scouting. By the beginning of the 1990s, there

Campo Las Palmas, the Dodgers' Dominican academy,
designed by Rafael Ávila and opened in 1987. (*Major League
Baseball*)

were thirteen academies; by 2000, nearly every one of MLB's thirty teams
had either contracted with a Dominican training facility or built its own.[62]

During this period, academies became the central institutions of a talent
development strategy characterized by what some have referred to as the
"boatload mentality." In a 1996 interview, Colorado Rockies vice president
Dick Balderson described the approach in terms of a hypothetical scouting
investment of $100,000: with that amount of money a team could either
land four U.S. prospects, or "sign twenty [Dominican] guys for five thousand dollars each."[63] The "boatload" impulse driving the Dominican academy system developed as a response to other trends in MLB scouting after
the institution of the amateur draft in 1965. In his illuminating 1984 study,
*Dollar Sign on the Muscle*, Kevin Kerrane describes how U.S. scouting underwent sweeping changes in the draft era, as teams centralized and stream-
lined older talent development practices. The "logical extension of central-
ization and bureaucracy" was the Major League Scouting Bureau (MLSB),
established in 1974, through which teams pooled resources and scouting
data.[64] With the draft and the MLSB in place, the Dominican academy

system became a way for teams once again to stake out territory that was all their own. Characterizing views expressed by Pat Gillick, Kerrane suggests that for Toronto's general manager, "the Caribbean basin was an emblem of the open market, a reminder of what scouting had been like in the States before the draft era."[65]

Cultivating an "open market" for scouts did not mean expanding freedom for players. On the contrary, the academies constituted the latest development in a history of moves to limit young athletes' bargaining power. Before the introduction of the draft in 1965, all amateur players—except those from territories where MLB executives recognized other leagues' privileges (Mexico after 1955, for example)—were technically free agents, eligible to be signed by any interested MLB team. Then, for the first twenty years of the draft, all "foreign" players were excluded, since top young prospects—particularly those from Caribbean nations—could be signed for significantly less money than their counterparts in the continental United States. In the mid-1980s, MLB owners began a series of rule changes designed to limit signing costs by incorporating new categories and regions within the draft. In 1985, foreign players attending school in the United States became draft-eligible. In 1989, Puerto Rican amateur players were made subject to the draft for the first time, and two years later, Canadian amateurs were incorporated, as well.[66]

Recent years have brought increasing calls for a "worldwide" draft, a movement within the industry that reflects a steady rise in signing bonuses secured by top Dominican players. In an effort to protect their own competitive advantages, representatives of MLB teams with deep investments in Dominican scouting have long resisted such a change.[67] The history of MLB scouting and talent development practices suggests, however, that when a strong majority of MLB team owners come to see a rule change as being in their own economic interest, they will move to adjust their industry's rules and practices accordingly. The 2011 collective bargaining agreement between MLB teams and the MLBPA empowered a new committee to examine several possible changes in talent acquisition practices, including making players from more territories subject to the draft. The agreement also established a "bonus pool" system, placing limits on each team's total budget for global talent development while retaining flexibility for every club to develop and pursue its own territorial strategies.[68]

In addition to the industry's internal rules and regulations, U.S. immigration law has played a central role in determining the place of Dominican scouting in the baseball world. The academy system was shaped in significant ways by restrictions on U.S. work visas for "foreign" athletes. Before 2007, professional baseball in the United States operated under a two-tiered visa system, with players on major league rosters eligible for P-1 visas and minor leaguers restricted to H-2B visas, of which only a limited number were available each year. The academies and Dominican Summer League enabled teams to develop Dominican players without securing work visas for more than the most elite prospects. New legislation passed by the U.S. Congress and signed by President George W. Bush in late 2006—the so-called Compete Act—made P-1 visas available to minor leaguers. The product of lobbying by MLB owners, the new system of visas was a response to the extraordinary increase in the numbers of Latin American—and particularly Dominican—players on MLB teams' minor league rosters, as academies sent more and more prospects to the higher levels of professional ball.[69]

Academies have become fundamental territories in baseball's age of free agency, not simply entry points into the profession but as themselves dynamic sites in the sport's labor history. In order to understand the work that takes place in the Dominican academies, it is important to note that not all of them operate on the same model. The anthropologist Alan Klein draws the helpful distinction between what he terms "halfway houses" and "full-service facilities," suggesting that in the former model, more common in the early days of the academy system, "players' movements were harder to control, resulting in more problems."[70]

One of the key elements of the academies, especially those of the "full-service" variety, is their emphasis on life skills that players will need if they make it to higher levels of professional baseball. Academy players receive training in a number of "fundamentals" beyond the playing field, such as English language skills, media relations basics, and strategies for negotiating U.S. cultural norms. In this way teams use their academies to initiate athletes into the particular forms of workplace and cultural knowledge specific to the industry, disciplining young ballplayers into new "citizens" of the baseball world. Even as they receive training for careers in baseball, most athletes in residence at academies will never make it to the next level, ultimately serving as competition for more promising contemporaries, bound for other territories and teams further up the sport's developmental ladder.[71]

Though MLB teams control the larger political economy of the academy system, Dominicans perform the overwhelming majority of its work.[72] Some of the most prominent scouts and coaches in the academy system were part of the first major wave of Dominican MLB stars in the 1960s. For example, after the end of his playing career Juan Marichal became director of Latin American scouting for the Oakland A's and was one of the main forces behind the team's Dominican academy. The facility opened in 1994 as Campo Juan Marichal.[73] While working for the A's, Marichal helped train dozens of future MLB players, including stars like Miguel Tejada, and he cites his work in this area as one of his major career accomplishments.[74]

The language training and cultural preparation that players receive in academies reflects the great influence that Marichal and his generation have had on the subsequent development of their sport in the Dominican Republic. Just as the bigotry that Curt Flood encountered throughout his experience in the U.S. minor leagues informed his eventual public stand in fighting for a more equitable profession, Dominican stars of the same era have drawn on their own encounters with racism and exclusion in U.S. professional ball, working to ensure that subsequent generations of their nation's top ballplayers have more training and resources at their disposal. "Before the academies, when kids got sent to the minors, it could be very hard for them," Marichal notes. "They might not have a teammate who spoke Spanish. If they stayed at the academy for two years, they learned English, how to eat in the United States, and how to understand some of American society and culture."[75]

The fact that Dominicans have figured prominently in building and operating the academy system provokes important questions about the meaning of Dominican agency within a system designed to serve the interests of Major League Baseball. Alan Klein has addressed the issue of agency in his analysis of so-called *buscónes,* independent scouts, some of whom have built academies of their own. Such figures have played increasingly central roles since the 1990s in finding and training young Dominican players prior to their entry into the MLB-run academies. Klein argues that "*buscónes* occupy a somewhat counterhegemonic position: they are local entrepreneurs, difficult to control, and indispensable to the commodity chain."[76] Furthermore, as Klein suggests, there are pitfalls of "progressive ethnocentrism" in failing to account for the ways in which Dominicans have both shaped and negotiated the power relations of the modern baseball industry.[77] The academy era has seen significant changes, however, in the terms of Dominican agency in the baseball world. Whereas in the 1960s and 1970s Dominican athletes led collective efforts to establish national baseball institutions, player agency in the academy era has taken more isolated, individual form, and has been enclosed within an increasingly MLB-dominated system.

In recent years MLB officials themselves have entered into public discussions of power and agency in Dominican baseball in the face of growing public scrutiny over its operations. In 2008, in the wake of a major scandal involving accusations that MLB scouts had taken kickbacks from *buscónes* and otherwise profited unethically from the growing market in Dominican prospects, Lou Melendez, MLB's vice president for international operations, told the *Boston Globe:* "You're not going to change the system. All you can do is try to manage it to make sure there is no abuse as it applies to [MLB] clubs."[78] Indeed, even though Major League Baseball established a Santo Domingo office in 2000 in an effort to better regulate scouting practices, the stakes of securing a signing bonus and a chance at a career in baseball, no matter how long the odds, are more than high enough to fuel an informal economy based on young ballplayers' potential.[79]

But also striking in Melendez's statement is what it reveals about the utility of claims to Dominican agency within MLB officials' own approach to power relations in the baseball world. By pointing out that key dimensions of Dominican scouting exist beyond the reach of their power, MLB executives can renounce responsibility for the conditions their industry has helped feed. Such comments reinforce the borders—rhetorical and real—that have structured baseball's labor history. The success of the academy system as a profitable talent development model stands as the product of MLB teams' construction and maintenance of such borders—practices of territorial politics fundamental to the political economy of the baseball industry.

The issue of Dominican agency appeared in particular relief in the cases of "age fixing" that received substantial press attention in the early years of the twenty-first century. In the eyes of baseball scouts everywhere, a player's youth can be an especially valuable attribute. This fact was evident in the early history of the academy system, which saw teams inking younger and younger players until outcry over the Blue Jays' signing of fourteen-year-old Jimy Kelly in 1984 led to a key reform: prospects now had to be at least seventeen.[80] The history of age fixing constitutes another dimension of baseball's political economy of youth. In small, individual acts of market manipulation, some Dominican prospects have fudged their age, representing themselves as younger than they really are. For a player to have a team think he is seventeen instead of nineteen can make all the difference. For athletes as well as for agents, *buscónes,* and others with a stake in signing bonuses and contracts, age fixing has been a means to extract a larger share of the industry's profits than MLB teams might otherwise offer.

An especially prominent revelation of age fixing concerned Miguel Tejada, who came up through the Oakland Athletics' academy and minor league system to become one of the great power-hitting shortstops of his era. In 2008, while a member of the Houston Astros, Tejada sat for an interview with ESPN reporter Tom Farrey, who surprised him by producing a birth certificate that showed him to be two years older than he had previously claimed to be. Stunned, Tejada walked out of the interview, the footage of which ESPN featured in its long-form investigative news show, *E:60*. In a subsequent press conference, Tejada explained the circumstances of his path into professional baseball: "I was a poor kid. I wanted to sign a professional contract, and that was the only way to do it. I didn't want or mean to do anything wrong."[81] ESPN's televised spectacle of accusation framed a complicated reality in individual terms, eliding the industry's deep structural inequalities through a simple theatrics of shame. The topic would remain a common feature of U.S. sports journalism in the wake of the Tejada case, as reporters and broadcasters frequently speculated about Dominican players' real ages, thus erecting further symbolic barriers to full citizenship in the baseball world.[82]

One of the most visible transformations in Dominican baseball during the academy era has occurred in the nation's winter league. Although U.S. teams continue to use LIDOM and similar leagues as developmental circuits, this practice has declined considerably since the 1980s. Turning away from the older model of deep personnel investment in Caribbean winter ball, Major League Baseball has created new minor leagues in which to train players during the off-season. Chief among these has been the Arizona Fall League, established in 1992. As Mike Port, the circuit's first president, put it: "The kids playing in the Arizona league don't have to deal with a different culture and they don't have to lose playing time to 'local heroes' as they might in the Caribbean. You can bet that American shortstops and second basemen love it in Arizona. In San Juan or Santo Domingo or Caracas, they might never get to play."[83] Whereas working agreements with winter league teams had once represented Major League Baseball's primary institutional scouting connection to the Caribbean, the new academy system eliminated key incentives for MLB teams to maintain robust relationships with circuits like LIDOM.

As a result of MLB teams' declining investment in Caribbean winter leagues, LIDOM teams began featuring more Dominican players. One clear sign of the shift in the composition of LIDOM's rosters is a change in the design of the league's annual All-Star Game, which for decades has been organized by FENAPEPRO. In 1970, in the context of FENAPEPRO's organizing for reduced numbers of imported players and more opportunities for native players in LIDOM, the All-Star Game pitted a team of imports against one of top Dominicans.[84] This model, which existed for years, symbolized one of the circuit's defining tensions—that between its identity on the one hand as a developmental body for MLB and on the other as the Dominican Republic's own "major" league. Reflecting the change in LIDOM's identity in the academy era, FENAPEPRO began collaborating with players' associations in other Caribbean winter circuits to organize interleague All-Star matches, in place of the exhibitions pitting imports against native stars.[85]

Since 1970 the culmination of the LIDOM season has been the annual Serie del Caribe. Although the most famous Dominican players tend to opt out of competition during much of the winter regular season, recovering from their long summers in MLB, some join their LIDOM teams for the tournament, viewing the games as opportunities both to prepare for spring training and to represent their country against top competition from other Caribbean leagues. For fans in many countries the World Baseball Classic, first staged in 2006, has represented a new opportunity to cheer for their nation's best ballplayers against those of other nations, but for Dominican observers the contest simply rearticulates a regular mode of baseball spectatorship.

As the Dominican Republic has become known throughout the baseball world as a major center of talent development, boosters in other countries have created their own models of recruiting academies. In addition to the Liga Mexicana's facilities, erected first in Pasteje and later in El Carmen, examples of academies elsewhere in Latin America include one that opened in Nicaragua in 2011, the Academia de Béisbol Nicaragüense, with a staff including former MLB star Denis Martínez training young prospects with the goal of attracting the interest of MLB scouts.[86] The country with the most developed academy system after the Dominican Republic is Venezuela, where many MLB teams moved to establish operations in the wake of the Houston Astros' groundbreaking success with their academy in Valencia, which opened in 1989. After considerable expansion during the 1990s, however, MLB team officials' concerns about the security of their investments under the government of Hugo Chávez—in light of the nationalization of companies in other industries—limited the development of an academy system in Venezuela on the same scale seen in the Dominican Republic.[87]

Puerto Rico has been home to one of Major League Baseball's most important academy projects. Having seen Puerto Rican representation in the majors decline since the incorporation of the island's players into the amateur draft in 1989, former White Sox and Rangers pitcher Edwin Correa secured funding from MLB to create the Puerto Rico Baseball Academy and High School. Different from the Dominican academies in that it includes intensive baseball instruction as part of a larger secondary school curriculum, it nonetheless builds on the model established by Guerrero and Ávila. Correa worked as a coach at Campo Las Palmas in 1999, an experience that influenced his decision to push for a Puerto Rican academy. Dozens of players from the school were selected in MLB's annual amateur draft over its first decade in operation, and in 2012 one of the academy's graduates, shortstop Carlos Correa (no relation), was the first overall selection, signing with the Houston Astros.[88]

The Dominican Republic itself has been the site of multiple academy projects, including a facility run by the Hiroshima Toyo Carp of the Japanese Central League. Team owner Kohei Matsuda invested in the academy, which opened in 1990 on the outskirts of San Pedro de Macorís, after seeing the success that MLB clubs had enjoyed with their Dominican operations.[89] Under the leadership of academy director Mitsunori Ueno, the Hiroshima club developed its facility along similar lines to the MLB academies—in addition to intensive baseball training, young prospects receive Japanese language instruction, as well as preparation for the transition to life in Japan.

A product of the Carp academy, Alfonso Soriano, went on to play a pivotal role in baseball's transnational labor history. After beginning his training at the facility in March 1995, Soriano played professionally in Japan in 1996 and 1997 (mainly in the minor leagues, but also in limited action with the Carp). Soriano came to be regarded as a top prospect during his two years in Japan, and began to attract attention from MLB scouts. Taking advantage of his apparent value on baseball's market for top talent, Soriano retired from NPB in the spring of 1998. He was advised through this process by Don Nomura, a player agent who had assisted pitcher Hideo Nomo in his own controversial departure from Nippon Professional Baseball three years earlier. NPB officials mounted a challenge to MLB clubs' ability to recruit Soriano, but the player was eventually allowed to pursue a career move across the Pacific. In September 1998 he signed a four-year, $3.1 million contract with the New York Yankees and soon became an All-Star second baseman in the Bronx.[90]

Soriano's case was a primary motivation for MLB and NPB owners to establish a new agreement governing player contracts, revising the "treaty" signed in 1967 in the wake of the dispute involving Masanori Murakami. The "posting" system that the officials agreed to in December 1998 became a critical element in the industry's elaborate configuration of routes and borders to transnational free agency. Under the terms of the posting system, NPB teams may solicit sealed bids for players on their rosters from all MLB teams interested in their services. The MLB team with the highest offer is then free to negotiate with the player. When the team and player come to an agreement, the player's NPB team receives the amount of the winning bid, or "posting fee." Several NPB players have moved to MLB in the years since 1998 via the posting system, including prominent Japanese stars Ichiro Suzuki and Daisuke Matsuzaka.[91]

Soriano's successful navigation through the contractual systems of both Nippon Professional Baseball and Major League Baseball is one of the more remarkable stories of the baseball world in the age of free agency, and demonstrates the seemingly limitless possibilities of transnational stardom available to the top echelon of Dominican ballplayers. Soriano is, however, one of the comparatively few Dominican professional players to succeed in rising to the top of the sport. For every Alfonso Soriano there are thousands more athletes who never play professional baseball beyond the academies. Soriano's success, like that of the academy system, depends on the labor of vast numbers of players who have little chance of joining him as major league free agents.

## Sugar

For decades, Dominican fans have played witness to the complex professional identities of their nation's baseball stars, following the careers of figures from Marichal and Alou to Tejada and Soriano across a range of local and transnational circuits. Interest among other fans and observers in the stories of Dominican athletes has grown considerably in recent decades, as the academy system has expanded in size and impact, bringing more and more of the nation's players to center stage in the baseball world. In addition to an increasing body of scholarship and investigative journalism on the treatment of Dominican athletes, other forms of cultural representation have emerged as well. If the expansion of Dominican scouting in the 1980s registered in texts such as W. P. Kinsella's "The Battery," the continued development of the academy system as one of the baseball industry's fundamental territorial forms in the early years of the current century was represented in a much more nuanced text—Anna Boden and Ryan Fleck's 2008 feature film *Sugar*. The story centers on the experience of Miguel "Sugar" Santos, a prospect with the fictional Kansas City Knights who shows great promise in the team's Dominican academy before facing significant challenges—on and off the field—as a minor leaguer in the United States.[92]

*Sugar* marked the film debut of Algenis Pérez Soto, whose performance as Santos stands as one of the most compelling in the history of baseball cinema. "Discovered" by the filmmakers while playing a pickup baseball game with friends, Soto had only recently given up his own dream of a career as an infielder and was working in a hotel in San Pedro de Macorís.[93] The film's narrative follows Sugar Santos through intensive practice sessions at the academy, weekend celebrations in Consuelo, the working-class community built around a sugar mill on the outskirts of San Pedro, and the unfamiliar social spaces of spring training in Arizona.

One of the most striking aspects of *Sugar* is its portrayal of Santos's experience as a member of a minor league team in the fictional Iowa community of Bridgetown. Santos stays with the Higgins family, diehard fans who proudly open their home every summer to a member of the Bridgetown Swing, while understanding little of their guests' lives and cultural backgrounds. Through the scenes set in and around the Higgins' farmhouse, the filmmakers integrate the story of Dominican athletes' professional and personal struggles into a landscape familiar to fans of other baseball movies. By placing Santos's professional coming-of-age amid the Iowa cornfields, the filmmakers draw a clear connection to *Field of Dreams*, the Kinsella-derived narrative of baseball nostalgia that remains one of the most iconic sports films in Hollywood history.

While revisiting familiar landscapes, *Sugar* stands apart from most sports movies in its refusal of traditional forms of heroism. Santos ultimately enacts an unexpected form of agency, choosing to step away from professional baseball. The pitcher rejects the isolating and debilitating experience that his job has become over the course of his first season in the United States, and sets his sights on a different future. Leaving Bridgetown and his one-time dream behind, he becomes part of a community of low-wage immigrant service workers in New York City. The film's concluding scene shows Santos joining a weekly amateur baseball league at the Roberto Clemente

Ballfield, a public city diamond where he plays alongside other former MLB prospects, who are themselves making their way beyond the bright lights of nearby Yankee Stadium.

Ultimately, the film's account of professional baseball in the academy era is a story about the forms of belonging and loss that define the larger experience of immigrants and their communities in the age of neoliberal globalization. As *Sugar* reminds us, even if the overwhelming majority of the athletes who make up the Dominican academy system will never appear in an MLB game, their stories are essential chapters in the history of free agency.

# 5

# Constructing Ichiro's Home Field

*Seattle, the Mariners,*
*and the Politics of Location*

I N   A   S P O R T  whose history is marked and measured by individual achievements, relatively few Major League Baseball players have earned single-name status. The early months of the 2001 season saw this elite cohort, led by such larger-than-life stars as Babe, Jackie, Reggie, and Fernando, welcome a new member: Ichiro. Like Valenzuela two decades earlier, Ichiro Suzuki made it onto the cover of *Sports Illustrated* before the end of May of his rookie year. Playing right field and batting leadoff, MLB's first Japanese position player helped lead the Seattle Mariners to 116 victories, eclipsing the 1998 New York Yankees' record for the most wins in a season by an American League team.[1]

As the *Sports Illustrated* cover story noted, from his growing legions of supporters in the stands at Seattle's Safeco Field to the enormous television audiences of passionate followers in Japan, fans of MLB's new sensation knew him simply as Ichiro. His special status was even reflected on the back of his jersey. According to a Mariners press release distributed in mid-May, Ichiro preferred that his uniform display his given name instead of his surname, carrying on a practice he began with his former team, the Orix Blue-Wave of Japan's Pacific League.[2] Over the course of the next decade, Ichiro's singular star power allowed the Mariners to become one of Major League Baseball's most recognizable global brands.

Like Reggie Jackson and Fernando Valenzuela before him, Ichiro was recruited and signed not simply for his athletic skill but also for his potential as a cultural icon. As an established star in Japan from his years in Nippon Professional Baseball, he held even greater promise for MLB marketing and licensing than players from other parts of the world. In contrast to Latin American baseball hotbeds like the Dominican Republic, which MLB executives continued to treat primarily as territories for the cheap and efficient development of a large, exploitable labor pool, team owners and league officials saw Japan as a vast market for the cultivation of new fans. With his extraordinary talent, slick style of play, and impeccable public image, Ichiro would have been a dream come true for any team's marketing department. But his national identity made him especially valuable to the Mariners, a franchise that by 2001 had come to see Japanese players as keys to a new business model based on a Pacific Rim team identity. Although not unique in featuring a player from Japan, Ichiro's Mariners were the first MLB team to construct an entire brand image around a Japanese star.

Ichiro's great debut season was a watershed moment in baseball history, and not simply because it marked the arrival of an alluring new business model for major league teams. Transcending a cold calculus of dollars and cents, Ichiro's play captured the collective imagination of the Mariners' growing fan base. "Ichiromania," visible in all sorts of phenomena—from fans toting homemade signs and Japanese flags to the ballpark, to the massive international media presence that followed the superstar's every move—rivaled Fernandomania in its scale, its frenetic energy, and its connection to the larger ethnic and transnational identity of its major league city. As a Japanese star working in Seattle, Ichiro seemed to many to embody his new hometown's high-tech Pacific Rim globalism. In a piece for the *New York Times Magazine* in September 2001, the Seattle-based writer David Shields likened Ichiro's displacement of former star players in the hearts of local fans to the eclipse of older corporations by the region's new technology firms. Shields mused that one fan's handmade sign, " 'Ichi-ro Heart Out, A-Rod and Junior' . . . perfectly captures the current Seattle zeitgeist: good riddance to stats-obsessed behemoths Alex Rodriguez, Ken Griffey Jr. and Boeing; nervous optimism about the continued health of Microsoft and Amazon; and a rapturous embrace of Ichiro's Pacific Rim virtues—modesty and understatement masking a fierce devotion to precision and success."[3]

Shields's assertion of Ichiro's "Pacific Rim virtues" is a striking regional caricature, and in this way evokes a common theme in popular narratives about baseball. Throughout the sport's history, star ballplayers and their teams have been cast as representational figures for constructed notions of local identity. A great deal of baseball storytelling has been built around ideas about how particular clubs embody the psyche, attitude, and history of their city or region. A quick glance at the local bookstore's sports section reveals baseball's powerful linkage between team and place, with volume after volume highlighting the ways in which Jackie Robinson's Dodgers represented postwar Brooklyn, the long-cursed Red Sox embodied a Calvinist New England worldview, and the "Bronx Zoo" Yankees enacted a cultural politics of crisis and celebrity emblematic of late 1970s New York City, to cite three prominent examples.[4] Baseball matters, these works suggest, because it tells us stories about the places we imagine ourselves to be from.

The ability of teams to frame their players, games, and ballparks as expressions of local identity has been an essential element of baseball's endurance as a powerful, profitable industry. The history of ballpark development in particular has been marked by teams' success in extracting public subsidies for construction and other costs through the threat of relocation. As a monopoly business with a limited number of franchises, Major League Baseball relies on local boosters' desires for their cities to secure "major league" status. Particularly for smaller cities like Seattle, attracting and keeping big league sports teams has become an especially high-stakes game in recent decades, with leagues more than willing to entertain the possibility of moving franchises to emerging media markets endowed with willing and wealthy local partners. Baseball is thus defined by a pervasive politics of location, which the residents and other stakeholders of cities and their neighborhoods must negotiate. The history of Major League Baseball in Seattle, from the 1970s to the turn of the twenty-first century, presents a particularly revealing case study.

The Mariners' transformation in the Ichiro era followed decades of conflict over the team's relationship to its city. The team's arrival in the 1970s brought stiff resistance from residents of the International District, Seattle's working-class Asian American neighborhood. A social movement of district residents became galvanized in opposition to plans for the Kingdome, the nearby stadium built to attract an MLB team. Then, in the early 1990s, a different kind of territorial power struggle took shape as Major League Baseball officials and other team owners attempted to prevent an executive from the Nintendo Corporation from buying the Mariners, arguing that a "foreign" owner should not hold a controlling interest in the so-called national pastime.

The tensions over local identity that structured the history of Major League Baseball in Seattle from the 1970s to the 1990s provide an illuminating backdrop for Ichiro's emergence as a figure through which the Mariners could enact a politics of location ideally suited to the age of globalization. Throughout his record-setting career in Seattle, Ichiro personified the baseball world's version of what the cultural theorist Aihwa Ong has termed a "flexible citizen," a mobile body capable of strategic repositioning amid the shifting market-based terrain of neoliberalism.[5] Repositioned as the star of the Seattle Mariners, Ichiro transformed his team's identity, playing a leading role in the ongoing development of Major League Baseball's politics of location.

## Laying the Groundwork for the Mariners

The history of professional baseball in Seattle dates to 1890 and the inaugural season of the Seattle Hustlers, who represented the city in the Pacific Northwest League. In 1903 a new Seattle team—the Indians—became a charter member of the Pacific Coast League (PCL), which grew to be the premier "minor" league on the West Coast. In 1937 Emil Sick, owner of the Rainier Brewing Company, bought the struggling Indians franchise, changed the team's name to the Rainiers, and moved the club into a new Art Deco–style facility called Sick's Stadium. Despite their unfortunately named ballpark, the Seattle Rainiers thrived in the heyday of the PCL, which, until the postwar emergence of televised MLB broadcasts and subsequent franchise expansion, enjoyed what amounted to "major" status for baseball fans in the Pacific Northwest. The Rainiers, however, like the rest of the league, suffered a devastating blow when the Giants and Dodgers moved from New York to begin play in two key PCL cities, San Francisco and Los Angeles, in 1958. In the years that followed, the PCL was forced to function like other minor leagues, with its primary identity as a "farm" for Major League Baseball. This model failed to attract significant numbers of fans in Seattle, a city whose residents had become accustomed to the top-quality professional baseball of previous decades. Instead of cheering on the Rainiers, more and more Seattle sports fans joined in a new rallying cry, calling for measures to attract an MLB team.[6]

Rainiers general manager Dewey Soriano led an early campaign for a joint city-county-state-owned stadium, trumpeting the possibility of drawing an MLB franchise with such a facility. Voters dealt Soriano's plan a temporary blow, rejecting a $15 million stadium bond issue in November 1960.[7] Members of the city's downtown business elite who supported a new stadium as a means of stimulating metropolitan investment and development were undeterred. For many such boosters, plans for a sports facility grew naturally out of the agenda unveiled at Seattle's World's Fair, otherwise known as the Century 21 Exposition, which ran from April through October 1962. As both a showcase for Space Age marvels and an opportunity for new material investment in the downtown area, the event announced ambitions for Seattle to become a major industrial and commercial hub—a "city of the future."[8]

In the wake of the World's Fair, city planers and business leaders made building a new stadium a top priority. Given the region's notoriously rainy climate, and in light of growing hopes that football and baseball franchises might both be lured to town, boosters sought public financing for an indoor, domed facility that could host events year-round. After voters again rejected a stadium bond issue in 1966, the state legislature passed a bill the following year that authorized King County to defer a percentage of hotel sales taxes for the purpose of paying off stadium construction bonds, a pivotal measure that Governor Daniel Evans then signed into law. Civic leaders then attached plans for the domed stadium to a massive public funding initiative called "Forward Thrust," which promised a range of other projects from parks and community centers to rapid transit.[9]

With a public vote on "Forward Thrust" scheduled for February 1968, American League team owners awarded a franchise to Seattle at their October 1967 convention. Baseball's power brokers made the franchise award contingent on Seattle's ability to provide "suitable baseball facilities." David Cohn, the head of the city's delegation to the meeting, reported that the MLB owners had authorized him "to tell the electorate that if the bond issue was approved, the franchise in the American League would follow."[10] At a subsequent meeting in December, Major League Baseball formally awarded the franchise to Pacific Northwest Sports, Inc., a group headed by Dewey Soriano (who was now president of the Pacific Coast League) and his brother Max, and largely bankrolled by William R. Daley, the former owner of the Cleveland Indians. Voters approved the funding the following February, prompting American League president Joe Cronin, who had campaigned for the stadium bill alongside other prominent baseball figures, to tell the Associated Press: "It will mean so much to the community. . . . I'm so happy about it."[11]

As planning for the team's new domed facility proceeded, the Seattle Pilots joined the American League in 1969, playing in Sick's Stadium, with a hastily constructed addition to the outfield bleachers designed to convert the minor league field into a suitable temporary home for a big league team.[12] Pilots fans had little to celebrate that summer, as the team slumped to a record of 64–98, though the campaign lives on in baseball history as the backdrop for pitcher Jim Bouton's controversial 1970 memoir *Ball Four.* Bouton's book would turn out to be the Pilots' most enduring legacy, since the team failed to last another season. With the team's owners declaring bankruptcy, in early 1970 MLB officials backed the franchise's sale to a group led by Bud Selig, a major automobile dealer based in Milwaukee.[13] Baseball fans in that city had seen their previous club, the Braves, depart for Atlanta after the 1965 season. The Pilots franchise—renamed the Brewers—found a long-term home in Milwaukee, and Selig became one of the most influential executives in the sport's history, serving as "acting commissioner" beginning in 1992 before being officially elected to Major League Baseball's top post by his fellow team owners in 1998.[14]

The Pilots' departure was one of the most abrupt franchise moves in the history of professional baseball—so much so that Brewers logos had to be sewn onto Seattle's old uniforms in a mad dash before the opening game of the 1970 season.[15] With plans for the new domed stadium well under way, the city of Seattle, King County, and the state of Washington sued Major League Baseball, arguing that funding for the facility had been approved based on the promise of a franchise. The legal case, which alleged fraud and antitrust violations, loomed in the background of ongoing negotiations with MLB officials for a new team. The parties finally resolved the dispute in early 1976 when Major League Baseball awarded Seattle an expansion franchise—the Mariners—that would begin play the following year.[16] The territorial dynamics that shaped the short history of the Pilots and the birth of the Mariners, distinguished by the interplay between public resource allocation and private franchise mobility, would continue to define Major League Baseball's place in Seattle in the decades that followed.

As part of the 1967 taxation bill that had preceded "Forward Thrust," a new State Stadium Commission (SSC) was charged with overseeing a public site selection and review process for what would become the King County Multipurpose Domed Stadium, popularly known as the Kingdome. After considering a variety of locations, the SSC proposed building the stadium at the Seattle Center, the site of the 1962 World's Fair. This proposal met with significant opposition, led by real estate developer Frank Ruano, who achieved notoriety in the Pacific Northwest for leading a series of fights against the public financing of sports facilities. Ruano's Committee to Save the Seattle Center organized a referendum campaign, and voters rejected the SSC's plan. After further study, in December 1970 the commission announced a new recommendation: the so-called King Street site, located at the western edge of the International District. Though Ruano and other opponents—now organized as Citizens Against Stadium Hoax, or "CASH"—again collected enough signatures to place the issue on the ballot, stadium supporters won a legal challenge, preventing another public vote on the stadium's location. Kitsap County Superior Court Judge Oluf Johnsen blocked CASH's strategy on the grounds that voters' 1968 approval of the stadium project as part of "Forward Thrust" amounted to a mandate to build the facility, and that therefore the planning process itself could not be made subject to referendum. This ruling, issued in March 1972, allowed plans for construction at the new site to go forward.[17]

Upon selection of the King Street site, stadium backers consistently championed the project's potential to transform both the immediate neighborhood and the broader region. Such potential was the theme at a meeting of the SSC on December 21, 1970, featuring a formal presentation by Charles Hope, the lead consultant on the team the commission hired to evaluate possible locations. Hope proclaimed that building the stadium at the King Street site "would encourage more rapid redevelopment of the surrounding area and would serve as an anchor to the southern part of the [Central Business District]. . . . The location provides the opportunity for such a facility to be an entire new focal point for the King County metropolitan area."[18] While planners cast the project as the basis for an imagined new Seattle, residents of the working-class immigrant neighborhood adjacent to the proposed site saw the stadium as a very real danger to their community. Nearly two years later, when the project's backers finally assembled for a groundbreaking ceremony, activists from the International District were there to greet them, and were already busy making the Kingdome the "focal point" of a transformative chapter in their neighborhood's history.

## The International District

The International District developed over succeeding generations of immigration to Seattle and out of the collective work of the city's Chinese, Japanese, and Filipino residents beginning in the late nineteenth century. Doug Chin, the author of an excellent short book on the neighborhood's history, has called the district "the most successful experiment in pan–Asian Americanism on the U.S. mainland."[19] Chinese labor migration to Seattle started in the late 1860s. Within a decade, Chinese merchants and workers had established a vibrant settlement to the east of Pioneer Square, the city's oldest and most central neighborhood. By the turn of the twentieth century, Japanese immigrants had built a community east of Chinatown, and by 1930 a large Filipino population had established roots in the area. In addition, the International District became home to a thriving African American community. In the decades before World War II some of Seattle's most popular jazz clubs, such as the Black and Tan and Basin Street, opened in the area, registering the increasingly important place of black culture in downtown Seattle.[20]

Baseball was itself central in the development of the International District. The sport was an especially important component of social life for Seattle's Japanese immigrant community in the decades before World War II, with many children and adults alike playing in casual games as well as organized leagues. The neighborhood supported multiple teams that both competed in local circuits and staged regular contests against clubs from as far away as Vancouver. Beginning in 1928, the neighborhood's Asahi team participated in the annual North American Pacific Northwest Baseball Championship. As historian Sayuri Guthrie-Shimizu details in her valuable study *Transpacific Field of Dreams,* such established clubs and leagues reflected the growth of Japanese communities in Seattle and elsewhere in the Pacific Northwest. Baseball also represented an important form of transnational connection and exchange during these years. Tokyo's Waseda University team made multiple trips to Seattle, and the Asahi club traveled from Seattle to Japan in 1914 and 1921. Indeed, residents of the International District were playing trans-Pacific baseball long before the Mariners.[21]

Although baseball was especially popular in Seattle's Japanese community, the sport has a larger multiethnic history in the International District. In his memoir *Hum Bows, Not Hot Dogs!* Bob Santos offers a valuable perspective on the place of baseball in the neighborhood's development. The child of Macario Santos, who emigrated from Manila by way of the U.S. Navy, and Virginia Nicol, a Filipina American who grew up in Seattle, Bob Santos played baseball, football, and basketball as a child growing up in the district. "Playing sports was always a way for our neighborhood kids to live out their daydreams of being athletic heroes," he recalled.[22] According to Santos, baseball often took the form of pickup games in local public parks. Later, while working in the Boeing Company's hammer shop as a young man, he regularly attended games at Sick's Stadium, cheering on Filipino outfielder Bobby Balcena and his fellow Rainiers.[23]

World War II marked a critical period of rupture and change in the district. While the boom in wartime production brought a substantial migration of African American families to the neighborhood, the policy of Japanese internment tore other community members from their homes and businesses. Some families did return to the area at the end of the war, but internment left a deep and lasting impact, and the International District lost its identity as a major Japanese American residential enclave.[24] Nonetheless, Japanese American businesses remained among the area's most prominent establishments into the twenty-first century. Chief among these was the Uwajimaya Market, one of the district's central commercial landmarks since it opened (having relocated from Tacoma, Washington) following World War II.[25] Over the course of the second half of the twentieth century, the International District served as a commercial center for a range of ethnic communities, a residential neighborhood populated largely by older Chinese, Japanese, and Filipino Seattleites, and a first area of settlement for new immigrants.

The name International District had its origins in multiethnic community organizing and political work during the immediate postwar period. The Jackson Street Community Council, an interracial "grassroots self-help group," was formed in 1946 and for the next two decades played a key role in neighborhood politics by helping to unite the area's at times disparate interests. Council leaders began using the designation "international" to promote local businesses and highlight the area's diverse identities, employing such place-names as "International Area" and "International Settlement." In 1951 Mayor William F. Devin adopted the wording that community leaders had employed, officially recognizing the area as Seattle's "International Center," in order to underscore contributions from "Chinese, Japanese, Filipino, and Negro" residents.[26] By the mid-1960s community members and neighborhood organizations had begun referring to the area as the International District.

These years brought a series of profound challenges to the neighborhood's identity, most ominously with construction of U.S. Interstate 5, which divided the area in half. The district suffered substantial population loss and multiple building closures in the 1960s, and remaining area residents lacked many basic social services. In the wake of the highway project, new community organizations emerged, including the International District Improvement Association (Inter*Im), founded in 1968 by a multiethnic group of business and community leaders. Inter*Im became a key conduit of federal Model Cities resources and a leading force for improved services for neighborhood residents.[27] For some community members, the

International District designation that was widely adopted during these years represented an imposed identity, erasing the name Chinatown, which had recognized a specific, long-standing ethnic community. As Jeffrey Hou and Isami Kinoshita note, while "many celebrated the multiethnic character of the district, others argued that those who came first have the right to claim its identity."[28] Today, the names International District and Chinatown–International District are both used, reflecting the neighborhood's complex history of struggle over survival and identity.[29]

As in any neighborhood with diverse interests and constituencies, there remained tensions and divides; but beginning in the early 1970s, the International District became a site of powerful community mobilization. The most significant galvanizing force in the modern history of the neighborhood was the plan to build the Kingdome on the district's western edge. As plans for the King Street stadium site took shape, district residents saw the Kingdome, like the interstate highway that preceded it, as a threat to their community. Fears that homes would be plowed under for parking lots only escalated in the early months of 1972, when city officials announced the closure of a number of the district's aging single-room-occupancy hotels, citing fire code violations.[30] It was in this context that a new coalition formed, first to oppose the stadium project, and ultimately to insist that the International District would not disappear in the shadow of the Kingdome.

## Hum Bows, Not Hot Dogs!

On November 2, 1972, Asian American students and other activists confronted city, county, and state officials at the official groundbreaking ceremony for the Kingdome project. Chanting "Down with the Dome!" the activists hurled balls of mud at the assembled officials and dignitaries. As Bob Santos later recalled, "We had sent a message to our political leaders: you may have your Kingdome, but don't forget about the [International District]."[31] In the wake of the mudslinging protest one of the government officials who had been splattered, King County executive John Spellman, commented, "For every small group which has opposed the stadium, there are hundreds of thousands who will attend when it is completed."[32] While leading politicians, the downtown business elite, and their MLB partners framed territorial claims around imagined fans and consumers, the movement that emerged in the International District enacted a different kind of spatial politics. District residents organized for new public commitments to

Anti-Kingdome activists marching to the office of the U.S. Department of
Housing and Urban Development, Seattle, November 14, 1972. (*Courtesy
Wing Luke Museum*)

their community, including investment in affordable housing for the area's
elderly Asian American population and preservation of the neighborhood's
pan-ethnic identity.

Twelve days after the protest at the groundbreaking ceremony, 150 members of a new organization, Concerned Asians for the International District,
marched on the U.S. Department of Housing and Urban Development's
Seattle office, carrying signs with such messages as "A Parking Lot Is Not
a Home" and "Hum Bows, Not Hot Dogs!"[33] The latter—referring to the

pork-filled steamed buns featured at many of the International District's family-run restaurants—became one of the movement's most distinctive slogans. The phrase "Hum Bows, Not Hot Dogs" succinctly captured the community-based politics of location that activists mobilized in opposition to Kingdome backers' territorial claims.

In uniting interests from the district's Chinese, Japanese, and Filipino communities, the anti-Kingdome movement reflected an emerging model of pan-Asian organizing. Local activists' construction and mobilization of pan-ethnic solidarity in places like the International District in the late 1960s and early 1970s marked the rise of the modern Asian American movement. Such coalition building grew out of a complex history of racial formation, as evidenced in the historical struggles over the name of the International District itself. Yen Le Espiritu suggests that Asian American pan-ethnicity be understood as a product of intertwined historical dynamics: dominant white interests' imposition of the category "Asian American" onto multi-ethnic communities, and the multiple constituencies in such communities coming to see their struggles as inextricably linked. Together with other local efforts, such as the famous campaign by a pan-Asian coalition to save San Francisco's International Hotel, the struggle in Seattle constituted a key chapter in one of the most important social movements in the second half of the twentieth century.[34]

A defining feature of the anti-Kingdome organizing from the start, and of the Asian American movement more broadly, was a new articulation of intergenerational solidarity. One particularly noteworthy instance early on in the campaign involved the Concerned Filipino Residents of the International District (CFRID), a group of elderly community members who, with assistance from young organizers, attempted to block stadium construction. Announcing plans to bring legal action, CFRID issued a statement in June 1972 that articulated members' collective feelings for the neighborhood they called home: "It is no place else in the city. It is our American experience." The statement went on to express the sentiments of the broader movement inspired by the imposition of the Kingdome: "We foresee an endless pasture of asphalt parking lots, interrupted only by luxury hotels and restaurants. Nowhere in this future do we see ourselves."[35] In filing the lawsuit, CFRID sought an injunction against stadium construction on the grounds that planners had failed to complete the environmental impact assessment required under state law. Assisted by lawyers from the city's Legal Services Center, they claimed that the project had already caused substantial "environmental impact" in the International District, citing the recent closures of six residential hotels. The legal case ultimately failed—a judge dismissed the suit in September—but the intergenerational collaboration it represented would continue to shape the fate of the neighborhood.[36]

University of Washington law student Peter Bacho, who would later become an important figure in Filipino American literature, served as a liaison between the residents of the International District and the lawyers working on the case.[37] In the process, he developed a friendship and a working relationship with Chris Mensalvas. A contemporary and friend of Filipino author and activist Carlos Bulosan, Mensalvas was a longtime organizer and former president of Local 37 of the International Longshore and Warehouse Union, which represented cannery workers, many of whom lived in the district. Together, Bacho and Mensalvas led CFRID's campaign for the rights of elderly Filipino residents, forming part of a broader movement uniting New Left student activists with Seattleites of their parents' and grandparents' generations.[38]

Protests like the mud-throwing action and the HUD march escalated in the wake of CFRID's lawsuit, and although the Kingdome project went forward, activists' organizing profoundly shaped the neighborhood's identity, spawning new alliances and lasting community institutions. In the years after the first anti-stadium mobilizations of the early 1970s, neighborhood residents and their allies pursued a broad agenda: securing resources and public services for community members, expanding employment and business opportunities for area residents and other Asian Americans, and ensuring self-determination in the material use of the International District, particularly around issues of traffic, parking, and waste—in short, the notion that the area's own interests should not be placed second to Kingdome fans' need to park their cars and dispose of their trash.[39] Developing new forms of political power became essential to this work. In his history of the neighborhood, Doug Chin highlights the "well-organized and politically astute community network" that grew out of the anti-Kingdome organizing, which helped area residents "gain recognition and access to local government resources and funding."[40]

One of the key institutional forms that such resources took was the Seattle Chinatown International District Preservation and Development Authority (SCIDPDA). Beginning in 1975, the SCIDPDA served as the district's chief manager and developer of affordable housing (overseeing a number of residential hotels), as well as of office and commercial space, with tenants including the Wing Luke Asian Museum (later renamed the Wing Luke Museum of the Asian Pacific American Experience) and the Northwest

Asian American Theatre.[41] Also as a direct result of the anti-stadium mobilizations, the neighborhood gained recognition from the city as a historic district, with a special board empowered to review development plans to ensure that it retained its historical identity.[42]

Among the other lasting accomplishments of the movement that anti-stadium activists built is the district's progressive community newspaper, the *International Examiner*. Writing in 2004, Ron Chew, who grew up in Seattle and attended the University of Washington before becoming one of the paper's longtime editors from its origins in the mid-1970s, recalled the anti-stadium organizing as a defining struggle: "Would this neighborhood, a cradle of Asian American history, a place I considered home, survive? If it did, would it advance into something cold and unrecognizable? I wanted to witness this for myself and collaborate with others—especially other student activists—in developing an active pipeline of news and information."[43] After building the *International Examiner* into one of the district's vital cultural institutions, Chew went on to serve as executive director of the Wing Luke Asian Museum.[44] Ron Chew is just one of many whose participation in the anti-Kingdome organizing of the early 1970s led to further work ensuring that the experiences and voices of the International District's residents remain valued as central to Seattle's past, present, and future. As the history of the district's galvanization suggests, movements formed in opposition to teams' territorial claims represent vital—if often overlooked—sites of community formation in the baseball world.

### The Territorial Politics of Team Ownership

Beginning with their inaugural 1977 season, the Seattle Mariners earned a reputation as one of Major League Baseball's least successful teams, failing to post a winning record until 1991. Over the course of that period, however, the Mariners franchise (as with all major league teams) grew astronomically in value. As the economist Andrew Zimbalist details, George Argyros purchased the club in 1981 for $13 million, a figure that effectively doubled the team's expansion price from just four years earlier. In 1985, by threatening to move the Mariners to another city, Argyros leveraged new public subsidies in the form of breaks on the team's rent at the Kingdome. In 1990 he sold the club to Jeffrey Smulyan, founder and CEO of Indianapolis-based Emmis Communications, for $77.5 million. Factoring in the $12 million in liabilities that Smulyan assumed from Argyros, the team's market value quintupled over the course of nine years.[45]

Almost immediately after taking ownership of the Mariners, Smulyan began pressuring city, county, and state officials for an increase in public subsidies. Smulyan was successful, in part because of his threat to pursue an "opt-out" clause in the team's twenty-year Kingdome lease, specifying that the Mariners could escape the agreement if attendance fell below 90 percent of the league average. Despite the King County Council's purchase of $200,000 worth of tickets in order to meet the 90 percent threshold, at the conclusion of the 1991 season Smulyan repeated his threat either to sell the team or to move it to a more lucrative location. His oft-quoted comment that he was "pouring money down a rat hole" seemed to sum up his feelings toward his franchise's hometown.[46] With the encouragement of Republican senator Slade Gorton, a new group of potential investors willing to purchase the team emerged, led by Nintendo president Hiroshi Yamauchi.[47] Nintendo, a Japanese video game manufacturer with North American operations based in nearby Redmond, Washington, was one of a group of new corporations transforming the economy of greater Seattle. Like software giant Microsoft, Nintendo had come to occupy a prominent position in a region increasingly distinguished as a hub for new technology firms. Making a public pitch for the Nintendo-led ownership group, Senator Gorton characterized Yamauchi's interests in philanthropic terms: "Mr. Yamauchi's motives are to thank the people of the State of Washington and the Pacific Northwest for their generosity, their welcome to him, and for the success of Nintendo of America. Puget Sound Country, he said, has been wonderful to him and he wants to give something back."[48]

Yamauchi's offer came at the height of what the historian Dana Frank has characterized as a "feeding frenzy of economic nationalism and Japan-bashing."[49] Some saw the Mariners' potential sale to a Nintendo executive as part of a larger trend of national decline, viewing with trepidation the specter of Japanese capitalists buying major U.S. businesses and cultural institutions. (Rockefeller Center and Columbia Pictures were the most frequently invoked in this category.) Popular works of the period further articulated nationalist fears through racist representations of Japanese people and capital—none more so that Michael Crichton's novel *Rising Sun,* which imagined a warlike invasion of Asian corporate power, beginning in Los Angeles and spreading across the county. Crichton included an afterword in order to state more succinctly the main idea of his accompanying fiction: "The Japanese have invented a new kind of trade—adversarial trade, trade like war, trade intended to wipe out the competition."[50]

Joining this "frenzy," MLB commissioner Fay Vincent responded to the

Nintendo-led group's intentions by proclaiming that MLB had a "strong policy against approving investors from outside the U.S. and Canada."[51] While Vincent's announcement struck many as just the latest articulation of racialized anxieties about the perceived threat of Asian capital, it also invited speculation that the commissioner and the team owners he represented had other motives, and were simply appealing to the discourse of the day while pursuing an effort to move the Mariners to Florida.[52] Such suspicions certainly appeared to have some merit. Between the mid-1980s and mid-1990s, the owners frequently invoked St. Petersburg, with its publicly financed Florida Suncoast Dome (later named Tropicana Field), as a potential destination for their teams, as they pushed for more favorable stadium deals in such existing MLB cities as San Francisco, Chicago, and Baltimore.[53] Whatever their motivations, MLB executives' initial refusal of "foreign" ownership set off a flurry of heated public pronouncements and negotiations.

The Seattle City Council unanimously adopted a resolution deploring "anti-Japanese and ethnocentric biases being used as criteria for the approval of the sale of the Seattle Mariners." The council emphasized "the strength of [the city's] Asian trade relationships and the vibrancy of Seattle's own Asian-American Community," and cautioned that "the consequences of an anti-Japanese bias by Major League Baseball has serious racial overtones and will generate negative feelings and impacts not only toward Japan, but Americans of Asian descent."[54] Many community leaders in Seattle shared the council's unanimous opinion, including Susan Mochizuki, executive director of the Japan-America Society of Washington State, who commented, "On the surface, it really looks like racism."[55]

The anti-Japanese rhetoric circulating in the baseball world had a particular impact in the International District. Speaking to a reporter from the *International Examiner,* Terry Nakano, the owner of the 300 Café, spoke out against the racism he and other community members sensed in the public discourse: "I've heard a lot of bigoted people on the radio. They bring up Pearl Harbor and Buy American and all this stuff. But I think that during this time, they should put all that aside in terms of the other people it affects." For Nakano, the issue included not only the racist rhetoric but also the specter of an empty stadium looming over the International District and its struggling small businesses: "If all those dates are vacant in the Kingdome . . . it will have a ripple effect all the way down."[56]

Against the backdrop of heated public debate over the Mariners' future, local public officials (including the mayor of Seattle and the governor of

Washington) made their case to Fay Vincent and other owners' representatives at a meeting in early February 1992. Significantly, the political leaders used the meeting to hint at the possibility of approving resources for a new stadium in the event the sale went through. In his talking points for the meeting, King County Council member Greg Nickels noted, "While the Kingdome is still an excellent facility, only 17 years old, we're examining the feasibility of a new sports facility with a retractable roof." He went on to highlight "available" land south of the Kingdome and the possibility of passing special taxation legislation to help finance the project.[57]

Members of the local business community contacted Vincent as well. John F. Clearman, the head of N.C. Machinery ("the Caterpillar dealer for Washington and Alaska") and chair of Seattle and King County's Economic Development Council, warned that "to reject this offer by this high quality investor group would be a colossal step backwards for baseball and would represent a blindness to the reality of the global marketplace."[58] Mayor Norman Rice thanked Clearman for sending the letter, likening the campaign in support of the Nintendo-led ownership group to an earlier struggle: "Once upon a time baseball couldn't see its way clear to allow African American players to play in the 'major leagues.' This opportunity is indeed a chance for the owners to move baseball into a world sport. It will take the same kind of courage Branch Rickey had. I hope they have that courage."[59] Rice also wrote to the members of the proposed ownership group, thanking them for their "personal leadership and commitment . . . to keep the Mariners" in Seattle, adding: "From our unique position as America's gateway to the Pacific Rim, we may have a vantage point on the future that others may not have. We can see how old-fashioned notions like national boundaries have been shattered by communications, trade, and independence. We recognize diversity as a value to be celebrated and promoted, rather than a threat to be feared."[60]

Facing threats of legal action and growing calls for congressional review of their industry's antitrust exemption, Major League Baseball's ownership committee finally approved the sale in June 1992. The committee insisted, however, that Yamauchi's investment constitute less than half the total purchase price of approximately $100 million, and that the Seattle-based chairman of the ownership group, Puget Sound Power and Light CEO John Ellis, have ultimate authority over the club's operating budget.[61] As Andrew Zimbalist points out, there was a historical irony to the condition that Yamauchi not hold a majority stake in the team. In 1970 a group of local investors had assembled a bid to buy the Pilots and keep them in Seattle, but then-commissioner Bowie Kuhn killed the deal on the grounds that the group's offer represented "too much of a spread of local ownership," with no single investor putting up at least 51 percent of the funds.[62] While the 1992 controversy over "foreign" capital clearly demonstrates the xenophobic hysteria particular to that historical moment, it also provides evidence of a longtime feature of Major League Baseball—the industry's construction and legitimation of local franchise identity.

Within years of threatening to prevent the Nintendo-led ownership group from introducing unwanted foreign interests into the national pastime, Major League Baseball officials would come to value the Mariners' unique status as a Pacific Rim franchise. As more and more MLB clubs began to appreciate the unrealized potential of Japanese consumer markets, the Mariners emerged in new light, becoming a trend-setting model of transnational branding. Over the course of the decade that followed the controversy of 1992, the team developed a distinctive territorial identity, erecting a state-of-the-art ballpark to replace the Kingdome, and making it home to a new band of global Mariners, led by one of the most transformative figures in baseball history, Ichiro Suzuki.

## Safeco Field and Ichiromania

Soon after purchasing the Mariners, the new ownership group began to campaign in earnest for a publicly financed replacement for the Kingdome.[63] The Mariners' lease at the stadium expired in 1996, a fact invoked frequently in an elaborate public relations campaign that raised the distinct possibility of the team pulling up stakes for greener pastures. In 1994 the team produced a glossy brochure that made the case explicitly, proclaiming in large type on its cover page, "A new ballpark is absolutely essential to the future of Major League Baseball in Seattle." Sent to public officials as part of the team's outreach strategy, the document described the club's ownership as "local people" who "came forward and bought the Mariners when they were headed elsewhere." Even while emphasizing such strong regional ties, the Mariners' campaign made it clear that "without a new ballpark and a chance to be competitive with the best teams in baseball," the team's owners would "have no choice but to consider outside offers to buy and move the team when the current lease expires."[64]

As part of the same public relations campaign, team officials presented architectural plans showing what a new home for Major League Baseball in Seattle could look like. The sketches for "New Century Park" outlined a host of exciting features, highlighted by a retractable roof to allow for outdoor baseball when the weather cooperated. The team emphasized that such a facility would be "uniquely suited to both the environment and the spirit of the Pacific Northwest" and would "reflect the international and technological leadership of this region."[65] If the ballpark campaign of the 1960s had deployed the language of aspiration, proclaiming that a domed stadium would help make Seattle a major league city, the attempt to win public support for a new facility three decades later appealed to Seattleites' growing sense of their hometown as a thriving center of the new global economy.

The greater Seattle community was sharply divided on the question of whether or not to provide further public subsidies for the Mariners. But despite considerable opposition to the project, public officials soon met the team's demands, spurred along by the Mariners' first playoff appearance in 1995, in which they defeated the New York Yankees in an epic opening round that enlivened interest in the team. After voters narrowly rejected a ballot measure that September to approve public financing for a new baseball-only facility, team officials made their case directly to lawmakers. Bowing to pressure from Mariners executives in the form of an October 30 deadline either to fund a new stadium or see the team put on the market, the state legislature approved a $320 million funding package, to be paid for with new consumer taxes.[66]

Having successfully navigated their territorial struggle for public subsidies, team officials turned their focus to the design process for what would eventually become Safeco Field, which opened just south of the Kingdome during the middle of the 1999 season. From the beginning, Seattle's ballpark designers were eager to create a facility consistent with the "retro" trend that swept Major League Baseball beginning with the opening of Baltimore's "Oriole Park at Camden Yards" in 1992. In aesthetic rebellion against the bland multipurpose stadiums of the Kingdome era, Camden Yards incorporated architectural elements of ballparks from the first decades of the twentieth century in a modern design that provided ample space for luxury seating attractive to corporate clients. Baltimore's new ballpark found considerable acclaim, earning high marks from baseball "purists" who longed for the idiosyncratic playing fields and close-up seating of an earlier era, while also attracting corporate investment from the emerging power centers of the city's transforming postindustrial economy. "If you crossed Fenway Park with a Hyatt Regency hotel," one early review suggested, "you'd get something resembling Baltimore's spanking new baseball stadium."[67] In the wake of the Orioles' success, several other MLB cities erected retro parks,

seeing Baltimore's approach to baseball urbanism as a promising development strategy.

The wave of retro ballparks that began in Baltimore became one of Major
League Baseball's most distinctive territorial developments in the age of free
agency. As Daniel Rosensweig elegantly argues in his analysis of Cleveland's
Jacobs Field, built in 1994 (renamed Progressive Field in 2008), designers
went to great lengths to construct, or to conjure, local nuance for fans to
consume: "From the creation of a sense of regional variation, to architectural gestures highlighting the uniqueness of a particular location, to simulat-
ed urban promenades and the injection of thousands of relics or souvenirs
of a previous order, these stadiums offer a link to an increasingly elided past
which is nonetheless perceived to be more stable and authentic than the
present."[68] Indeed, one of the most striking characteristics of the parks that
Seattle's design team looked to as models was their aesthetic investment in
imagined urban pasts, inviting baseball fans to feel at home by experiencing
nostalgia for versions of cities that never existed in the first place.

The members of the Public Facilities District Board, the planning committee charged with overseeing ballpark design, visited the new parks in
Baltimore and Cleveland, as well as Coors Field in Denver, as instructive
examples of the retro style. On December 18, 1995, the board adopted a
vision statement for the Mariners' new home: "The stadium is expected to
combine the look and feel of traditional ballparks with the convenience,
amenities and revenue-generating features of a modern state-of-the-art
facility." Moreover, it "should have a look that fits into the urban environment of its surrounding community."[69] Among the gestures toward the
"traditional" that made their way into the final Safeco Field design were a
hand-operated scoreboard in left field and the incorporation of the sound
of passing train whistles into the park's aural experience. Along with such
old-fashioned accoutrements, Safeco Field's brick and exposed-steel ex-
terior, expansive dining options (including tacos, stir-fry, and sushi), and
state-of-the-art retractable roof made the ballpark legible as a very different
kind of place from the Kingdome.[70]

Like other multipurpose stadiums built in the years between the great
postwar boom and the fiscal crises of the mid-1970s, the Kingdome was a
monument to its era's brand of urban liberalism. It was defined by its imposing late-modernist aesthetic and by its proclamation of metropolitan
identity, named as it was for King County, the place it called home. Safeco
Field, though built with taxpayer money like the facility it replaced, carried
the name of a corporation. Safeco Insurance paid the Mariners $40 million

A view of Safeco Field, the Kingdome, and downtown Seattle from the south, 1999. The International District lies northeast of the Kingdome. (*Reuters/CORBIS*)

for the naming rights, and while some Seattleites formed a grassroots organization—"Seattle Can Say No"—to oppose the private branding of a publicly financed park, many others accepted the transaction as an inevitable part of the baseball business.[71] By the first years of the twenty-first century ballparks across the continent, from Safeco Field in Seattle to Citi Field in New York (which replaced Shea Stadium in 2009), helped make corporate claims to public culture a regular feature of the North American built environment. On rare occasions facilities' names presented problems, as in the case of Houston's Enron Field, which existed in scandal-imposed limbo before being rebranded as Minute Maid Field in the summer of 2002. For the most part, however, hosting teams named for cities in parks named for corporations became an almost unremarkable practice, constituting one of the most basic elements of Major League Baseball's politics of location in the age of free agency.

Soon after purchasing the Mariners in 1992, the Nintendo-led ownership group began exploring marketing connections to Japan. Many of their early ideas in this area, such as transnational broadcasting and merchandising, staging exhibition games against Japanese teams, and organizing tours to

Seattle for Japanese fans, would become central to the club's focus over the next decade.[72] In an effort to bring life to this emerging business model, in the spring of 1998 Mariners executives brokered a working agreement with the Kobe-based Orix BlueWave. Over forty years earlier, in the summer of 1957, Seattle and Kobe (sharing identities as key Pacific Rim port cities) had formed a "Sister City" relationship, collaborating on cultural exchanges, in an example of the Cold War–era "people-to-people" version of international diplomacy. Mariners officials described the 1998 agreement as a "baseball extension" of the ties established and nurtured through the Sister City program. Under the terms of the arrangement, the Mariners and BlueWave would pursue joint marketing efforts, as well as share coaches, staff, and scouting resources.[73]

The most essential figures in the Mariners' construction of a new Pacific Rim identity were Japanese players. Pitcher Hideo Nomo's success with the Los Angeles Dodgers beginning in 1995, after having retired from Nippon Professional Baseball to pursue a career across the Pacific, suggested transnational possibilities for other Japanese players. The posting system that league officials established in 1998, after Alfonso Soriano left NPB and signed with the Yankees, became one possible route—if a Japanese team offered up the rights to a player's contract, he could have the opportunity to negotiate with an interested MLB club. Nippon Professional Baseball's limited system of free agency, first established in 1993 and later revised in 1998, represented another possible path to MLB. As part of this system, veteran players (initially those with ten years of experience; nine after the 1998 revision) could become free agents and entertain offers from MLB teams.[74] One such veteran, star relief pitcher Kazuhiro Sasaki, signed with the Mariners in late 1999. Led by new general manager Pat Gillick, Mariners brass worked hard to woo Sasaki. A specially designed recruiting tour of Seattle included a visit to the International District's Uwajimaya Market. Weeks later, when team officials and their new prized pitcher held a press conference in Kyoto to announce the contract, Hiroshi Yamauchi was in attendance, in what media outlets reported as the Nintendo executive's first public appearance on official Mariners business.[75] Sasaki immediately established himself as one of MLB's top relievers, winning the American League's Rookie of the Year award in 2000, and setting the stage for an even more dramatic debut the following season—that of Ichiro Suzuki.

Ichiro began to make waves during his 1994 breakout NPB season. Setting a Japanese record with 210 hits (in just 130 games) on the way to the first of seven consecutive batting titles in the Pacific League, he quickly be-

came one of the most accomplished and popular players in Nippon Professional Baseball. By the middle of the 1994 season he was already enough of
a standout with the Orix BlueWave to have achieved the one-name status
that he would bring with him to the Mariners.[76] His fame reverberated well
beyond the diamond, as evidenced by a cover story in *Newsweek International* in the summer of 1996 that proclaimed: "He's hot. He's hip. He's the
new face of Japan."[77] Even as he was anointed the "new face of Japan," Ichiro
saw the opportunity to play in the United States as an attractive next step,
especially after spending two weeks training with the Mariners in the spring
of 1999, during a special exchange facilitated under the terms of the working agreement. With the BlueWave struggling despite their star's great play,
team executives embraced the opportunity to recoup value from the rights
to his contract via the new posting system. Seeing Ichiro as a perfect fit
for right field at Safeco, the Mariners submitted a winning bid of over $13
million for the rights to negotiate with him. Ichiro became a Mariner in
November 2000, signing a $14 million three-year contract.[78]

From the very beginning of his time in Seattle, Ichiro was an absolute
sensation. His batting style, in which he seemed to be already moving toward first base at the moment of contact with the ball, was a revelation to
fans and writers who had not seen him play in Japan. As an outfielder Ichiro
turned heads, as well. Television footage of him throwing out Oakland's
fleet-footed Terrence Long attempting to advance from first base to third
on a routine single went viral, as fans, commentators, players, and coaches
alike quickly recognized the Mariners' new right fielder as the owner of
one of the game's strongest arms. Prowess in the field complemented utter
dominance at the plate, earning him the American League's Most Valuable
Player and Rookie of the Year honors, the first time someone had captured
both awards since Boston's Fred Lynn in 1975. But Ichiro's first MLB season
drew even loftier statistical comparisons than Lynn's legendary campaign.
He was the first major leaguer to lead his league in both batting average and
stolen bases since Jackie Robinson accomplished the feat with the Brooklyn
Dodgers in 1949.

As had been the case the previous season, when Kazuhiro Sasaki was the
American League's Rookie of the Year, as well as in 1995, when Hideo Nomo
won the honor in the National League, Ichiro's status as a "rookie" aroused
controversy. Some influential observers suggested that established players
from Japan shouldn't be considered for an award intended to honor young
stars just up from the minors. "When they put the Rookie of the Year Award
in," Indians general manager John Hart argued (while making the case for

Cleveland's C. C. Sabathia as more deserving), "nobody thought they'd be bringing in 30-year-old guys from Japan."[79] ESPN's Jayson Stark, one of the most prominent baseball journalists of the era, cast the issue in slightly different light two years later in an online column during the rookie season of another breakout Japanese star—Hideki Matsui of the New York Yankees. A member of the Baseball Writers' Association of America, the organization responsible for voting on awards such as Rookie of the Year, Stark wrote:

> It's time we start treating Japanese baseball for what it is—a third "major" league. It would be a farce to adopt that stance just to keep foreign players from being the Rookie of the Year. We should adopt it to respect and honor the accomplishments of the Ichiros, the Matsuis and the Nomos in Japan—in *every* way. Those accomplishments, those stats belong in their listings in the baseball encyclopedias and registers. Those feats should be part of those players' credentials when we consider their Hall of Fame worthiness. And all we ask, as we lend them that respect, is that it means they *shouldn't* be eligible for Rookie of the Year awards.[80]

The fact that influential writers like Stark found themselves reevaluating the comparative "major" status of U.S. and Japanese professional baseball was yet another measure of the extraordinary impact that Ichiro and other Japanese stars had on the sport. Fans of Major League Baseball, an enterprise that for a century had dubbed its annual championship the World Series, now confronted complicated questions about the sport's assumed international hierarchy. In the years following his historic rookie season, Ichiro continued to rewrite Major League Baseball's record books, an effort highlighted by his remarkable ten consecutive campaigns with 200 or more hits. Ichiro's production at the plate reached an astounding peak in 2004, when he set the record for hits in a single season with 262, breaking George Sisler's mark (257) from 1920. Few athletes have made as great an impact on their sport over the course of a decade—by any measure—as Ichiro did with the Mariners beginning in 2001.

Ichiro's cultural impact carried well beyond the typical bounds of the baseball world, even inspiring multiple songs by Seattle-area musicians, including hip-hop artist Xola Malik's "Ichiro!" ("popcorn / Cracker Jack / c'mon Ichiro, swing that bat") and indie rocker Ben Gibbard's "Ichiro's Theme" ("go, go, go, go Ichiro / rounding third and heading for home"). Although by any estimation a pop culture superstar, and the subject of constant interest from members of the U.S. and Japanese media, Ichiro distinguished himself as one of MLB's most elusive personalities, rarely engaging in extended or revealing interviews. Particularly for fans who had access to his words only as they were interpreted and made available to the English-language press, his persona remained something of a mystery. As evidence of the fact that fans on both sides of the Pacific hungered for greater access to Ichiro, at the height of the hysteria during his rookie season a number of media outlets reported the rumor that a Japanese magazine was prepared to pay $2 million for a nude photograph of the transnational superstar.[81]

During Ichiro's debut year in MLB, the Seattle-based novelist and essayist David Shields—in addition to profiling him for the *New York Times Magazine*—published *"Baseball Is Just Baseball": The Understated Ichiro*, an "unauthorized collection" of the player's published comments. The book has a pseudo-philosophical quality, thanks to the sparseness of its pages, each containing a short quotation, in most cases consisting of just one or two sentences. With Shields as a guide, readers encounter such kernels of wisdom as "If your feet are healthy, you're healthy" and "Failure is the mother of success."[82] Shields came to the project after finding himself eagerly opening the Seattle newspapers each morning in anticipation of whatever brief, unorthodox comment from Ichiro might appear. "He never boasted in the way that I was accustomed to athletes doing," says Shields, "or if he did, he seemed to do so in a way that was fresh and funny in its uncluttered assertion of neutral fact."

That a ballplayer could inspire a book consisting of brief "sayings and naysayings," culled from the daily sports pages and presented as "provocative and inspiring," is an index of just how captivating a cultural figure Ichiro became. In the book's introduction, Shields reflects on his own cultural framework for interpreting and representing Ichiro in this way: "Maybe the words acquired a lyrical glamour as they got translated from Japanese to English? Perhaps it was the translators themselves who were turning Ichiro's ordinary statements into haunting aphorisms? Maybe it was a cultural-transmission issue: maybe what were to my Western ears Zen koans were, to Ichiro, self-evident truths, the only gestures available? I could analyze it to death, but I'd rather not."[83] As Shields begins to acknowledge, the book enters a long history of representation in the baseball world that figures individual stars as embodiments of essentialized notions of racial, ethnic, and national identity. Evoking an Orientalist genre of Western cultural production about Asian bodies and cultures, Shields's celebration of Ichiro registers the ballplayer's status as a commodified transnational icon.

As Ichiro himself recognized, the fact that most fans in Seattle heard his words only through interpreters contributed to his status as a somewhat enigmatic superstar. "What I can't express in words, because of the language

Ichiro getting ready to hit, Shea Stadium, June 2008. (*Photo by Andrew J. Klein, reprinted with permission*)

barrier, I hope to show . . . with my performance on the field," he told interviewer Narumi Komatsu in 2004. "I don't know if in these past three years I've repaid all [the Mariners'] investment in me, but I'm confident I've made a contribution. I want to help the team win, of course, but also I want to be an appealing sort of player myself."[84] Ichiro's success as a remarkably "appealing sort of player" in Seattle did more than justify his team's investment in his contract. His captivating performance allowed Major League Baseball to enlist his team in an elaborate global marketing strategy.

Under a policy that dates back to the years of MLB's first globetrotting postseason barnstorming teams, all revenue that major league teams generate from international broadcasting, marketing, and licensing goes into a shared pool.[85] This means that Major League Baseball as a whole was invested in the transnational commodification of Ichiro Suzuki, and in the broader construction of the Mariners as a team that Japanese fans could call their own. Major League Baseball Japan, a division of Major League Baseball International (MLB's global marketing wing), entered the 2005 season with fourteen corporate sponsorship agreements. Exemplifying the industry's focus on the marketability of stars, MLB International's April 2005 newsletter announced a new partnership with Japanese telecommunications giant NTT that would "focus on corporate advertising, highlighting [NTT's] relationship with MLB and Seattle Mariners outfielder Ichiro Suzuki."[86] The star also joined his fellow members of the Major League Baseball Players Association in promoting and profiting from the global sale of Ichiro memorabilia, from replica jerseys to bobblehead dolls. Through the organization's ongoing licensing program, and partnerships in such new initiatives as the World Baseball Classic, the MLBPA helped further Ichiro's status as one of the most prominent—and profitable—figures in the baseball world.

With Ichiro's arrival in 2001, Safeco Field itself became an innovative site of transnational cultural production and commodification. The team built a permanent broadcast booth for NHK, the major Japanese television network, enabling a trans-Pacific audience to enjoy every Mariners game. Ichiro's commanding presence on the diamond drew advertisements targeted to fans tuning in from Japan, as well as Japanese visitors to the ballpark. Team officials marketed Mariners games as destination events for the Pacific Northwest's growing Asian tourism industry, and luxury tour packages soon featured excursions to Safeco Field. Stadium guides printed in Japanese were included in Mariners official game programs, and the team hired bilingual staff members to assist Japanese fans.[87] Indeed, for all the ballpark's gestures toward a situated urban experience built on tradition and nostalgia, from the brick façade to the sounds of train whistles, Safeco Field's most distinguishing identity during Ichiro's years there was as a stage for one of Major League Baseball's most transcendent stars.

Known throughout the baseball world as Ichiro's home turf, Safeco Field also served as a constant structuring presence for residents of the International District. The ballpark was erected immediately south of the old Kingdome site, where—after the dome's demolition in 2000—a football stadium for the Seattle Seahawks, the Mariners' former co-tenants at the Kingdome, appeared in its place. As Doug Chin notes, community organizations did not mobilize against the second generation of sports stadiums on nearly the same scale as they had decades earlier, in part because area residents had "become accustomed" to the daily annoyances of stadium traffic and noise. Chin also points to the successes of community organizing during the Kingdome era in creating structures through which area residents and stakeholders could participate in planning the new facilities.[88] Nevertheless, a number of district constituents did mount a campaign against the Safeco Field project, echoing the concerns of the earlier era of anti-dome protests.[89] On June 28, 1996, over one hundred community members assembled, chanting "Social Programs, Not Souvenir Programs" and "Congee Not Congestion."[90] With their allusions to the "Hum Bows, Not Hot Dogs!" slogan of 1972, these chants voiced the enduring legacy of neighborhood mobilization.

As he did for communities and constituencies throughout greater Seattle, Ichiro generated a great deal of enthusiasm and pride among many of the International District's residents and business owners. At the height of Ichiromania, the ballplayer's image was a common sight in the neighborhood, as it was throughout the region. In light of the International District's history of organizing for the preservation of Asian American cultural identity in opposition to the Mariners' designs on the area, the fact that the new face of the franchise belonged to one of the most famous Japanese athletes in modern sports history took on special significance. As a regional nexus of Asian culture and commerce, home to such retailers as the Uwajimaya Market and the Kinokuniya Bookstore, the International District was uniquely situated for Ichiromania. Commenting on a display of books and other products in both English and Japanese at Kinokuniya, the *International Examiner* asked: "What is an Asian bookstore without an Ichiro section? Here, it looks more like a shrine in honor of Seattle's favorite outfielder."[91]

In the spring of 2003, as the baseball season was getting under way, a new exhibit opened at the Wing Luke Asian Museum—*Playing for Keeps: Asian Pacific Americans in Sports*. Situating stories of athletic achievement within larger histories of race, immigration, and community formation, the exhibit framed contemporary professional athletes like Ichiro in light of the work done by previous generations of transnational migrants, both on and off the playing field.[92] Vibrant cultural institutions like the community newspaper and museum ensured that the neighborhood could critically embrace the achievements of Ichiro's Mariners and still retain a community identity beyond the shadow cast by Safeco Field.

The International District's history of community mobilization resonates with that of other neighborhoods in the second half of the twentieth century. Dating back to the struggles over Los Angeles's Chavez Ravine in the era of MLB's postwar expansion, poor and working-class communities have been threatened by Major League Baseball's territorial claims. A more recent and lesser-known campaign occurred in Philadelphia in the late 1990s. At the same time that residents of the International District were confronting the reality of another stadium, a community coalition successfully organized against a proposed ballpark for the Philadelphia Phillies in their city's Chinatown neighborhood. Forming the Stadium Out of Chinatown Coalition, community members and stakeholders pushed back against the plans of the city's political and business leaders, making persuasive arguments about the potential impact on the neighborhood's survival that recalled the struggle against the Kingdome.[93] The histories of eviction at Chavez Ravine and community mobilization in Philadelphia's Chinatown, like the history of struggle in Seattle's International District, stand as illuminating events in Major League Baseball's construction of place-based affiliation. Ballparks like Safeco Field may invite spectators to revel in a shared identity as baseball fans, but the history of their development reveals a more complex, contested politics of location.

Selling the Ichiroll at Safeco Field, August 2006. (*Photo by author*)

During the 2001 season, Safeco Field's sushi bars began featuring a new culinary creation: the Ichiroll. Fans at Mariners games, whether tourists from Japan or young urban professionals working in Seattle's new technology industries, could, for a cool $9, savor a perfect complement to the action on the field.[94] The Ichiroll can be seen as an emblem for the ways in which Japanese ballplayers have joined with athletes from Mexico, the Dominican Republic, and elsewhere to remake Major League Baseball, negotiating their own transnational commodification as cultural icons. In the broader context of the Mariners' relationship with their city, however, the branded spicy tuna roll stands as a more complicated component of the ballpark experience. International District residents' long struggle for resources and recognition in the shadow of the Mariners' stadium projects represents a very different story of collective identity from the one enacted and sold at Safeco Field. For while the Ichiroll was not a hot dog, neither was it a hum bow.

# Epilogue

ICHIRO'S PHENOMENAL DEBUT season in Seattle, in which he led his team to a runaway division title and a showdown with the Yankees in the American League Championship Series, helped Mariners fans get over the departure of the previous face of the franchise: star shortstop Alex Rodriguez. Following the 2000 season, "A-Rod," widely considered one of the best players of his generation, signed a ten-year $252 million free agent contract with the Texas Rangers. For Seattle fans this marked the second consecutive winter of catastrophic loss, coming on the heels of Ken Griffey Jr.'s departure for his hometown of Cincinnati after the 1999 campaign. When Rodriguez returned to Seattle for the first time with his new team in April, sellout crowds at Safeco Field greeted the former Mariner with thunderous boos. Some in attendance even showered the field with fake $100,000 bills, protesting the player's apparent choice of money over loyalty to his first major league home.[1]

There was a certain irony in the spectacle of Seattle's baseball fans mocking A-Rod while rallying behind Ichiro, who himself had only recently changed jerseys in pursuit of a lucrative opportunity in a new city. As the Safeco Field crowd's alternate booing and cheering suggests, fans and players alike have had to become increasingly adept at the art of flexible affiliation. To connect with their teams, communities must engage in nimble acts of fiction writing, embracing each year's roster of athletes as hometown heroes, in spite of the crude reality of MLB's marketplace of athletic talent.

Fans' collective revisions of local identity, like the annual acts of player mobility and roster replenishment with which they are inextricably linked, have come to define Major League Baseball in the age of free agency. New practices—and politics—of flexibility lie at the heart of three of the baseball industry's most significant developments in the early years of the twenty-first century: the growth of the World Baseball Classic, the increasing popularity of fantasy baseball leagues, and the public revelation of players' use of banned performance-enhancing substances.

One of the most conspicuous developments in the baseball industry in recent years has been the World Baseball Classic (WBC). Held for the first time in 2006, reprised in 2009 and 2013, and scheduled to be repeated at four-year intervals thereafter, this round-robin tournament pits national teams against one another in a format modeled on soccer's World Cup. Reflecting the balance of power in the industry's labor relations, the MLBPA has been a core partner in the WBC from the beginning.[2] While one long-term ambition for the contest is to develop new territories of baseball interest, the event relies first and foremost on fan investment from established national strongholds.

One nation that has figured especially prominently in the early history of the WBC is Cuba, making the tournament a relatively rare instance in which the country's athletes have competed against the rest of the baseball world's top professional players. Cuba advanced to the championship game in 2006 with hard-fought wins over both Venezuela and Puerto Rico, showcasing the exemplary play that has long defined Cuban teams' performance in international amateur competition. But the Cubans ultimately fell in the championship game to a great team from Japan, led by Ichiro Suzuki. The iconic Mariner and his fellow Japanese stars continued their WBC dominance in 2009, this time besting South Korea in the final game. In the wake of their back-to-back victories, Japanese players campaigned for a larger share of WBC revenue. In July 2012 the Nippon Professional Baseball Players Association announced that its members would sit out in 2013 unless the tournament's profits could be distributed more equitably. The players did not back down until Nippon Professional Baseball officials negotiated a new agreement on sponsorship rights with WBC organizers.[3]

Seeking audiences across the baseball world, the WBC builds on a signature element of Major League Baseball's transnational business model: tapping into communities of fans through the popularity of local stars. But the tournament has at times placed athletes' multiple identities and constituencies in conflict. Ichiro, for example, faced criticism in 2009 from some members of the Seattle sports media over whether his commitment to winning a WBC championship for Japan might hinder his preparation for the upcoming MLB season.[4] Alex Rodriguez confronted scrutiny of a different sort as he struggled to decide which national team to join. Born in New

York City, Rodriguez spent parts of his childhood in both Santo Domingo and Miami. In this way he exemplified the complex transnational identity shared by millions of Dominican Americans. WBC rules allow players to represent either their own or their parents' native country, and in 2006 Rodriguez labored over his decision before announcing that he would play for the U.S. team, drawing rebuke from multiple quarters. An injury forced him to sit out the 2009 WBC, but not before he had declared his intention to join the Dominican team, inviting a new wave of criticism.[5] The public controversies over the terms of players like Ichiro and A-Rod's participation in the World Baseball Classic underscored how central flexible citizenship had become to the sport by the first decade of the twenty-first century.

Fantasy baseball, in which fans draft and manage imaginary teams composed of major league players, competing against other "owners" to compile the best statistics over the course of the season, has become exceedingly popular in recent decades.[6] Writer Daniel Okrent and his fellow members of the Rotisserie League (named for La Rotisserie Française, the Manhattan restaurant where early league meetings took place) have been credited with devising the first version of modern fantasy baseball in the late 1970s. By the early 1990s, millions of fans were competing in leagues with the help of the expanded publication of statistics in print forums such as *USA Today*. But what had been a craze among a committed subculture of baseball nuts exploded into a much larger Internet-based phenomenon in the late 1990s and early 2000s, as dedicated websites processed pitch-by-pitch results from MLB games into real-time score updates for growing numbers of fantasy leagues.[7]

The proliferation of fantasy leagues in the Internet era spurred MLBPA leaders and MLB officials alike to assert property rights to the player statistics essential to this growing offshoot of the baseball business. Starting in the 1990s, the MLBPA signed licensing agreements with a number of fantasy content providers. The union's approach in this area grew naturally out of the long, profitable history of collective licensing that dated back to Marvin Miller's first years as MLBPA executive director. In 2005, MLB's division for Internet-based business initiatives, Major League Baseball Advanced Media (MLBAM), signed a $50 million five-year deal with the union to acquire players' licensing rights for fantasy leagues and related online content. When in short order MLBAM declined to ink a deal with St. Louis–based CBC Distribution and Marketing, a fantasy content provider with which the MLBPA had worked since 1994, a legal fight ensued. Faced with the prospect of being shut out of its own industry, CBC brought a successful suit against both MLBAM and the MLBPA. CBC won the case by arguing that player statistics, which have long been widely available through newspapers and other media, are in the public domain.[8]

The CBC court fight was a significant development in the baseball business, and not just for its implications for the future viability of fantasy content providers. The fact that Major League Baseball's players and team owners were positioned on the same side of a legal battle over property rights was a sign—like their joint investment in the World Baseball Classic—of the MLBPA's power in the industry. Union–management collaboration in marketing and licensing initiatives such as branded fantasy content and the WBC unfolded in an era of relative labor peace which distinguished baseball from the other major professional sports in the United States. That baseball's owners and union officials hammered out a new collective bargaining agreement without a great deal of rancor in the fall of 2011 was notable in light of the bitter lockouts that rocked professional football (2011), basketball (2011), and hockey (2012–13) during the same period. The MLBPA's strong and stable position in the industry, particularly when seen against the backdrop of tense struggles faced by athletes and their organizations in other sports, provides further evidence of ballplayer unionism's enormous impact over the four decades since Marvin Miller visited spring training camps for the first time.

Fantasy baseball matters not simply as an important feature of MLB as a business but also as an increasingly widespread form of spectatorship. Unlike some fans, whose interest in baseball news might not extend far beyond their favorite team, committed fantasy leaguers depart from conventional place-based forms of engagement, keeping tabs on every MLB player and top prospect. Allowing fans to organize their own "home" teams, and requiring neither physical proximity to the ballpark nor access to local broadcasts, fantasy baseball lends itself especially well to the cultivation of fans who fall outside MLB's traditional arrangements of territorial identity. Just as significant, the enterprise privileges a form of spectatorship centered on individual athletes' "metrics" rather than on MLB teams' collective accomplishments.

With its growing legions of imaginary executives, the fantasy phenomenon resonates with a larger trend in baseball storytelling. As personnel transactions have become more and more a part of the drama of Major League Baseball in the age of free agency, general managers have themselves become stars. Consider the 2011 feature film *Moneyball*, starring Brad

Pitt as Oakland A's general manager Billy Beane. Based on Michael Lewis's best-selling account of Beane's innovative approach to reappraising under-valued talent, *Moneyball* marked a key development in films about baseball, making the front office the center of the action.[9] Nominated for an Acade-my Award, Pitt's portrayal of Beane may prove as iconic for new generations of baseball fans, who have grown up playing in fantasy leagues and tracking off-season free agent transactions, as Gary Cooper's Lou Gehrig and Robert Redford's Roy Hobbs were in their own day.[10] Though contractual dramas have figured in popular baseball narratives since the nineteenth century, free agency has engendered a heightened attention to the work of evaluat-ing, recruiting, and managing athletic talent.

For many baseball fans, the turn of the twenty-first century will always be known principally by one designation: the steroid era. Whispers and rumors about doping in baseball had circulated since the late 1980s, but the first decade of the new century saw a cascade of public scrutiny when performance-enhancing drugs became the subject of tell-all memoirs, con-gressional investigations, and collective bargaining between major league players and their teams. In response to the scandal, league officials imple-mented mandatory random testing, first in the minors and later—following a 2002 agreement with the union—in MLB.[11] The results of the drug testing programs quickly pointed up a striking global division in the impact of per-formance enhancement.

Since the beginning of baseball's anti-doping program, Latin American athletes have represented a disproportionate number of those testing posi-tive, at both the major and minor league levels. Players from the Dominican Republic in particular have tested positive for steroids at a noticeably high rate, accounting for 38 percent of positive tests between 2005 and 2009, while representing only 17 percent of all players at the time.[12] The large number of Dominican athletes among sanctioned players is a product of their nation's position in the political economy of the contemporary base-ball world. The rise of the Dominican Republic as a key site of MLB talent development has created powerful dreams for many young Dominican ball-players from impoverished backgrounds, for whom the baseball academies promise a shot at a better life than seems possible working in the nation's tourist industry, free trade zones, or informal economy. With the stakes so high, many young players—and those around them with a financial interest in their future careers in the big leagues—are willing to put their bodies at risk for a chance at a contract. With steroids available both over the counter and under the table, their use has grown widespread throughout Dominican baseball, even as MLB officials have instituted testing in the academies and the Dominican Summer League.

Players who use performance-enhancing drugs without medical supervision assume deadly risk. In 2001, two Dominican prospects died after taking veterinary steroids. Eighteen-year-old William Felix succumbed to a heart attack after several months of self-administered shots. Lino Ortiz, age nineteen, perished three days after injecting himself in advance of his third tryout with an MLB team, reportedly out of desperation to improve his chances of impressing the scouts.[13] In the years since these tragic deaths, especially in the wake of the larger steroid controversy in Major League Baseball, U.S. baseball executives have responded to pressure by advocates for Dominican player safety with increased drug testing and additional resources for education and prevention among the nation's prospects. There are, however, substantial limits to such reform efforts. MLB's academy system, in which work contracts and signing bonuses are awarded on the basis of scouts' assessments of the potential contained in young athletes' bodies, presents powerful incentives for gaining every possible physical advantage.

While the stories of young men like William Felix and Lino Ortiz stand as reminders of the inequalities that structure baseball as a transnational culture industry, the most prominent episodes in the steroid controversy in recent years have centered on stars. Some of Major League Baseball's most famous players, including Mark McGwire, Barry Bonds, Roger Clemens, and Alex Rodriguez, have had their remarkable achievements on the diamond called into question by allegations (and, in some cases, admissions) that they used steroids or human growth hormone. A distinguishing characteristic of the public response to baseball's steroid era has been an intense focus on individuals, and on individual guilt. From José Canseco's bombshell memoir, *Juiced*, to Major League Baseball's own internal investigation headed by former U.S. senator George Mitchell, to the series of congressional hearings on the matter, the public has been invited to reckon with the steroid era through rituals of naming names.[14]

The widespread focus on personal culpability is closely tied to the privileged place that individual records occupy in baseball history. Commentators and fans have expressed outrage that Mark McGwire and Barry Bonds, star players linked to steroid use, hold the iconic home run records previously set by Babe Ruth and Hank Aaron. But there is more at stake in the outrage over performance enhancement than respect for the statistical accomplishments of earlier heroes. Stars' alleged use of steroids threatens to undermine a core cultural identity attached to athletes more broadly—their ability to stand as ideal representations of individual agency. It is a measure of our powerful cultural investment in individualism that the most dominant response to the steroid era has been to scorn players like McGwire and Bonds as "cheaters" or betrayers of fair play, rather than to call into question the larger structures of power and ideologies of competition under which they labor.

It remains to be seen whether a deeper cultural conversation about the political economy of athletic performance can grow out of baseball's steroid era. The successive waves of accusations and revelations have certainly brought new focus to the laboring bodies of star athletes. While the drugs in question help build muscle, they also help heal. Like Jim Bouton's "greenies" and the other substances that generations of professional athletes have taken to allow them to go back out on the field, day after day, steroids are as much performance enabling as they are performance enhancing. In this sense the sport's doping controversies have revealed some of the physical pain and abuse that elite athletes must endure on the job in order to make Major League Baseball what it is. This is not to suggest that players are powerless victims. On the contrary, the forms of player power that have shaped the modern baseball industry have likewise done much to establish the stakes and debates of the steroid era. That is, as a union defined by its commitment to a labor politics of free market individualism, the MLBPA has helped set the stage for the performances of accusation and guilt that have done so much to define recent baseball history. Although star power has clearly served MLB players well in many respects, the measures of personal risk and solitary blame that athletes continue to bear suggest some of the limits and contradictions of a workplace ethic of individual exceptionalism.

Even in the wake of the steroid scandals and through the lean years of the "Great Recession," Major League Baseball has remained extraordinarily popular. Fans throughout the baseball world continue to find value and meaning in the work that big league players perform. While some athletes have seen their reputations profoundly tarnished by allegations of drug use, others have been held up as unimpeachable examples of principled hard work. For every Alex Rodriguez, forced to carry the burden of blame for his industry's widespread culture of performance enhancement, there is an Ichiro Suzuki, singled out as a model of clean play. Although no longer leading the American League in hits every year, after more than a decade with the Mariners, Ichiro remained one of the sport's most celebrated stars.

Ichiro's iconic status made July 23, 2012, an especially dramatic day in the baseball world, when the Mariners traded their longtime star to the New York Yankees, in exchange for two minor league pitching prospects. Having played for more than ten years in MLB, and over five with the same team, Ichiro was protected against being traded under the "ten–five" rule, which team owners and the union had agreed to in the wake of Curt Flood's historic challenge to the reserve clause. In the immediate aftermath of the move, Mariners officials announced that the player had come to them earlier in the season to request a trade if it could improve the team's prospects for rebuilding into a World Series contender once more. Joining a new team might also provide Ichiro with the opportunity to pursue his primary remaining objective in MLB: to play in a World Series himself. An additional factor was the growing sense—unimaginable just a few years earlier—that there would be at least a measure of public support for a deal. Ichiro still showed flashes of his former brilliance, but by 2012 his skills had slipped to the point where some Seattle sports commentators—including his former teammate Jay Buhner—registered their strong conviction that the team should move on without the player whom many regarded as worthy of eventual recognition in Cooperstown.[15]

On the day of the trade, before he assumed his new role with the Yankees, Ichiro held a press conference to bid farewell to Seattle and reflect on his career with the Mariners. "Thank you for the last eleven and a half years," he said through his interpreter. Speaking slowly, with emotion audible in his voice, the star player went on to describe his choice to request a trade as a difficult but necessary next step for himself and his now former team.[16] Seen in the larger context of Major League Baseball's labor history, his comments are especially meaningful. Thanks to the struggles of earlier generations of athletes like Curt Flood, Ichiro had been able to exercise substantial agency in determining his professional future.

Hours after his press conference, Ichiro played for the first time as a visitor at Safeco Field. He received an enormous standing ovation before his first at-bat in the gray Yankees uniform, taking two deep bows in response to the crowd's loud, sustained cheers. The moment became an opportunity for an imagined community of baseball fans to honor a departing hero. Ichiro's leaving occurred under far more compelling circumstances than those of other Seattle players in earlier years, including his new teammate Alex

Rodriguez, who after moving from the Mariners to the Rangers in 2000 had since been acquired by the Yankees, in another blockbuster trade. But much more than a matter of celebrating one athlete in comparison to others, the crowd's ovation was a form of collective reckoning with historical change, a shared acknowledgement of the end of an era. For fans who had rooted for Ichiro's Seattle Mariners, his first at-bat with the Yankees presented a rare chance to say good-bye, not only to a great player but also to a period in their own cultural history.

Baseball remains a captivating cultural form because we continue to celebrate athletes for the labor they perform on behalf of the communities they represent, in spite of the dollar signs attached. Perhaps the powerful applause at such moments as Ichiro's farewell registers as an index of longings for collective purpose in the face of the free market individualism that has defined our era, however elusive such dreams may be. Does the future hold a world—baseball or otherwise—in which more people enjoy real freedom and agency in their own lives, with the opportunity to leave their mark as part of something larger than themselves? If baseball teaches us anything, it is to have faith that history remains to be written, and that there is always hope for what the next season may bring.

# NOTES

## Introduction

1. As Warren Goldstein argues, "the experience of baseball play cannot be understood apart from the experience of work—inside as well as outside the game." Warren Goldstein, *Playing for Keeps: A History of Early Baseball* (Ithaca: Cornell University Press, 1989), 155.

2. See, for example, John F. Kasson, *Amusing the Million: Coney Island at the Turn of the Century* (New York: Hill and Wang, 1978); and Kathy Peiss, *Cheap Amusements: Working Women and Leisure in Turn-of-the-Century New York* (Philadelphia: Temple University Press, 1986).

3. W. P. Kinsella's fiction contains extended meditations on this aspect of the sport. See, in particular, *The Iowa Baseball Confederacy* (Boston: Houghton Mifflin, 1986).

4. Warren I. Susman, "Culture Heroes: Ford, Barton, Ruth," in *Culture as History: The Transformation of American Society in the Twentieth Century* (New York: Pantheon, 1984), 146.

5. For an insightful formulation of the relationship between sport's material and symbolic content, see Michael Oriard, *Reading Football: How the Popular Press Created an American Spectacle* (Chapel Hill: University of North Carolina Press, 1998).

6. See Richard Ben Cramer, *Joe DiMaggio: The Hero's Life* (New York: Simon and Schuster, 2000), 66–67.

7. Jayson Stark, "Angels Shock the Baseball World," ESPN.com, December 9, 2011.

8. My use of "the baseball world" as an analytical term draws on work by scholars of world-systems theory and global cultural studies. In particular, see Immanuel Wallerstein, *World-Systems Analysis: An Introduction* (Durham: Duke University Press, 2004) and Pascale Casanova, *The World Republic of Letters* (Cambridge: Harvard University Press, 2004). For a valuable discussion of baseball's transnational identity, see William W. Kelly, "Is Baseball a Global Sport? America's National Pastime as Global Field and International Sport," *Global Networks* 7.2 (2007): 187–201.

9. David Harvey, *The Condition of Postmodernity: An Enquiry into the Origins of Cultural Change* (Cambridge: Blackwell, 1990), vii.

10. Ibid., 124; Aihwa Ong, *Flexible Citizenship: The Cultural Logics of Transnationality* (Durham: Duke University Press, 1999).

## 1. The Roots of Free Agency

1. Leonard Koppett, "Shea Stadium Opens with Big Traffic Jam," *New York Times,* April 18, 1964; Arthur Daley, "History Is Made," *New York Times,* April 19, 1964.

2. Prior to the Brooklyn Dodgers' move to Los Angeles, Moses had championed the Flushing site as an ideal location for a modern municipal baseball stadium, a proposition that team owner Walter O'Malley rejected. See Neil J. Sullivan, *The Dodgers Move West* (New York: Oxford University Press, 1987).

3. "The Fair Makes It Easy for Tireless Met Fans," *New York Times*, May 9, 1964.

4. "Text of President Johnson's Speech at Dedication," *New York Times*, April 23, 1964. On the stall-in, see Brian Purnell, "'Drive Awhile for Freedom': Brooklyn CORE's 1964 Stall-In and Public Discourses on Protest Violence," in *Groundwork: Local Black Freedom Movements in America*, ed. Jeanne Theoharis and Komozi Woodard (New York: New York University Press, 2005), 45–75.

5. On the beginnings of baseball in the United States, see Warren Goldstein, *Playing for Keeps: A History of Early Baseball* (Ithaca: Cornell University Press, 1989); and Harold Seymour, *Baseball: The Early Years* (New York: Oxford University Press, 1989).

6. On baseball in Cuba, see Roberto González Echevarría, *The Pride of Havana: A History of Cuban Baseball* (New York: Oxford University Press, 1999); Louis A. Pérez Jr., "Between Baseball and Bullfighting: The Quest for Nationality in Cuba, 1868–1898," *Journal of American History* 81.2 (September 1994): 493–517, and *On Becoming Cuban: Identity, Nationality, and Culture* (Chapel Hill: University of North Carolina Press, 1999); Peter C. Bjarkman, *A History of Cuban Baseball, 1864–2006* (Jefferson, N.C.: McFarland, 2007); and Milton H. Jamail, *Full Count: Inside Cuban Baseball* (Carbondale: Southern Illinois University Press, 2000).

7. Donald Roden, "Baseball and the Quest for National Dignity in Meiji Japan," *American Historical Review* 85.3 (June 1980): 518 and 520.

8. Rob Ruck, *The Tropic of Baseball: Baseball in the Dominican Republic* (1991; repr., Lincoln: University of Nebraska Press, 1999), 4. The presence of corporations was critical in the early transnational development of baseball. Sugar mills were key sponsors of Caribbean baseball, and the expanding railroad industry was an important conduit for early baseball in Mexico. See William H. Beezley, *Judas at the Jockey Club and other Episodes of Porfirian Mexico* (Lincoln: University of Nebraska Press, 1987).

9. Joseph A. Reaves, *Taking in a Game: A History of Baseball in Asia* (Lincoln: University of Nebraska Press, 2002), 116.

10. For an overview of baseball's development around the world, see Peter C. Bjarkman, *Diamonds around the Globe: The Encyclopedia of International Baseball* (Westport, Conn.: Greenwood Press, 2005). On the history of Mexican baseball, see Alan M. Klein, *Baseball on the Border: A Tale of Two Laredos* (Princeton: Princeton University Press, 1997); and Pedro Treto Cisneros, *The Mexican League: Comprehensive Player Statistics, 1937–2001* (Jefferson, N.C.: McFarland, 2002).

11. Albert G. Spalding, *America's National Game* (1911; repr., Lincoln: University of Nebraska Press, 1992).

12. On the controversy surrounding the Chicago White Sox and the fixing of the 1919 World Series, see Eliot Asinof, *Eight Men Out: The Black Sox and the 1919 World Series* (1963; repr., New York: Henry Holt, 2000), and Daniel A. Nathan, *Saying It's So: A Cultural History of the Black Sox Scandal* (Urbana: University of Illinois Press, 2005). Warren Susman's essay "Culture Heroes: Ford, Barton, and Ruth," from *Culture as History: The Transformation of American Society in the Twentieth Century* (New York: Pantheon, 1984), remains one of the best treatments of the cultural meaning of baseball in the age of Babe Ruth. Other key works include Robert W. Creamer, *Babe: The Legend Comes to Life* (New York: Fireside, 1974); and Harold Seymour, *Baseball: The Golden Age* (New York: Oxford University Press, 1989).

13. See Neil Lanctot, *Negro League Baseball: The Rise and Ruin of a Black Institution* (Philadelphia: University of Pennsylvania Press, 2004).

14. Reaves, *Taking in a Game*, 67–69.

15. Jules Tygiel, *Baseball's Great Experiment: Jackie Robinson and His Legacy* (New York: Oxford University Press, 1983), 26–27. On barnstorming, see also Gaspar González-Monzón,

"Barnstorming American Culture: Traveling Entertainment as Work and Performance" (Ph.D. diss., Yale University, 1999).

16. Two excellent one-volume accounts of the development of professional baseball in the United States are Charles C. Alexander, *Our Game: An American Baseball History* (New York: Henry Holt, 1991); and Benjamin R. Rader, *Baseball: A History of America's Game* (Urbana: University of Illinois Press, 2002).

17. Tygiel, *Baseball's Great Experiment*, 15.

18. Neil J. Sullivan, *The Minors: The Struggles and the Triumph of Baseball's Poor Relation from 1876 to the Present* (New York: St. Martin's, 1990), 42–46.

19. As Lee Lowenfish notes, the rise of the farm system as the predominant form of major-minor affiliation was apparent enough in early 1937 that a *Sporting News* editorial described "a baseball world that has been entirely 'Rickeyized.'" *Sporting News*, January 14, 1937, quoted in Lowenfish, *Branch Rickey: Baseball's Ferocious Gentleman* (Lincoln: University of Nebraska Press, 2007), 279. For a detailed discussion of the farm system, see Sullivan, *The Minors*.

20. Reaves, *Taking in a Game*, 79.

21. Adrian Burgos Jr., *Playing America's Game: Baseball, Latinos, and the Color Line* (Berkeley: University of California Press, 2007). Burgos argues persuasively that rather than being exceptions to a binary Jim Crow system, players from what he terms the "Spanish-speaking Americas" played central roles in baseball's complex racial hierarchy: "in the face of African Americans' outright exclusion, Latinos were the main group used to test the limits of racial tolerance and to locate the exclusionary point along the color line" (12).

22. Tygiel, *Baseball's Great Experiment*, 86–87.

23. Ibid., 86–90.

24. Quoted in Burgos, *Playing America's Game*, 184–85.

25. Quoted in Tygiel, *Baseball's Great Experiment*, 299.

26. Lanctot, *Negro League Baseball*, 317.

27. Quoted ibid., 386.

28. Adrian Burgos Jr., *Cuban Star: How One Negro-League Owner Changed the Face of Baseball* (New York: Hill and Wang, 2011), 187.

29. Branch Rickey, "Survey of Work, Jobs, Conditions, etc. Now Facing the New York Club," 1961, box 37, folder 2, Branch Rickey Papers, Manuscript Division, Library of Congress, Washington, D.C. (hereafter Rickey Papers).

30. Quoted in Donn Rogosin, *Invisible Men: Life in Baseball's Negro Leagues* (1983; repr., Lincoln: University of Nebraska Press, 2007), 31.

31. "Ex-Outfielder Reveals He Took $60,000 Bribe from Baseball," *Los Angeles Times*, February 27, 1966. On the 1946 controversy and its aftermath, see Rob Ruck, *Raceball: How the Major Leagues Colonized the Black and Latin Game* (Boston: Beacon Press, 2011), 118–42; and Klein, *Baseball on the Border*, 82–107. Mark Winegarder's novel *The Veracruz Blues* (New York: Viking, 1996) is a perceptive fictionalized account of these events.

32. "Mexican League Emissary Asks Tieup with O.B.," *Sporting News*, January 26, 1955; Ray Gillespie, "Mexican Loop in O.B., Eyes Major Hookups," *Sporting News*, February 2, 1955.

33. See Klein, *Baseball on the Border*; and Cisneros, *The Mexican League*.

34. González Echevarría, *Pride of Havana*, 44, 22, 47–49.

35. Ibid., 53–54.

36. "Majors Can Aid Latin-American Unity," *Sporting News*, December 10, 1947.

37. "Caribbean Pacts Killed Outlaws, Reports Finch," *Sporting News*, December 8, 1948.

38. Bjarkman, *Diamonds around the Globe*, is an excellent English-language source on the Serie del Caribe. For more on the history of winter ball in the postwar period, see Lou Hernández, *The Rise of the Latin American Baseball Leagues, 1947–1961: Cuba, the Dominican Republic, Mexico, Nicaragua, Panama, Puerto Rico, and Venezuela* (Jefferson, N.C.: McFarland, 2011).

39. Cuban players were not outnumbered by Puerto Ricans until 1972. Data from the *Baseball Almanac*, www.baseball-almanac.com/players/birthplace.php.

40. See Bjarkman, *History of Cuban Baseball*, 240–42.

41. Ruck, *Tropic of Baseball*, 74–75.

42. According to the *Sporting News*, Happy Chandler had agreed to the dual-contract system as a concession to Caribbean league officials in negotiations in the wake of the Liga Mexicana challenge. Dan Daniel, "Dual O.B.—Caribbean Player Pacts Ended," *Sporting News*, August 24, 1955.

43. "Maduro Named Baseball Liaison to Latin Leagues," *Washington Post*, December 9, 1965; "Segar, Maduro Accept Jobs in Eckert Cabinet," *Sporting News*, December 18, 1965. Maduro was a key figure among the group of baseball businessmen who brought Cuba into the orbit of "organized baseball" in the postwar period. Roberto González Echevarría describes Maduro as being from a wealthy family with "strong ties to American interests" (*Pride of Havana*, 17).

44. Pedro Galiana, "Desde el Bull-Pen," *El Universal*, December 17, 1965; Shirley Povich, "To Whom It May Concern," *Washington Post*, December 12, 1965.

45. The National Association required deposits from affiliated winter leagues for payment of fines and various other contingencies. LIDOM secretary Aristides Alvarez Sánchez wrote an extensive account of the events, "Los Casos de Demeter y Northrup," published in four parts in *El Caribe*, July 11, 12, 13, and 16, 1967.

46. " 'Lamenta' Rompimiento con Beisbol Organizado," *El Caribe*, July 9, 1968.

47. Arturo Industrioso, "El Presidente Mejía Feliú Está Dispuesto Renunciar; Licey Dice 10 Refuerzos Conlleva Gastos Fuertes," *El Caribe*, September 6, 1968; "Liga Resuelve Jugar el Campeonato con Importados," *El Caribe*, September 16, 1968.

48. Alvaro Arvelo, "La Decisión de la Liga," *El Caribe*, July 4, 1968.

49. Duilio Digiacomo, "Apuntes: El Beisbol Latino ante el Comisionado Eckert," *El Universal*, August 11, 1968.

50. See Reaves, *Taking in a Game*, 80–83.

51. See Robert K. Fitts, *Remembering Japanese Baseball: An Oral History of the Game* (Carbondale: Southern Illinois University Press, 2005), 1–10.

52. Donald S. Connery, "A Yank in Japan," *Sports Illustrated*, June 25, 1962; Edward Prell, "Stanka Pitches Sox into Global Feud," *Chicago Tribune*, February 1, 1961; "Stanka Stays in Orient; Buys Sox Contract," *Chicago Tribune*, January 31, 1962.

53. "U.S., Japan O.K. Trading Pact—In Baseball," *Chicago Tribune*, October 29, 1962.

54. On Murakami, see Alan M. Klein, *Growing the Game: The Globalization of Major League Baseball* (New Haven: Yale University Press, 2006), 131–33; and Robert Whiting, *The Meaning of Ichiro* (New York: Warner Books, 2004), 73–78.

55. Quoted in Fitts, *Remembering Japanese Baseball*, 89.

56. Ibid.

57. Bob Stevens, "Murakami Debuts; Giants Lose," *San Francisco Chronicle*, September 2, 1964.

58. "Murakami Case Threatening Buc Japan Tour, Says Frick," *Sporting News*, March 13, 1965.

59. See Rader, *Baseball*, 194–95.

60. See Steve Treder, "Open Classification: The Pacific Coast League's Drive to Turn Major," *Nine* 15.1 (Fall 2006): 88–109.

61. In 1946 the San Francisco Seals drew 670,563, a minor league attendance record that would last for decades. By way of comparison, the St. Louis Browns (the MLB team with the lowest attendance that year) drew 526,435, and the Philadelphia Athletics (the next lowest) drew 621,793. Five PCL teams (including the Seattle Rainiers, who drew 548,368) brought in over 500,000 fans in 1947, significantly more than that year's least popular MLB team, the Browns (320,474 fans). Paul J. Zingg and Mark D. Medeiros, *Runs, Hits, and an Era: The Pacific Coast League, 1903–58* (Urbana: University of Illinois Press, 1994), 110–12; Dan Raley, "A Man Named Sick Made Seattle Well," in *Rain Check: Baseball in the Pacific Northwest*, ed.

Mark Armour (Cleveland: Society for American Baseball Research, 2006), 57; John Thorn, *Total Baseball* (Toronto: Sport Media Publishing, 2004), 2421.

62. See Rader, *Baseball*, 188.

63. According to Neil J. Sullivan, the 1962 Player Development Plan, which established new forms of MLB financial aid for the minors as well as a new classification system, "epitomized the triumph of the farm system over the independents" (*The Minors*, 254).

64. James Edward Miller, *The Baseball Business: Pursuing Pennants and Profits in Baltimore* (Chapel Hill: University of North Carolina Press, 1990), 80–82. See also David Pietrusza, *Major Leagues: The Formation, Sometimes Absorption, and Mostly Inevitable Demise of Eighteen Professional Baseball Organizations, 1871 to Present* (Jefferson, N.C.: McFarland, 1991).

65. Walter Shannon to Al Fleishman, July 28, 1960, box 40, folder 6, Rickey Papers.

66. Harold E. Goodnough, "Selling Baseball in Your Territory," box 39, folder 18, Rickey Papers.

67. Barney Kremenko, "Betty King Is Queen of Mets' Promotions for Feminine World," *Sporting News*, March 5, 1966.

68. See Goldstein, *Playing for Keeps*, 38–39.

69. Eric Avila, *Popular Culture in the Age of White Flight: Fear and Fantasy in Suburban Los Angeles* (Berkeley: University of California Press, 2004), 145–84. See also Thomas S. Hines, "Housing, Baseball, and Creeping Socialism: The Battle of Chavez Ravine, 1949–1959," *Journal of Urban History* 8.2 (February 1982): 123–43.

70. Statement, May 18, 1960, box 37, folder 2, Rickey Papers.

71. "Nixon Advocates 3D Major League," *New York Times*, July 9, 1959. Nixon had gone on the record previously, in October 1958, in favor of an international expansion for MLB. "There should be a team in Mexico City," Nixon had said. "Caracas is big enough, and Havana and Canada should have two teams." Citing the emergence of jet travel, he also suggested that adding a Japanese franchise was now a viable option. "Nixon Forecasts Majors' Growth," *New York Times*, November 1, 1958.

72. William Shea, in a meeting with CL and MLB officials on August 18, 1959, noted pessimistically with respect to San Juan as a possible location, "Of course, the problem we face with them is the economy of the dollar that they get, as to whether they can support it." Minutes, Meeting of the Commissioner of the American-National League and the Continental League, box 36, folder 2, Rickey Papers. In a more positive report to fellow CL officials the next month (dated September 28, 1959), Rickey observed that the San Juan group "continues to be the most ardent applicant, with qualifying assurances in every respect." "Continental League Report No. 3," box 40, folder 14, Rickey Papers.

73. Ted Smits, "Canada Preferred over Japan, Mexico, for Foreign Expansion of Big Leagues," *Washington Post*, March 6, 1966.

74. Henry Luce, "The American Century," *Life*, February 17, 1941.

75. The *Sporting News* first published Harwell's piece on April 13, 1955, and printed it again every year for the next decade.

76. A representative example appeared in a 1966 story about Cleveland's Luis Tiant, featuring "quotes" from the pitcher about his off-season training regimen: "No work at regular job, but work alla-time on getting in goood condition. I theenk I peetch better because I lose alla weight, but it is too early for me to tell." Russell Schneider, "Tiant Tantalizes Tribe by Cutting Down on Weight," *Sporting News*, March 12, 1966.

77. On Gillette's corporate history, see Gordon McKibben, *Cutting Edge: Gillette's Journey to Global Leadership* (Boston: Harvard Business School Press, 1998); and Russell B. Adams Jr., *King C. Gillette: The Man and His Wonderful Shaving Device* (Boston: Little, Brown, 1978).

78. Maury Allen, "A Letter from Venezuela," *New York Post*, November 26, 1965.

79. Eduardo Moncada, "Bearnarth, Pítcher del Valencia, Escribe Horrores sobre Venezuela," *El Nacional*, December 15, 1965.

80. "Trataron de Línchar a Bearnarth" and "Protegido por la Policía, Salió Bearnarth del Estadio," *El Nacional,* December 17, 1965. Bearnarth wrote about his experience in an article titled "The Amazing Adventures of a Met in Venezuela," published in the April 1966 issue of *Sport.*

81. Roger Angell, *The Summer Game* (New York: Viking, 1972); John Updike, "Hub Fans Bid Kid Adieu," *New Yorker,* October 22, 1960.

82. William Faulkner, "Kentucky: May: Saturday," *Sports Illustrated,* May 16, 1955.

83. "An Artist's Ball Game," *Sports Illustrated,* April 6, 1956.

84. "Memo from the Publisher," *Sports Illustrated,* August 16, 1954.

85. Although MLB team owners had viewed the emergence of radio as a popular entertainment medium in the 1920s as a potential threat to live attendance, by the mid-1930s they were enjoying substantial amounts of broadcasting revenue. With the rise of television, broadcasting proceeds increased even more substantially, expanding from just 3 percent of the industry's total receipts in 1946 to 28 percent by 1970. Andrew Zimbalist, *Baseball and Billions: A Probing Look inside the Big Business of Our National Pastime* (New York: Basic Books, 1992), 48. See also James R. Walker and Robert V. Bellamy Jr., *Center Field Shot: A History of Baseball on Television* (Lincoln: University of Nebraska Press, 2008).

86. Roger Kahn, *The Boys of Summer* (New York: Harper and Row, 1972).

87. *San Francisco Chronicle,* September 2, 1964.

88. Stan Isaacs, "Louisiana in Dark Showing Through," *Newsday,* July 23, 1964.

89. Franklin E. Whaite, "El Manager Oscuro," *El Nacional,* August 17, 1964. Whaite's column was reprinted in the Dominican daily *Listín Diario* on August 30.

90. Advertisement published in *El Caribe,* May 29, 1964; Carlos José Lugo and Juan Marichal, interviews by author, San Pedro de Macorís, January 5, 2006, and Santiago, Dominican Republic, January 8, 2006, respectively.

## 2. A Piece of Property

1. *Sports Illustrated,* August 19, 1968, cover.

2. Flood was traded along with Cardinals Tim McCarver, Joe Hoerner, and Byron Browne for Phillies Dick Allen, Cookie Rojas, and Jerry Johnson.

3. Quoted in Leonard Koppett, "Kuhn Denies Flood's Request to 'Free' Him for Other Offers Besides Phils," *New York Times,* December 31, 1969. Curt Flood published the exchange in his autobiography (with Richard Carter), *The Way It Is* (New York: Trident Press, 1971), 194–95.

4. For more on Major League Baseball's modern labor history, see Charles P. Korr, *The End of Baseball as We Knew It: The Players Union, 1960–1981* (Urbana: University of Illinois Press, 2002); Lee Lowenfish, *The Imperfect Diamond: A History of Baseball's Labor Wars* (New York: Da Capo, 1991); John Helyar, *Lords of the Realm: The Real History of Baseball* (New York: Ballantine, 1995); and Robert F. Burk, *Much More Than a Game: Players, Owners and American Baseball since 1921* (Chapel Hill: University of North Carolina Press, 2001).

5. Quoted in Lowenfish, *Imperfect Diamond,* 141.

6. William Marshall, *Baseball's Pivotal Era, 1945–1951* (Lexington: University Press of Kentucky, 1999), 64–65.

7. Along with Lowenfish, *Imperfect Diamond,* and Marshall, *Baseball's Pivotal Era,* for more on Murphy and the ABG, see Burk, *Much More Than a Game.*

8. Lowenfish, *Imperfect Diamond,* 183–88.

9. "Players Organize and Retain Lewis," *New York Times,* July 13, 1954; Dan Daniel, "Dual O.B.—Caribbean Player Pacts Ended," *Sporting News,* August 24, 1955.

10. Lowenfish, *Imperfect Diamond,* 188–91; Helyar, *Lords of the Realm,* 83.

11. Marvin Miller, *A Whole Different Ballgame: The Sport and Business of Baseball* (Secaucus, N.J.: Carol Publishing Group, 1991), 8; Helyar, *Lords of the Realm,* 69.

12. Robin Roberts to William Eckert, January 12, 1966, box 3, folder 32, Marvin J. Miller Papers, Tamiment Library/ Robert F. Wagner Labor Archives, New York University (hereafter Miller Papers); Burke, *Much More than a Game,* 149.

13. Korr, *The End of Baseball,* 28–35.

14. See Nelson Lichtenstein, *State of the Union: A Century of American Labor* (Princeton: Princeton University Press, 2002), 98–99.

15. Korr, *The End of Baseball,* 35.

16. See Miller, *Different Ball Game,* 19–20; Helyar, *Lords of the Realm,* 17.

17. Miller, *Different Ball Game,* 21. Miller's organizing experience with the machinists' union proved to be excellent preparation for much of what his job entailed in the early years of his tenure with the MLBPA. Marvin J. Miller, telephone interview by author, February 24, 2007.

18. See Miller, *Different Ball Game,* 21–32.

19. Marvin J. Miller, "The Long Range Sharing Plan," 1963, box 1, folder 8, Miller Papers. Miller also helped engineer a similar agreement at Alan Wood Steel Company.

20. A. H. Raskin, in "Making Strikes Obsolete," *Atlantic Monthly,* June 1966, 49, described Miller as "the most creative of all [the United Steelworkers'] technicians."

21. "First Report by the National Labor-Management Panel to the Director of the Federal Mediation and Conciliation Service," July 23, 1964, box 1, folder 4, Miller Papers.

22. Miller, *Different Ball Game,* 31–32.

23. Marvin J. Miller to Robin Roberts, December 30, 1965, box 3, folder 52, Miller Papers.

24. Dave Brady, "Player Rep Friend Raps Proposal That Athletes Form Labor Union," *Sporting News,* August 3, 1963.

25. Miller, *Different Ball Game,* 33–34.

26. According to pitcher Jim Bouton, most ballplayers viewed their association as something very different from a labor union. "Most of the guys didn't care about politics," Bouton later recalled. "They were mostly conservative guys from small towns who grew up in houses where people were very conservative and unions were a bad word, and that's why the players' union never called themselves a union. Players wouldn't join a union—unions were bad. An association—now that's a little different." Jim Bouton, telephone interview by author, July 25, 2005.

27. Victor Riesel, "Meany is Against Athletes' Union," *Commercial Appeal* (Memphis), March 13, 1966, box 3, folder 52, Miller Papers.

28. Dick Kaegel, "Miller Confident Despite Players' Noisy Opposition," *Sporting News,* March 26, 1966.

29. Quoted in Korr, *End of Baseball,* 42.

30. Flood, *The Way It Is,* 163.

31. "Year of the Holdouts," *Ebony,* June 1966.

32. Directed by Buzz Kulik and starring David Janssen, *Warning Shot* was released in 1967.

33. "Drysdale, Koufax to Make Film; Continue Their Dodger Holdout," *New York Times,* March 18, 1966; "The Super-Holdouts," *Newsweek,* March 28, 1966.

34. According to Frick: "If an American player has his release, that's different, but a contract says he may not play with any other club, and the reserve clause is as binding in Japan as in the United States. I am sure the Japanese are happy with our working arrangements and have no desire to impair them." Bob Hunter, "Drysdale Faces Ban If He Plays Baseball in Japan," *Sporting News,* September 25, 1965.

35. "The Super-Holdouts," *Newsweek,* March 28, 1966.

36. Quoted in Peter Bart, "Koufax–Drysdale Pitch: A Fight against 'Slavery,'" *New York Times,* March 27, 1966.

37. As the editors of *Life* put it in their coverage of the holdout, "An entire infield, even an entire team, might demand to be signed as a unit—or not at all." "New Union's Million-Dollar Pitch," *Life,* April 1, 1966. The team initially offered Koufax $100,000 and Drysdale $85,000;

the pair signed for a reported $120,000 and $105,000, respectively. Bill Becker, "Koufax and Drysdale Agree to One-Year Contracts Totaling over $210,000," *New York Times,* March 31, 1966.

38. According to Miller: "The Taft-Hartley Act, [the owners] said, prohibited the payment of money by an employer to an employees' organization. . . . Not until I was elected did they call down the letter of the law." Miller, *Different Ball Game,* 68.

39. Ibid., 68–74, 91.

40. Although the new plan abandoned the language of the previous "60 percent" scheme, Miller later asserted that in his years as executive director, players never received less than the original formula would have produced. Ibid., 78.

41. Ibid., 97.

42. Helyar, *Lords of the Realm,* 29 and 234.

43. Joe King, "New Contract Form and Reserve Clause Sought by Players," *Sporting News,* August 12, 1967; Victor Riesel, "Baseball Players Hurl 'Union' Demands at Clubs," *Milwaukee Sentinel,* October 2, 1967; Leonard Koppett, "Baseball Players Seek Increase in Base Pay, Voice on TV Pacts," *New York Times,* August 1, 1967.

44. Flood, *The Way It Is,* 168.

45. American League of Professional Baseball Clubs, "Uniform Player's Contract," 1964, section 2(c), National Baseball Hall of Fame Library, Cooperstown, N.Y., Contracts file.

46. Jack Herman, "Small Print in Pact Ends Redbird Gripe," *Sporting News,* April 2, 1966; Flood, *The Way It Is,* 182–83.

47. Marvin Miller to Bowie Kuhn, October 30, 1970, pt. 1, box 94, folder 10, Arthur J. Goldberg Papers, Manuscript Division, Library of Congress, Washington, D.C. (hereafter Goldberg Papers).

48. Jerome Holtzman, "Leave Umps under League Direction," *Sporting News,* May 29, 1971.

49. "Night Schedule Will Grow for World Series in 1972," *New York Times,* May 7, 1971.

50. Miller, *Different Ball Game,* 203–23.

51. "No Alternatives to Strike—Peters," *Boston Globe,* April 1, 1972.

52. Cincinnati Reds, press release, "Statement by Bob Howsam," April 6, 1972, National Baseball Hall of Fame Library, Cooperstown, N.Y., Marvin Miller file.

53. Furman Bisher, "A Charm That's Dangerous," *Atlanta Journal,* March 8, 1970.

54. Miller, *Different Ball Game,* 142–52; Helyar, *Lords of the Realm,* 89–91.

55. Pete Axthelm, "The Great National Bore," *Newsweek,* October 14, 1968.

56. Leonard Sloane, "Baseball's Promotional Pitch," *New York Times,* August 8, 1968.

57. Major League Baseball Players Association, "Memorandum," November 21, 1978, box 3, folder 40, Miller Papers.

58. *Baseball,* dir. Ken Burns (Florentine Films, 1994); Brad Snyder, *A Well-Paid Slave: Curt Flood's Fight for Free Agency in Professional Sports* (New York: Viking, 2006).

59. Frank Robinson, Vada Pinson, and Joe Morgan also grew up in Oakland. See Paul Kilduff, "Bay Area a Taproot of Baseball's Family Tree," *San Francisco Chronicle,* September 24, 2004.

60. Flood, *The Way It Is,* 34–39.

61. It was clear to Flood and his African American teammates that their manager's racism informed his distribution of playing time. Cardinals players did not lack evidence of Hemus's views about race. In one instance, the manager unapologetically announced to the team that he had used a racial epithet in a confrontation with an opposing player. Ibid., 70.

62. In 1947 a number of Cardinals players vocally opposed Jackie Robinson's integration of the National League, reportedly threatening to strike rather than share the field with a black ballplayer. See Jules Tygiel, *Baseball's Great Experiment: Jackie Robinson and His Legacy* (New York: Oxford University Press, 1983), 185–89. The team did not feature its first African American player (Tom Alston) until 1954. The city, the southernmost in all of Major League

Baseball until the expansion era, had a reputation throughout the sport of being hostile to African American athletes. The Chase Hotel in St. Louis, where every visiting team stayed, remained segregated until 1954, requiring black players on opposing teams to commute to the ballpark from separate accommodations. As late as the mid-1960s, black players were restricted to rooms without views, so they could not be seen from outside. Jules Tygiel, *Extra Bases: Reflections on Jackie Robinson, Race, and Baseball History* (Lincoln: University of Nebraska Press, 2002), 111.

63. Elston Howard integrated the Yankees in 1955, Ozzie Virgil the Tigers in 1958, and Pumpsie Green the Red Sox in the middle of the 1959 season, more than twelve years after Jackie Robinson played his first game with the Brooklyn Dodgers. The Philadelphia Phillies were the third-slowest team to desegregate, waiting until 1957 to add John Kennedy to the roster.

64. Quoted in George Cantor, *The Tigers of '68: Baseball's Last Real Champions* (Lanham, Md.: Taylor Trade, 1997), 210. For a discussion of the place of the *South End* in the radical politics of late 1960s Detroit, see Dan Georgakas and Marvin Surkin, *Detroit: I Do Mind Dying* (1975; repr., Boston: South End Press, 1998).

65. "Brushback!!," *Baltimore Afro-American*, June 19, 1965.

66. Bob Gibson with Phil Pepe, *From Ghetto to Glory: The Story of Bob Gibson* (New York: Popular Library, 1968), 148.

67. Arnold Rampersad, *Jackie Robinson: A Biography* (New York: Knopf, 1997), 363.

68. In 1968 Gussie Busch described Flood in glowing terms: "The best damned centerfielder in baseball, and he paints, too." William Leggett, "Not Just a Flood, but a Deluge," *Sports Illustrated*, August 19, 1968.

69. Neal Russo, "Richie Seen as Hepped-Up Cardinal," *Sporting News*, October 25, 1969.

70. Snyder, *Well-Paid Slave*, 10.

71. "Vida's Blues," *Time*, March 27, 1972; *Sports Illustrated*, March 27, 1972, cover.

72. Bob Gibson, player representative for the Cardinals during the holdout, discussed the standoff between the players and owners on the *Tonight Show*. Gibson suggests that Busch's tirade was inspired in part by his television appearance. See Bob Gibson and Lonnie Wheeler, *Stranger to the Game* (New York: Viking, 1994), 210–11.

73. St. Louis Cardinals, "A Statement by August A. Busch, Jr. to Cardinal Players," National Baseball Hall of Fame Library, August Busch file; Flood, *The Way It Is*, 228–36; "Many Requests for Copy of Busch Talk to Players," *Sporting News*, April 26, 1969.

74. Dick Young, "First 100 Days: Kuhn Here to Stay," *Sporting News*, May 17, 1969; Edgar Munzel, "Allyn Delivers Busch-Type Speech, Warning Pale Hose of Attitudes," *Sporting News*, April 12, 1969.

75. Flood, *The Way It Is*, 172–74.

76. Though he eventually settled for a $90,000 contract, published reports suggested that he had previously told general manager Bing Devine that he would refuse to sign for less than $100,000. Bob Broeg, "Redbirds' Balky Stars Now Find Situation Devine," *Sporting News*, March 15, 1969.

77. Flood, *The Way It Is*, 175.

78. Miller, *Different Ball Game*, 173–76 and 180–90.

79. Ibid., 41.

80. For example, in 1967 Bowie Kuhn (then working as legal counsel for the National League) opined: "First, the integrity of the game and the freedom of its participants from suspicion depend upon the reserve clause. Secondly, there would be chaos without it—there is no other word for it. Take the reserve clause away and competition in a league structure would disappear." Joe King, "Cronin Answers Miller's Bad-Faith Charge," *Sporting News*, June 24, 1967.

81. Burk, *More than a Game*, 9 and 116–17.

82. On the draft, see Allan Simpson, *The Baseball Draft: The First Twenty-five Years, 1965–1989* (Durham, N.C.: American Sports Publishing, 1990); and W. C. Madden, *Baseball's First-Year Player Draft: Team by Team through 1999* (Jefferson, N.C.: McFarland, 2001).

83. Miller, *Different Ball Game*, 193.

84. Ibid., 98 and 182–83.

85. Writing to David Feller, a law professor at the University of California at Berkeley, with whom he consulted in preparation for his argument before the Supreme Court, Arthur Goldberg cited "the realistic view" that the owners were not prepared to bargain at all on the question of the reserve system and were simply "using the argument in the hope of retaining their immunity under the antitrust laws." Arthur Goldberg to David Feller, December 31, 1971, pt. 1, box 94, folder 11, Goldberg Papers.

86. Justice Lewis Powell recused himself, citing the fact that he owned Anheuser-Busch stock. See Snyder, *Well-Paid Slave*, 285–86.

87. Ibid., 294 and 303.

88. Red Smith, "The Buck Passes," *New York Times*, June 21, 1972.

89. The *New York Times* editorial ("Batter Up in Court," May 28, 1970) advocated "some modification" of the system. The *Wall Street Journal* editorial declared: "Like any other big business, baseball is going to have to work out reasonable ways to get along with its employees. It's a little silly that a $90,000-a-year outfielder has had to go to court to make that simple point" ("Curt Flood's Crusade," January 9, 1970).

90. "Out, Stretching the Law," *New York Times*, November 11, 1953. The editorial heralded the decision as "an outstanding victory for common sense."

91. For Flood this change came too late, as he would never reap the financial rewards of his battle with the baseball establishment. As Brad Snyder details, Flood faced a number of challenges in his life after baseball and died of cancer at the age of fifty-nine in 1997.

92. Snyder, *Well-Paid Slave*, 314.

93. Quoted in Hal Lebovitz, "How Far Would You Go for $110,000?," *Cleveland Plain Dealer*, March 11, 1970, box 3, folder 9, Miller Papers.

94. Flood, *The Way It Is*, 18.

95. Robert Lipsyte, "Crack in the Clubhouse Wall," *New York Times*, June 1, 1970.

96. David W. Zang, *SportsWars: Athletes in the Age of Aquarius* (Fayetteville: University of Arkansas Press, 2001), 3–7.

97. Ibid., 8.

98. "Terrorism on the Left," *Newsweek*, March 23, 1970.

99. In the wake of Miller's election, and with the prospect of a newly effective MLBPA, Bouton took the rare step of campaigning for the position of player representative, distributing a document detailing his qualifications and enthusiasm for the position. With election to the position of player rep still amounting to little more than a popularity contest, he was soundly defeated. Bouton, interview by author. A copy of Bouton's campaign document is in box 2, folder 14, Miller Papers.

100. Bouton, interview by author; "Spell of the Olympics," *Newsweek*, October 21, 1968.

101. "Inside Baseball," *Time*, June 15, 1970.

102. Bouton, *Ball Four* (1970; repr., New York: Wiley, 1990), 219.

103. David Halberstam, "American Notes: Baseball and the National Mythology," *Harper's*, September 1970, 24.

104. Dick Young, "Young Ideas," *Sporting News*, August 29, 1970.

105. Dick Young, "Young Ideas," *Sporting News*, June 20, 1970.

106. Bouton, interview by author.

107. "Boston Scribes Howl: TV in Bullpen," *Sporting News*, May 29, 1971; "Boston Writers Protest TV Bull Pen Invasion," *New York Times*, May 16, 1971; Jack Lang, "Kuhn Reports Progress toward Writer Demands," *Sporting News*, July 31, 1971.

108. Bouton himself briefly pursued a career in television—as a sports reporter at WABC-

TV in New York City. "Jim Bouton in TV Job," *New York Times*, September 9, 1970.

109. Jim Murray, "Baseball—An Age of Innocence Bent on Destruction," *Los Angeles Times*, April 6, 1972.

110. See Jane Hastings Ardell, *Breaking into Baseball: Women and the National Pastime* (Carbondale: Southern Illinois University Press, 2005), 204–5.

111. A notable exception came in the wake of Martin Luther King Jr.'s assassination. Roberto Clemente and other members of the Pittsburgh Pirates refused to open the season until after King's funeral. See David Maraniss, *Clemente: The Passion and Grace of Baseball's Last Hero* (New York: Simon and Schuster, 2006), 220.

112. Lowell Reidenbaugh, "Author Bouton Hits Jackpot—with Bowie's Assist," *Sporting News*, August 8, 1970.

113. Joe Falls, "Does He Have a Conscience?," *Sporting News*, June 20, 1970.

114. "Inside Baseball," *Time*, June 15, 1970.

115. David Harvey's study *A Brief History of Neoliberalism* (New York: Oxford University Press, 2005) offers a particularly valuable treatment of neoliberalism's relationship to broader notions of human freedom.

116. Red Schoendienst with Rob Rains, *Red: A Baseball Life* (Champaign, Ill.: Sports Publishing, 1998), 154.

117. "Baseball Players Learn They Face Cuts in 1969," *Washington Post*, November 8, 1968.

118. Matthew Frye Jacobson, "'Richie' Allen, Whitey's Ways, and Me: A Political Education in the 1960s," in *In the Game: Race, Identity, and Sports in the Twentieth Century*, ed. Amy Bass (New York: Palgrave Macmillan, 2005), 31.

119. Reggie Jackson with Bill Libby, *Reggie: A Season with a Superstar* (Chicago: Playboy Press, 1975), 41.

120. See Bruce Markusen, *A Baseball Dynasty: Charlie Finley's Swingin' A's* (Haworth, N.J.: St. Johann Press, 2002), 85–88. As Edward J. Reilly notes, the new uniforms "made the A's especially striking on color television." Edward J. Rielly, *Baseball: An Encyclopedia of Popular Culture* (Lincoln: University of Nebraska Press, 2005), 103.

121. See Helyar, *Lords of the Realm*, 141–59.

122. Dylan recorded "Catfish" during the sessions for his 1976 album *Desire*, but Columbia Records did not release the song until 1991, on *The Bootleg Series Volumes 1–3 (Rare and Unreleased), 1961–1991*.

123. On Seitz and the pivotal arbitration cases he heard, see Roger I. Abrams, *Legal Bases: Baseball and the Law* (Philadelphia: Temple University Press, 1998), 115–34.

124. Ron Fimrite, "He's Free at Last," *Sports Illustrated*, August 30, 1976.

125. Dick Young, "Young Ideas," *Sporting News*, October 25, 1975.

126. For an account of the Jackson-Munson dispute (and an insightful narrative about the place of Jackson's Yankees in late 1970s New York City), see Jonathan Mahler, *Ladies and Gentlemen, the Bronx Is Burning: 1977, Baseball, Politics, and the Battle for the Soul of a City* (New York: Farrar, Straus and Giroux, 2005).

127. Lee Lescaze, "For Reggie Jackson, the Sweet Taste of Success," *Washington Post*, February 23, 1978; "Standard Brands Inc. Unwraps its Reggie Bar," *Wall Street Journal*, February 23, 1978. At the first Yankees home game after the Reggie Bar's debut, at which tens of thousands of the foil-wrapped candies were distributed free to fans, Jackson hit a three-run blast on his first swing. The field was soon covered in foil Reggie wrappers, in tribute to the slugger. Red Smith, "Candy That Tastes Like a Hot Dog," *New York Times*, April 14, 1978.

## 3. Two Strikes

1. For an excellent discussion of Fernandomania, see Samuel O. Regalado, *Viva Baseball! Latin Major Leaguers and Their Special Hunger* (Urbana: University of Illinois Press, 1998), 170–92.

2. Pérez Avella had "loaned" the pitcher to another club, the Yucatán Leones, during the 1979 Liga Mexicana season. George Vecsey, "Valenzuela Shows Gifts of a Natural," *New York Times,* April 25, 1981.

3. Ross Newhan, "Castillo Gives It His Best Pitch," *Los Angeles Times,* March 30, 1978.

4. Phil Elderkin, "Baseball's El Toro: Mexican Mirage?," *Christian Science Monitor,* April 30, 1981.

5. Mark Heisler, "Valenzuela Adds New York to His Collection," *Los Angeles Times,* May 9, 1981.

6. Lowell Reidenbaugh, "Player of the Year Valenzuela is the King of Fan Appeal," *Sporting News,* December 19, 1981.

7. Regalado, *Viva Baseball!* 182.

8. Mike Littwin, *¡Fernando!* (New York: Bantam Books, 1981).

9. Steve Wulf, "No Hideaway for Fernando," *Sports Illustrated,* March 23, 1981.

10. Dave Kindred, "Valenzuela: Mexican Koufax a Heaven-Sent Gift to the Dodgers," *Washington Post,* October 14, 1981.

11. Mark Heisler, "Fernando Almost Throws It Away," *Los Angeles Times,* May 24, 1981.

12. Steve Marcus, "Mets Don't Speak His Language," *Newsday,* May 9, 1981.

13. "Valenzuela Hits the Road, 'Sorry' He Missed Parade," *Los Angeles Times,* November 4, 1981; Steve Harvey, "80,000 L.A. Fans Cheers on a Dodger Blue Day," *Los Angeles Times,* October 31, 1981; Ronald L. Soble, "Fernando Shows for His Hero's Role," *Los Angeles Times,* November 23, 1981.

14. Nancy Yoshihara, "Move over Farrah, Here Comes Famous Fernando," *Los Angeles Times,* May 21, 1981.

15. "Fernando to Pitch—Juice," *Los Angeles Times,* July 28, 1981; advertisement for Fernando Valenzuela coin, *Los Angeles Times,* September 20, 1981; Eugenio Pallares, "Televisa Contrata a Valenzuela," *Unomásuno,* June 20, 1981.

16. Ira Berkow, "Valenzuela's Back, and So Is Tumult," *New York Times,* March 25, 1982.

17. Stan Isle, "Caught on the Fly," *Sporting News,* March 27, 1982.

18. Jim Murray, "Fernando's Support Seems to Be Missing," *Los Angeles Times,* March 2, 1982.

19. Daniel H. Pink, *Free Agent Nation: How America's New Independent Workers are Transforming the Way We Live* (New York: Warner Books, 2001).

20. Ralph Ray, "Player, Owner Reps Agree on New Labor Pact," *Sporting News,* July 24, 1976. See also Charles P. Korr, *The End of Baseball as We Knew It: The Players Union, 1960–1981* (Urbana: University of Illinois Press, 2002), 168–85.

21. Dave Anderson, "The Oakland 9 Challenge Charles O.," and "The Orioles' 'Double Standard,'" *New York Times,* March 20, 1976, and May 13, 1976; Ralph Ray, "Player, Owner Reps Agree on New Labor Pact," *Sporting News,* July 24, 1976; Ross Newhan, "Baseball's Free Agent Scramble Is On," *Los Angeles Times,* November 5, 1976.

22. Daniel Okrent, *Nine Innings: The Anatomy of a Baseball Game* (1985; repr., New York: Houghton Mifflin, 2000), 157.

23. Pete Axthelm, "Baseball's Money Madness," *Newsweek,* June 28, 1976.

24. *Sports Illustrated,* August 11, 1975, cover; *Time,* April 26, 1976, cover.

25. John Helyar, *Lords of the Realm: The Real History of Baseball* (New York: Ballantine, 1995), 277; Red Smith, "Unwanted Strike," *New York Times,* February 27, 1981.

26. Helyar, *Lords of the Realm,* 279–80; *Sports Illustrated,* June 22, 1981, cover; "Let the Fans Strike," *Chicago Tribune,* July 15, 1981.

27. Korr, *End of Baseball,* 221–22.

28. John Helyar places special emphasis on the role of the Williams-led dissident bloc in the strike. See Helyar, *Lords of the Realm,* 274–307.

29. Bob Logan and Richard Dozer, "Latins Feeling Left Out: DeJesus," *Chicago Tribune,* July 28, 1981.

30. Marvin J. Miller, telephone interview by author, February 24, 2007; Marvin Miller, *A Whole Different Ballgame: The Sport and Business of Baseball* (Secaucus, N.J.: Carol Publishing Group, 1991), 216–17.

31. In 1992, Bernazard told the *Sporting News:* "There's still a long way to go. Right now we are trying to educate the Hispanics as to what the association can do for them in terms of adjusting and of what to expect in the U.S." Dave Nightingale, "Lost in America," *Sporting News,* August 3, 1992. Latino players continued to advocate for greater support from their union into the twenty-first century. For example, in 2003, Red Sox pitcher Pedro Martínez called for the MLBPA to ensure that translation resources be made available for players' conversations with the press. See Adrian Burgos Jr., *Playing America's Game: Baseball, Latinos, and the Color Line* (Berkeley: University of California Press, 2007), 254.

32. See Helyar, *Lords of the Realm,* 282–85.

33. Lee Ballinger, "View from the Mill on Baseball Strike," *New York Times,* May 24, 1981. See also Lee Ballinger, *In Your Face! Sports for Love and Money* (Chicago: Vanguard Books, 1981).

34. Jim Villani, "Baseball and Labor," *Pig Iron* 3 (1981): 4.

35. Michael Denning, *Culture in the Age of Three Worlds* (New York: Verso, 2004), 222. See also Josiah Bartlett Lambert, *"If the Workers Took a Notion": The Right to Strike and American Political Development* (Ithaca: Cornell University Press, 2005).

36. In a telephone interview by the author on February 24, 2007, Marvin Miller noted that there was never a concern among MLBPA leaders that the owners would attempt to employ replacement players to break the 1981 strike.

37. Ronald Blum, "Other Sports Learn Lessons from Football Strike," *Daily News of Los Angeles,* November 1, 1987. Fehr became executive director of the MLBPA in 1985, having served as the union's general counsel beginning in 1977.

38. On the 1994–95 strike, see Robert F. Burk, *Much More Than a Game: Players, Owners, and American Baseball since 1921* (Chapel Hill: University of North Carolina Press, 2001), 262–305.

39. See Leonard Koppett, "Background Given on Bums, Giants Pay-TV," *Los Angeles Times,* June 9, 1957; and James R. Walker and Robert V. Bellamy Jr., *Center Field Shot: A History of Baseball on Television* (Lincoln: University of Nebraska Press, 2008), 57–60.

40. Dave Brady, "Indians Lead Baseball into Pay TV," *Washington Post,* May 10, 1973; Dave Brady, "Yankees on First in Pay-TV Game," *Washington Post,* May 24, 1974.

41. Walker and Bellamy, *Center Field Shot,* 232.

42. "Baseball Broadcast Rights Total $90 Million for '81," *Sporting News,* April 11, 1981.

43. The Dodgers' 1981 schedule (before the strike limited the number further) included forty-six road games and fifty home games. "Dodgers to Televise Record 46 Road Games on KTTV," *Los Angeles Times,* April 7, 1981; "Western Airlines Joins Dodger Sponsors' Roster," *Los Angeles Times,* April 7, 1981. Following an untelevised Valenzuela start at Dodger Stadium in May, Jackson Gray of Encinco wrote in a letter to the editor of the *Los Angeles Times:* "The Dodgers' refusal to televise Fernando's home games is a cruel slap in the face of the millions of Southern Californians who have supported the team. Apparently, no amount of love and support by the fans can sway the decision-making apparatus of Dodger management" (*Los Angeles Times,* May 23, 1981).

44. In 1987, teams televised an average of 96 games (out of 162), and ten years later that figure had risen to 122. "Cable vs. Free: The Pastime Split," *New York Times,* April 7, 1987; Paul D. Staudohar, "The Symbiosis between Baseball and Broadcasting," in *Cooperstown Symposium on Baseball and American Culture, 2001,* ed. William M. Simons (Jefferson, N.C.: McFarland, 2002), 194.

45. See "Kuhn Doubts Lure of Pay Television," *New York Times,* October 26, 1974.

46. Walker and Bellamy, *Center Field Shot,* 167–69.

47. "Going Super with Ted," *Newsweek,* January 1, 1979. See also Porter Bibb, *It Ain't as Easy as It Looks: Ted Turner's Amazing Story* (New York: Crown, 1993).

48. William Taaffe, "He Spent a Lot to Save a Lot More," *Sports Illustrated*, February 11, 1985; "Baseball Bats over $300 Million in 1986," *Broadcasting*, March 3, 1986.

49. Wayne Minshew, "A 'Lifetime Contract' Binds Andy to Braves," *Sporting News*, April 24, 1976.

50. Helyar, *Lords of the Realm*, 191–92; Wayne Minshew, "Braves Names Not Same," *Atlanta Constitution*, May 2, 1976; Ron Fimrite, "Bigwig Flips His Wig in Wigwam," *Sports Illustrated*, July 19, 1976.

51. Minutes, MLBPA Executive Board Meetings, November 28–29, 1978, and July 16, 1979, box 2, folder 6, Miller Papers.

52. Minutes, MLBPA Executive Board Meeting, December 1–3, 1981, ibid.

53. Marvin J. Miller, "Miller: The Union's Strength Is Established," *New York Times*, August 16, 1981.

54. "Owners Ask Court to Tune Out MLPA," *Washington Post*, June 15, 1982; "Players Lose in Court," *New York Times*, March 24, 1987.

55. William Serrin, "Agreement is Acclaimed," *New York Times*, April 1, 1983.

56. Tom Paegel, "Screen Actors Approve Contract, End Walkout," *Los Angeles Times*, October 24, 1980; "Coast Musicians Going Back after Settling 5 1/2-Month Strike," *New York Times*, January 16, 1981; "Directors Guild OKs New Pact," *Chicago Tribune*, June 29, 1981. See also David F. Prindle, *The Politics of Glamour: Ideology and Democracy in the Screen Actors Guild* (Madison: University of Wisconsin Press, 1988), 124–32.

57. "Remarks by President Reagan before Convention of United Brotherhood of Carpenters in Chicago," *Daily Labor Report*, no. 171, September 3, 1981, F-1.

58. On collusion, see Helyar, *Lords of the Realm*, 354–87.

59. See Littwin, *¡Fernando!* 19.

60. Horacia Ibarra, *Héctor Espino: Un Hombre, Un Bat, ¡Una Leyenda!* (Monterrey, Mexico: Sociedad Cuauhtémoc y Famosa, 2001), 58.

61. Jorge Pasquel, the dominant figure among Liga Mexicana owners in previous years, died in a plane crash in 1955. Prior to his death Pasquel had continued to run the circuit's Veracruz club, although he stepped down as commissioner in 1949. See Alan M. Klein, *Baseball on the Border: A Tale of Two Laredos* (Princeton: Princeton University Press, 1997), 107.

62. Luis Suárez Fernández, *Alejo Peralta: Un Patrón sin Patrónes* (Mexico City: Editorial Grijalbo, 1992); Sam Dillon, "Alejo Peralta Díaz, 80, Is Dead; One of Mexico's Wealthiest Men," *New York Times*, April 10, 1997; "Obituary: Alejo Peralta," *Economist*, April 19, 1997.

63. "Se Inaugurará el Próximo Día 20 la Escuela de Beisbol," *Excelsior*, October 14, 1959; *Los Fabulosos Tigres, 1955–2005* (Mexico City: Fundación Ingeniero Alejo Peralta y Díez Caballeros), 38. On Peralta's emphasis on developing and featuring Mexican players, see also Klein, *Baseball on the Border*, 107; and Suárez Fernández, *Alejo Peralta*, 252.

64. Luis Tiant with Joe Fitzgerald, *El Tiante: The Luis Tiant Story* (New York: Doubleday, 1976), 20.

65. Pedro Treto Cisneros, *The Mexican League: Comprehensive Player Statistics, 1937–2001* (Jefferson, N.C.: McFarland, 2002), 3; Scott Ostler, "Bravo! Baseball!," *Los Angeles Times*, September 5, 1979.

66. David G. LaFrance, "Labor, the State, and Professional Baseball in Mexico in the 1980s," in *Sport in Latin America and the Caribbean*, ed. Joseph L. Arbena and David G. LaFrance (Wilmington, Del.: Scholarly Resources, 2002), 92.

67. José Luis Puertas, "Jorge Fitch, Aclara: 'Los Policías fueron Quienes nos Agredieron, No Nosotros al Público,'" *Unomásuno*, April 8, 1980; LaFrance, "Labor, the State, and Professional Baseball," 92–93. The two major accounts of the ANABE movement are LaFrance's essay and Benito Terrazas, *Casa Llena, Bola Roja: La Lucha de los Peloteros de la ANABE* (Mexico City: Editorial Leega, 1984).

68. Aaron N. Wise and Bruce C. Meyer, *International Sports Law and Business*, vol. 2 (The Hague: Kluwer Law International, 1997), 916–19.

69. Pitcher Eleno Cuen, for example, reported that he did not receive compensation when the Houston Astros purchased his contract. "No Queremos que nos Pase lo que a Nino Donoso, Subraya Eleno Cuen," *Unomásuno*, July 21, 1980. On Valenzuela's compensation from his contract's sale to the Dodgers, see Mike Littwin, "Teen-Age Beer-Drinker Is Now Dodger Stopper," *Los Angeles Times*, October 3, 1980.

70. LaFrance, "Labor, the State, and Professional Baseball," 94–96.

71. "Oquendo, Contra los Peloteros," *Unomásuno*, January 10, 1981.

72. LaFrance, "Labor, the State, and Professional Baseball," 97.

73. "Según CONPEPROCA, Empresarios Cancelaron Serie sin Escuchar a los Peloteros," *El Universal*, January 17, 1981.

74. LaFrance, "Labor, the State, and Baseball in Mexico," 98–99.

75. Terrazas, *Casa Llena*, 86; "Peloteros Crearán Liga Nacional," *Unomásuno*, February 18, 1981.

76. "Diamante," *Unomásuno*, June 10, 1981.

77. "La Seguridad Económica de los Mets con Aportaciones Solidarias," *Unomásuno*, July 21, 1981; LaFrance, "Labor, the State, and Baseball in Mexico," 99–100.

78. "Diácono Orea no Podrá Seguir en la Pelota," *Unomásuno*, October 30, 1980.

79. Benito Terrazas, "El Jab de JLP y el Screw de Valenzuela, a la Par en Palacio," *Unomásuno*, June 27, 1981.

80. Jaime Bravo, "Valenzuela, Flor en la Tumba del Beisbol," *Unomásuno*, June 28, 1981.

81. Francisco Ponce, "El Terrible Fer," *Proceso*, June 29, 1981.

82. Raúl Monge Amador, "Valenzuela, Convertido en un Objeto más del Tianguis Deportivo Profesional," *Proceso*, June 29, 1981.

83. Festival advertisement, *Unomásuno*, June 26, 1981; Benito Terrazas, "Histeria Infantil por Ver a Valenzuela," *Unomásuno*, June 29, 1981.

84. Francisco Ponce, "Esperanzas," *Proceso*, May 11, 1981.

85. LaFrance, "Labor, the State, and Professional Baseball," 102.

86. Ibid., 110.

87. There is a rich scholarly literature on the history of Mexican neoliberalism, including Louise E. Walker, *Waking from the Dream: Mexico's Middle Classes after 1968* (Stanford: Stanford University Press, 2013).

88. "Rechazan a Mexicanos en EU," *Unomásuno*, February 26, 1981; "La Asociación de Equipos Impide a los Anabistas se Contraten en Ligas Mayores," *Unomásuno*, March 11, 1981; Jaime Bravo, "Un Triunfo de Peralta en el Caso del Houston," *Unomásuno*, March 26, 1981; Terrazas, *Casa Llena*, 106–7.

89. " 'Espero que la Ley me Ampare,' Dice Houston," *Unomásuno*, March 20, 1981.

90. I have adopted the translation of the office's title from Kevin J. Middlebrook, *The Paradox of Revolution: Labor, the State, and Authoritarianism in Mexico* (Baltimore: Johns Hopkins University Press, 1995).

91. See Terrazas, *Casa Llena*, 107.

92. "Peloteros de la ANABE Rechazan Trato para Jugar en Estados Unidos," *Unomásuno*, April 2, 1981; "Equipos de Grandes Ligas Están Interesados en Ángel Moreno," *Unomásuno*, July 15, 1981.

93. Jaime Bravo, "Moreno, a los Serafines," *Unomásuno*, July 17, 1981.

94. Ross Newhan, "Angel of Angels Could Answer Pitching Prayer," *Los Angeles Times*, March 20, 1982.

95. "Diamante," *Unomásuno*, August 16, 1981.

96. Benito Terrazas, "Desertan 3 de Juárez, Líder Grupal," *Unomásuno*, June 19, 1981; Alfonso "Houston" Jiménez, interview by author, Yakima, Wash., August 30, 2006; Terrazas, *Casa Llena*, 107.

97. Jiménez, interview by author.

98. "We struggled really to get enough coaches, managers, business managers to run our

farm teams," Peralta said in explaining the impetus for the academy. "Then many players in the league, over-age players, had no future, and many were alcoholics, drug addicts. Mexican youngsters came up to this atmosphere and many were lost because of its influence. That's when I made up my mind we should give something better to the Mexican youngster." Skip Myslenski, "Broken Dreams, Bright Promises," *Chicago Tribune*, June 14, 1982.

99. "El Cuartel del Beisbol Hace Huir a Jóvenes; Fracaso de Patrones," *Unomásuno*, May 3, 1981; Salo Otero, "Baseball Academy in Mexican League," *Sporting News*, August 1, 1981; Fernando de León, "Peralta Habla, Ahora, de 'Mexicanizar el Beisbol,'" *Unomásuno*, February 14, 1983; *Los Fabulosos Tigres*, 162–63.

100. See Milton Jamail, "Put Baseball on the Free-Trade Agenda," *Washington Post*, October 26, 1991.

101. In 1980 MLB rosters included thirteen Mexican players. In 2000 the number was twenty-eight. During that same twenty-year period, the number of Dominican-born players in MLB increased from thirty-one to 116. Data from www.baseball-almanac.com/players/birthplace.php.

102. "Diamante," *Unomásuno*, May 10, 1981.

103. Elisabeth Malkin, "U.S. Sports Teams Tackle Sales in Mexico," *Advertising Age*, September 13, 1993.

104. Steve Popper, "Mexican Group is Latest to Seek to Draw the Expos," *New York Times*, August 5, 2003.

105. Raúl Martínez, interview by author, El Carmen, Mexico, July 27, 2009. At the time of the interview Martínez was the academy's director.

106. Mark Shaffer, "Béisbol Striking Out," *Arizona Republic*, June 1, 2004.

## 4. On the Borders of Free Agency

1. *Bull Durham*, dir. Ron Shelton (1988).

2. *Major League*, dir. David S. Ward (1989).

3. Adrian Burgos Jr., *Playing America's Game: Baseball, Latinos, and the Color Line* (Berkeley: University of California Press, 2007), 233; Allan Simpson, "Top Ten Players Drafted, 1986," www.perfectgame.org, April 11, 2007.

4. Joseph Durso, "Four Enter Baseball Hall amid Cheers and Tribute," *New York Times*, August 1, 1983; "Kuhn Tuvo Algunas Expresiones en Español para Juan Marichal," *La Opinión*, August 2, 1983.

5. Data from www.baseball-almanac.com/players/birthplace.php. Marichal was one of eleven Dominican players to appear in an MLB game in 1963. Over 10 percent (95 out of 856) of players on MLB rosters on the first day of the 2012 season were Dominican. See Joey Nowak, "Opening Day Rosters Reflect Global Growth," MLB.com, April 5, 2012.

6. "I saw a three line filler in a newspaper stating that the President of the Dominican Republic had bestowed some ludicrous title, like Knight Commander of the Blue Camellia, on Juan Marichal, to honour his induction into the Baseball Hall of Fame. From that grew the story 'The Battery.'" W. P. Kinsella, *The Thrill of the Grass* (New York: Penguin, 1984), xi. The *Toronto Globe and Mail* reported on January 19, 1983: "Dominican Republic president Salvador Jorge Blanco has awarded former major-league pitcher Juan Marichal the order of Great Knight Commander because of his recent induction into baseball's Hall of Fame." The Dominican daily *Listín Diario* reported that in naming Marichal "Gran Comendador con la Orden de mérito de Duarte, Sánchez y Mella," Blanco proclaimed that "through Juan Marichal, Dominican baseball, along with the rest of Latin American baseball, has entered the U.S. Hall of Fame." In accepting the Dominican national honor Marichal said, "I hope that the Dominican people feel as happy as I do, because this triumph is for the Dominican Republic and for all of Latin America." Tony Pérez, "Condecoran Marichal como Gran Comendador," *Listín Diario*, January 18, 1983.

7. W. P. Kinsella, "The Battery," in *The Thrill of the Grass*, 181.

8. *Field of Dreams*, dir. Phil Alden Robinson (1989).

9. Though Kinsella set "The Battery" in the Dominican Republic, he created an imaginary Caribbean nation—"Courteguay"—as the setting for later stories, as well as for the 2011 novel *Butterfly Winter*, which expanded on the narrative of "The Battery."

10. The expression "the land of shortstops" appears in Steve Wulf, "Standing Tall at Short," *Sports Illustrated*, February 9, 1987. American Airlines' in-flight magazine employed similar terminology in profiling the baseball culture of the Dominican city San Pedro de Macorís, while promoting the carrier's direct flights from New York to Santo Domingo. Tony Tedeschi, "Land of the Infielders," *American Way*, October 1, 1985, National Baseball Hall of Fame Library, Cooperstown, N.Y., Dominican Republic file.

11. Kinsella addressed his work's relationship with magical realism in a 1989 interview: "I finally read García Márquez's *One Hundred Years of Solitude*, which was fabulous. I wrote one story, "The Battery," under his inspiration, but most of the other South American fiction struck me as impenetrable." Liam Lacey, "Colleague's Attack Motivates Kinsella," *Toronto Globe and Mail*, December 21, 1989.

12. See Frances R. Aparicio and Susana Chávez-Silverman, eds., *Tropicalizations: Transcultural Representations of Latinidad* (Hanover: University Press of New England, 1997).

13. On the history and political economy of the Dominican Republic in the neoliberal era, see in particular Helen I. Safa, *The Myth of the Male Breadwinner: Women and Industrialization in the Caribbean* (Boulder: Westview Press, 1995); Denise Brennan, *What's Love Got to Do with It? Transnational Desires and Sex Tourism in the Dominican Republic* (Durham: Duke University Press, 2004); and Steven Gregory, *The Devil behind the Mirror: Globalization and Politics in the Dominican Republic* (Berkeley: University of California Press, 2007).

14. Juan Marichal with Lew Freedman, *Juan Marichal: My Journey from the Dominican Republic to Cooperstown* (Minneapolis: MVP Books, 2011), 24. On the history of Dominican amateur ball, see Alan M. Klein, *Sugarball: The American Game, the Dominican Dream* (New Haven: Yale University Press, 1991); and Rob Ruck, *The Tropic of Baseball: Baseball in the Dominican Republic* (1991; repr., Lincoln: University of Nebraska Press, 1999).

15. Juan Marichal, interview by author, Santiago, Dominican Republic, January 8, 2006.

16. Marichal, *Juan Marichal*, 25. See also Ruck, *Tropic of Baseball*, 64–74.

17. Klein, *Sugarball*, 23; Ruck, *Tropic of Baseball*, 34–41.

18. Juan Gautreau, "Desenfreno del 1937 Anima Directivos del Beisbol Actual," *El Caribe*, April 10, 1951.

19. Manuel Joaquín Báez Vargas, *Pasión Deportiva* (Santo Domingo: Editora Corripio, 1985), 249–58; "Hay Posibilidades de que se Juegue Beisbol Profesional," *El Caribe*, December 25, 1950. See also Klein, *Sugarball*, 29–31; and Ruck, *Tropic of Baseball*, 104.

20. Ruck, *Tropic of Baseball*, 74–75.

21. "Dedican al Presidente Trujillo Campeonato Profesional," *El Caribe*, April 21, 1951.

22. Clifford Kachline, "Dominican Loop Closes Doors to Stateside Talent," *Sporting News*, September 21, 1960. Kachline's piece appeared in *El Caribe* on September 20, 1960.

23. Orlando Inoa and Héctor J. Cruz, *El Béisbol en República Dominicana: Crónica de una Pasión* (Santo Domingo: Colección Cultural Verizon, 2004), 159.

24. Lauren Derby, *The Dictator's Seduction: Politics and the Popular Imagination in the Era of Trujillo* (Durham: Duke University Press, 2009), 5.

25. Arturo Industrioso, "Samuel: Un Bigleaguer," *El Caribe*, November 24, 1960.

26. "Estrellas Dominicanas en los Diamantes de BB del Caribe," ¡*Ahora!* January 1–15, 1963.

27. Felipe Alou with Herm Weiskopf, *My Life and Baseball* (Waco, Tex.: Word Books, 1967), 119.

28. Ibid., 119–20.

29. Joe King, "Latins Rhumba to Frick Tune—Fined $2,500," *Sporting News*, February 16, 1963.

30. Ibid.

31. "Stooping Low for Fast Buck," *Sporting News*, February 16, 1963.

32. King, "Latins Rhumba to Frick Tune."

33. On the Alou-Frick dispute and its larger context, see Rob Ruck, *Raceball: How the Major Leagues Colonized the Black and Latin Game* (Boston: Beacon Press, 2011), 160–64.

34. "Venezuela Acusada de Piratería por Peloteros de Santo Domingo," *El Universal*, December 17, 1965.

35. Alou, *My Life and Baseball*, 134–35; Fernando A. Vicioso, "Ace Marichal Sharp in Tune-up; Sitdown Staged by Felipe Alou," *Sporting News*, February 26, 1966.

36. Marichal, *Juan Marichal*, 173. See also "The Dandy Dominican," *Time*, June 10, 1966.

37. Ramón A. Reyes, "¿Será Marichal el Mejor Pagado?" *¡Ahora!* May 1, 1967.

38. Roosevelt Comarazamy, "Juan Marichal: El Pelotero y el Hombre," *¡Ahora!* April 28, 1975. In his 2011 autobiography Marichal addressed his decision to stop playing winter ball in order to rest during the MLB off-season: "I had to protect myself. . . . I had to, but it was hard because the people in the Dominican loved me and wanted to see me" (169).

39. "Federación Dicta un Paro 15 Minutos en 2 Estadios," *El Caribe*, October 23, 1970.

40. "Se Organizan los Peloteros Profesionales," *¡Ahora!* November 23, 1970. In 1956 there was one Dominican player (Osvaldo "Ozzie" Virgil) in MLB. Seventeen Dominicans appeared in MLB during the 1970 season. Data from www.baseball-almanac.com/players/birthplace.php.

41. Alvaro Arvelo, "Liga y Federación Logran Acuerdo Soluciona Crisis," *El Caribe*, January 19, 1971.

42. Alvaro Arvelo, "Disienten de Maduro," *El Caribe*, December 16, 1970.

43. "Dice El Chilote: El Beisbol Profesional Esta Desahumanizado," *¡Ahora!* November 9, 1970.

44. Felix Acosta Nuñez, "Forman Confederación Peloteros Profesionales del Caribe en PR," *Listín Diario*, February 10, 1971.

45. "Eligen Lantigua Presidente Confederación Peloteros," *El Caribe*, March 24, 1975. Lantigua remained involved in the leadership of FENAPEPRO into the 1980s.

46. "Bolas y Strikes," *¡Ahora!* April 25, 1977; Aridio Perdomo, "Ligas Verano Ayundan Deporte," *El Caribe*, March 22, 1978.

47. "Equipos Liga Verano Cibao Reducirán Sueldos Players," *El Caribe*, April 11, 1983; Ramón Rodriguez, "Fernández Muñoz Afirma Equipos Liga de Verano Reducirán Sueldos y Refuerzos en Próximo Torneo," *El Caribe*, May 25, 1984.

48. "Liga Cibao Anuncia Entrenamientos," *Listín Diario*, April 10, 1985; "Invitan Presidente Tirar Primera Bola," *Listín Diario*, May 3, 1985.

49. "Comienza Domingo Campeonato Beisbol," *El Caribe*, June 13, 1986; Mario Emilio Guerrero, "Inaugurarán el Día Primero Julio Torneo Beisbol de la Liga Verano," *El Caribe*, June 25, 1987.

50. Carlos A. Hernández, "Javier Critica Actual Sistema en Beisbol Verano en el País," *Listín Diario*, June 7, 1988.

51. Ruck, *Raceball*, 197.

52. Mario de Jesús, "Se Mueve la Liga de Verano del Cibao," *Listín Diario*, April 25, 2009; Jeffrey Nolasco, "Arroceros Toman Delantera Final Liga Verano Cibao," *Hoy*, September 4, 2009.

53. "Bolas y Strikes," *¡Ahora!* April 25, 1977.

54. Dave Nightingale, "Baseball's Secret Treasure," *Sporting News*, August 19, 1985.

55. Bill Brubaker, "The Envy, and Scourge, of the Latin Scouts," *Washington Post*, February 4, 1986.

56. Klein, *Sugarball*, 96–101.

57. Ibid., 64; fact sheet distributed at Campo Las Palmas, in author's possession.

58. Quoted in Klein, *Sugarball*, 64.

59. Until Campo Las Palmas opened, Ávila himself conceded that Guerrero's facility was the industry standard. Dave Nightingale, "Baseball's Secret Treasure," *Sporting News,* August 19, 1985; Klein, *Sugarball,* 65.

60. Manuel L. Medina, "Morales Troncoso Destaca Apertura Academia Beisbol," *El Caribe,* March 23, 1987.

61. Campo Las Palmas fact sheet.

62. Klein, *Sugarball,* 42; Ruck, *Raceball,* 197. See also Arturo J. Marcano Guevara and David P. Fidler, *Stealing Lives: The Globalization of Baseball and the Tragic Story of Alexis Quiroz* (Bloomington: Indiana University Press, 2002).

63. Quoted in Marcos Bretón and José Luis Villegas, *Away Games: The Life and Times of a Latin Baseball Player* (Albuquerque: University of New Mexico Press, 1999), 38.

64. Kevin Kerrane, *Dollar Sign on the Muscle: The World of Baseball Scouting* (1984; repr., New York: Simon and Schuster, 1989), 37.

65. Ibid., 41.

66. See W. C. Madden, *Baseball's First-Year Player Draft, Team by Team through 1999* (Jefferson, N.C.: McFarland, 2001), 11–12; James Davidson, "Baseball Draft: Canadians Unlikely to Have Big Impact," *Toronto Globe and Mail,* June 1, 1991.

67. Alan Schwarz, "Pressure Building for Draft of Players from Outside U.S.," *New York Times,* July 13, 2008.

68. "2012–2016 Basic Agreement," available at www.bizofbaseball.com; Jonathan Mayo, "Game of Signing International Talent to Change," MLB.com, December 2, 2011.

69. Kathy Kiely, "Legislators Open Loopholes in Immigration Law," *USA Today,* May 1, 2007.

70. See Alan M. Klein, *Growing the Game: The Globalization of Major League Baseball* (New Haven: Yale University Press, 2006), 97.

71. In March 2000, Boston Red Sox general manager Dan Duquette described the academy system this way: "The idea is to sign a number of talented players, let them play, and then invite the best players over to the States. The ones who aren't good enough to come—you let them go, and sign another batch." Sean McAdam, "Baseball Is More than a Game in the Dominican Republic," *Providence Journal,* March 20, 2000.

72. According to a 2003 study conducted by MLB teams, their combined annual impact on the Dominican economy totaled $76 million, and their operations in the country employed 1,200 people. "Dominican Economy Gets $76 Million from Baseball," *San Jose Mercury News,* July 25, 2003.

73. Bretón and Villegas, *Away Games,* 69–72.

74. Marichal, interview by author. See also Marichal, *Juan Marichal,* 204–12.

75. Marichal, *Juan Marichal,* 210. See also Ruck, *Raceball,* 211–12.

76. Alan M. Klein, "Dominican Republic: Forging an International Industry," in *Baseball without Borders: The International Pastime,* ed. George Gmelch (Lincoln: University of Nebraska Press, 2006), 132.

77. Alan M. Klein, "Progressive Ethnocentrism: Ideology and Understanding in Dominican Baseball," *Journal of Sport and Social Issues* 32.2 (May 2008): 121–38.

78. Bob Hohler, "It's Not Just Hitters Taking Cuts," *Boston Globe,* September 16, 2008.

79. Steve Fainaru, "MLB Looks to Regulate Dominican Agents," *Washington Post,* September 17, 2003.

80. To be eligible to sign, players must turn seventeen by the end of that year's summer season. See Ruck, *Raceball,* 213.

81. "Tejada Admits to Being Two Years Older Than He Had Said," ESPN.com, April 17, 2008.

82. For an example of media speculation about players' ages, see Dan Le Batard, "Miami Marlins' Expensive Experiment: Will MLB Work Here?" *Miami Herald,* November 20, 2011.

83. Dave Nightingale, "Off-Broadway Auditions," *Sporting News,* December 7, 1992.

84. "Organizan Juego Estrellas de Nativos e Importados," *El Caribe*, December 17, 1970.

85. See Enrique Rojas, "¿La Nueva Rivalidad?" ESPNDeportes.com, February 6, 2008.

86. Carlos A. Montealto, "La Academia de Denis Martínez: Un Sueño que Renace," *La Prensa*, January 25, 2011. Martínez, who was a star with the Orioles and later pitched a perfect game as a member of the Montreal Expos, is typically identified as "Dennis" in the English language press.

87. See Milton H. Jamail, *Venezuelan Bust, Baseball Boom: Andrés Reiner and Scouting on the New Frontier* (Lincoln: University of Nebraska Press, 2008), 215–22.

88. Rafael Hermoso, "Baseball and Books," *New York Times*, April 13, 2003; Benjamin Hoffman, "Astros Defy Expectations with the Top Overall Pick," *New York Times*, June 4, 2012.

89. Cody Monk, *Alfonso Soriano: The Dominican Dream Come True* (Champaign, Ill.: Sports Publishing, 2003), 61; Robert K. Fitts, *Remembering Japanese Baseball: An Oral History of the Game* (Carbondale: Southern Illinois University Press, 2005), 65.

90. Monk, *Alfonso Soriano*, 72–74.

91. See Robert Whiting, *The Meaning of Ichiro: The New Wave from Japan and the Transformation of Our National Pastime* (New York: Warner Books), 145–47.

92. *Sugar*, dir. Anna Boden and Ryan Fleck (2008).

93. Gina Piccalo, "'Sugar' Is Sweet for Algenis Pérez Soto," *Los Angeles Times*, March 29, 2009.

## 5. Constructing Ichiro's Home Field

1. To be a "position player" is to play a position other than pitcher. Another Japanese outfielder, Tsuyoshi Shinjo, began his Major League Baseball career in 2001, as well, appearing in his first game with the New York Mets one day after Ichiro's debut with the Mariners.

2. Jeff Pearlman, "Big Hit," *Sports Illustrated*, May 28, 2001.

3. David Shields, "Being Ichiro," *New York Times Magazine*, September 16, 2001. The piece later appeared in Shields's collection *Body Politic: The Great American Sports Machine* (New York: Simon and Schuster, 2004), 121–35.

4. See Roger Kahn, *The Boys of Summer* (New York: Harper and Row, 1972); Dan Shaughnessy, *The Curse of the Bambino* (New York: Dutton, 1990); and Jonathan Mahler, *Ladies and Gentlemen, the Bronx Is Burning: 1977, Baseball, Politics, and the Battle for the Soul of a City* (New York: Farrar, Straus and Giroux, 2005).

5. Aihwa Ong, *Flexible Citizenship: The Cultural Logics of Transnationality* (Durham: Duke University Press, 1999).

6. On the Pacific Northwest League, see Jim Price, "A Tale of Four Cities," in *Rain Check: Baseball in the Pacific Northwest*, ed. Mark Armour (Cleveland: Society for American Baseball Research, 2006), 4–11. For the history of the Rainiers and Emil Sick, see Dan Raley, "A Man Named Sick Made Seattle Well," ibid., 56–62. See also Paul J. Zingg and Mark D. Medeiros, *Runs, Hits, and an Era: The Pacific Coast League, 1903–58* (Urbana: University of Illinois Press, 1994), and Neil J. Sullivan, *The Minors: The Struggles and the Triumph of Baseball's Poor Relation from 1876 to the Present* (New York: St. Martin's, 1990), 219–29.

7. Bill Sears, "How the Dome Miracle Became Reality," *Kingdome Magazine*, March 1976, box 19, William A. Cunningham Papers, Center for American History, University of Texas at Austin.

8. Timothy A. Gibson, *Securing the Spectacular City: The Politics of Revitalization and Homelessness in Downtown Seattle* (Lanham, Md.: Lexington Books, 2003), 36. On the Seattle World's Fair, see also John M. Findlay, *Magic Lands: Western Cityscapes and American Culture after 1940* (Berkeley: University of California Press, 1992), 214–64.

9. Sears, "How the Dome Miracle Became Reality."

10. "A.L. to Expand by 1971: A's Move to Oakland OKd," *Los Angeles Times*, October 19, 1967.

11. Charles Maher, "Seattle Awarded A.L. Franchise," *Los Angeles Times*, December 2, 1967; "Seattle Voters Clear Way for Major Baseball," *Los Angeles Times*, February 15, 1968.

12. Nick Rousso, "An Exhilarating Big League Bust," in Armour, *Rain Check*, 120.

13. Among the key figures in the early history of the Brewers was team vice president Robert C. Cannon, who had previously worked as the adviser to the Major League Baseball Players Association, before the MLBPA hired Marvin Miller in 1966.

14. On Selig, see Andrew Zimbalist, *In the Best Interests of Baseball? The Revolutionary Reign of Bud Selig* (Hoboken, N.J.: Wiley, 2006).

15. Daniel Okrent, *Nine Innings: The Anatomy of a Baseball Game* (1985; repr., New York: Houghton Mifflin, 2000), 128.

16. Hy Zimmerman, "9-Month Recess Called in Seattle Suit," *Sporting News*, May 11, 1974; "Seattle Assured of Team in '77," *Sporting News*, February 28, 1976.

17. Larry Brown, "Initiative Out; Stadium Gets Go Ahead," *Seattle Times*, March 24, 1972; Sears, "How the Dome Miracle Became Reality." Ruano would continue to be a major opponent of public expenditures on stadiums in greater Seattle until his death in 2005. See Athima Chansanchai, "Frank Ruano, 1920–2005: Stadium Opponent was 'First Suburban Rebel,'" *Seattle Post-Intelligencer*, April 25, 2005.

18. Minutes, meeting of State Stadium Commission, December 21, 1970, box 3, folder 17, Baseball Litigation Records, Record Series 4402-02, Seattle Municipal Archives. Hope's comments responded to one of the SSC's main criteria for site selection, outlined at the outset of the process: the completed project's potential to "establish a focal point with which the community could identify in the same manner as it presently identifies with the Space Needle, Seattle Center, Mount Rainier, Lake Washington, etc." Hy Zimmerman, "Stadium Committee Picks 5 Possible Sites," *Seattle Times*, August 24, 1970.

19. Doug Chin, *Seattle's International District: The Making of a Pan–Asian American Community* (Seattle: International Examiner Press, 2001), 10.

20. Ibid., 13–17, 25–31, 45–51, 53, and 75.

21. Sayuri Guthrie-Shimizu, *Transpacific Field of Dreams: How Baseball Linked the United States and Japan in Peace and War* (Chapel Hill: University of North Carolina Press, 2012), 103. See also S. Frank Miyamoto, *Social Solidarity among the Japanese in Seattle* (1939; repr., Seattle: University of Washington Press, 1984), xvii–xviii; Samuel O. Regalado "'Play Ball': Baseball and Seattle's Japanese-American Courier League," *Pacific Northwest Quarterly* 87.1 (Winter 1995–96): 29–37; John Rosapepe, "A Pastime with a Past," *Seattle Times*, March 20, 2003.

22. Bob Santos, *Hum Bows, Not Hot Dogs! Memoirs of a Savvy Asian American Activist* (Seattle: International Examiner Press, 2002), 33.

23. Ibid., 34 and 41–42.

24. Monica Sone's memoir *Nisei Daughter* (1953; repr., Seattle: University of Washington Press, 1979) is a classic account of Seattle's Japanese American community before World War II.

25. "Today, the district serves the Japanese Americans only as a symbolic community, for very few reside or work there. Nonetheless, it stands for the integrated interethnic relationships among different Asian groups in Seattle and affects the perceptions of Japanese Americans about other Asian Americans." Yasuko I. Takezawa, *Breaking the Silence: Redress and Japanese American Ethnicity* (Ithaca: Cornell University Press, 1995), 12. On Uwajimaya, see the company website: www.uwajimaya.com/history.html.

26. Shelley Sang-Hee Lee, *Claiming the Oriental Gateway: Prewar Seattle and Japanese America* (Philadelphia: Temple University Press, 2012), 209; Santos, *Hum Bows, Not Hot Dogs,* 74–75.

27. Santos, *Hum Bows, Not Hot Dogs,* 74–77. After the Model Cities program ended in 1974, Inter*Im continued its work in the neighborhood as a grant-funded organization, and in 1979 became a 501(c)(3) nonprofit community development corporation.

28. Jeffrey Hou and Isami Kinoshita, "Bridging Community Differences through Informal Processes: Reexamining Participatory Planning in Seattle and Matsudo," *Journal of Planning, Education, and Research* 26.3 (March 2007): 305.

29. I use the former term, which was the place-name used most frequently by organizers and community groups both during and after the anti-stadium mobilizations of the 1970s.

30. Chin, *Seattle's International District*, 80.

31. Santos, *Hum Bows, Not Hot Dogs*, 81. Police arrested one of the demonstrators, although he was later released and the charges were dropped.

32. "Seattle Stadium Ceremony Disrupted," *Yakima Herald-Republic*, November 3, 1972, clipping scrapbook (1972–1974), Public Information Office files, Department of Stadium Administration, King County Archives, Seattle. According to this account (an Associated Press wire story), county councilman and former MLB player John O'Brien was hit with mud, and a ceremonial gold-plated home plate was "tarnished and scratched" during the demonstration. As King County's highest-ranking elected official, John Spellman was one of the most influential public officials involved in the stadium project.

33. Santos, *Hum Bows, Not Hot Dogs*, 81–82. Photographs show that both "Hum *Bow*, Not Hot Dogs" and "Hum *Bows*, Not Hot Dogs" appeared on signs at the HUD protest on November 14, 1972. See the collections of the Wing Luke Museum of the Asian Pacific American Experience (http://wingluke.org/collections.htm) and the Seattle Civil Rights and Labor History Project (http://depts.washington.edu/civilr/aa_kingdome.htm).

34. Yen Le Espiritu, *Asian American Panethnicity: Bridging Institutions and Identities* (Philadelphia: Temple University Press, 1992), 9–14.

35. Ray Ruppert, "Stadium Protest: 'Where Are We Going to Go?,'" *Seattle Times*, June 25, 1972, clipping scrapbook (1972–1974), Public Information Office files, Department of Stadium Administration, King County Archives.

36. While the case was under way, John Spellman expressed frustration that lawyers from the Legal Services Center, an organization largely funded by the federal Office of Economic Opportunity, were involved in an attempt to block a government project. "Spellman Irked at Latest Suit to Block Stadium," *Seattle Times*, August 2, 1972; "Stadium Work to Proceed as Judge Dismisses Lawsuit," *Seattle Times*, September 16, 1972.

37. Bacho's published works include the acclaimed novel *Cebu* (Seattle: University of Washington Press, 1991). See Peter Bacho, "A Life Well Lived," in *Dark Blue Suit and Other Stories* (Seattle: University of Washington Press, 1997), 81–90, for an account of his relationship with local activist Chris Mensalvas.

38. In addition to fighting the Kingdome project, Mensalvas was a mentor for a younger generation of leaders who organized a series of reforms within Local 37, making the union a powerful advocate not only of cannery workers' rights but also of international solidarity with working people in the Philippines. Two leaders of the movement within Local 37, Gene Viernes and Silme Domingo, were murdered in 1981, and the Philippine government of Ferdinand Marcos was eventually found responsible for the killings. See Thomas Churchill, *Triumph over Marcos* (Seattle: Open Hand Publishing, 1995), and Kieran Walsh Taylor, "Turn to the Working Class: The New Left, Black Liberation, and the U.S. Labor Movement" (Ph.D. diss., University of North Carolina at Chapel Hill, 2007), 198–245.

39. Issues of the *International Examiner* from the period provide an extensive record of these concerns. For example, Nemesio Domingo wrote an editorial for the October 1975 issue calling for community organizations to collaborate on a development plan that supported locally owned business. "The economic future of the ID depends on its ability to draw people and consumers for its own attraction," he urged. "It will be an odious epithet if the ID becomes a 'dumping ground' for post Stadium events."

40. Chin, *Seattle's International District*, 86.

41. Ibid., 84–86. See also Dean Wong, "PDA Celebrates Twenty Years of Community Service," *International Examiner*, October 3, 1995.

42. Chin, *Seattle's International District*, 83.

43. Ron Chew, "Memorable Years at the International Examiner," *International Examiner*, December 14, 2004.

44. See Ron Chew, "The Wing Luke Asian Museum," *Chinese America: History and Perspectives* 14 (2000): 62–68.

45. Andrew Zimbalist, *Baseball and Billions: A Probing Look inside the Big Business of Our National Pastime* (New York: Basic Books, 1992), 131.

46. Ibid., 131–34.

47. Other members of the proposed ownership group included John Ellis, CEO of Puget Sound Power and Light Company; Chris Larson, who led a collection of investors from Microsoft; Boeing CEO Frank Schrontz; and executives from McCaw Cellular. For a concise account of the Mariners' 1992 sale, see Art Thiel, *Out of Left Field: How the Mariners Made Baseball Fly in Seattle* (Seattle: Sasquatch Books, 2003), 55–75.

48. Slade Gorton, "Dream Team for a Major League City," *Seattle Times*, January 24, 1992.

49. Dana Frank, *Buy American: The Untold Story of Economic Nationalism* (Boston: Beacon Press, 1999), 214.

50. Quoted ibid., 229.

51. Thiel, *Out of Left Field*, 66.

52. George Will speculated, "Perhaps the hope and expectation was that no Seattle group would come up with [$100 million], thus enabling the American League to seize a share of the Florida market." Will, "Buyers on Deck," *Washington Post*, February 6, 1992.

53. Joanna Cagan and Neil deMause, *Field of Schemes: How the Great Stadium Swindle Turns Public Money into Private Profit* (Monroe, Me.: Common Courage Press, 1998), 72.

54. Seattle City Council, Resolution no. 28492, January 27, 1992, Seattle Municipal Archives.

55. Mark Potts, "Japan and Mariners: Quandary for Game," *Washington Post*, February 28, 1992.

56. Mary Akamine, "Chicken Fried Steak and the Mariners' Fate," *International Examiner*, February 5, 1992.

57. Notes for commissioner's meeting, February 1992, box 38, folder 5, Office of the Mayor, Norman B. Rice, Departmental Correspondence, Seattle Municipal Archive.

58. John M. Clearman to Fay Vincent, January 24, 1992, box 38, folder 4, ibid.

59. Norman B. Rice to John F. Clearman, February 5, 1992, ibid.

60. Norman B. Rice to Christopher R. Larson, January 28, 1992, ibid.

61. Tom Farrey and Joni Balter, "M's Sale Gets Go-Ahead," *Seattle Times*, June 9, 1992.

62. Zimbalist, *Baseball and Billions*, 130, 135.

63. In November 1993, Mariners officials announced that they no longer considered the Kingdome a viable long-term home, after reviewing the results of a facility survey they had commissioned from stadium design firm HOK. See Bob Finnigan, "M's Look Beyond Kingdome," *Seattle Times*, November 9, 1993.

64. In the same brochure, team CEO John Ellis noted: "The only reason the current ownership group came together and committed our resources was to save Major League Baseball here. We believed that the Mariners were a regional asset, and that we were acting for the benefit of the community. After investing millions of dollars, our conclusion is . . . [that] a new ballpark is needed to secure the future of Major League Baseball in the Pacific Northwest. We're willing to do our part to get it built, but now the community must show its commitment to help." Seattle Mariners, promotional brochure for proposed "New Century Park," 1994, King County Archives, County Council records, Councilmember Maggi Fimia, Issue files 1970–2001.

65. Ibid.

66. See Cagan and deMause, *Field of Schemes*, 163–65. In December 1996, when the project confronted massive cost overruns, the Mariners' owners again threatened to leave. Senator

Slade Gorton then brokered a deal for more public financing for the project. See also Thiel, *Out of Left Field*, 141–70.

67. George D. Moffett III and Peter Grier, "A New-Fangled, Old-Style Ballpark," *Christian Science Monitor*, April 9, 1992.

68. Daniel Rosensweig, *Retro Ball Parks: Instant History, Baseball, and the New American City* (Knoxville: University of Tennessee Press, 2005), 45.

69. The statement was printed in "Field of Dreams," *Mariners Magazine*, April 1996, 4. Joan Enticknap, an executive at Seafirst Bank, chaired the Public Facilities District Board. Other members included local business, labor, and nonprofit leaders.

70. Philip J. Lowry, *Green Cathedrals: The Ultimate Celebration of Major League and Negro League Ballparks* (New York: Walker and Company, 2006), 219–20; Kathleen Triesch Saul, "Buy Me Some Peanuts and Sushi," *Seattle Times*, July 28, 1999.

71. Samantha Shapiro, "The Name Game," *The Stranger*, July 16, 1998, box 14, folder 3, Legislative Department, Nick Licata files, Seattle Municipal Archives.

72. See Greg Brown, "Mariners Look East with Ideas," *Seattle Post-Intelligencer*, April 5, 1993.

73. Foreshadowing future developments, the announcement of the working agreement in the official team magazine was accompanied by a short, glowing piece about Ichiro Suzuki titled "Japan's Ken Griffey Jr." "Mariners—BlueWave," *Mariners Magazine*, April 1998, 26–27.

74. See Robert Whiting, *The Meaning of Ichiro* (New York: Warner Books, 2004), 91–95. As Whiting details, the union of NPB players—the Nippon Professional Baseball Players Association—has remained significantly weaker than the MLBPA.

75. Bob Finnigan, "M's Go All Out to Woo Sasaki," *Seattle Times*, November 21, 1999; Larry Stone, "Get Ready for 'Sasakimania,'" *Seattle Times*, December 25, 1999.

76. Whiting, *Meaning of Ichiro*, 16.

77. Quoted ibid., 18.

78. Ibid., 21–22; Dan Levitt, "Working the Free Market: How the Seattle Mariners Won 116 Games in 2001," in Armour, *Rain Check*, 125.

79. Quoted in Larry Stone, "Does 'Aged' Ichiro Have Unfair Edge?," *Seattle Times*, September 2, 2001.

80. Jayson Stark, "Change the Rules for Rookies," ESPN.com, September 5, 2003.

81. Sam Howe Verhovek, "Japan's Baseball Idol Wins Fans in Seattle," *New York Times*, April 24, 2001.

82. *"Baseball Is Just Baseball": The Understated Ichiro: An Unauthorized Collection Compiled by David Shields* (Seattle: TNI Books, 2001), 41, 109.

83. Ibid., 4–5.

84. Ichiro Suzuki, *Ichiro on Ichiro: Conversations with Narumi Komatsu*, trans. Philip Gabriel (Seattle: Sasquatch Books, 2004), 241–42.

85. In an interview on December 19, 2005, with Maury Brown, Mariners official Chuck Armstrong explained that in "the Far East marketing, with the phenomenon of Sasaki and Ichiro, everybody else gets as much of that revenue as we do. In fact, we don't really do any marketing over there. Major League Baseball Advanced Media and Major League Enterprises do a lot of that. We're helpful, and we think it's helpful that it spreads the Mariner name and . . . certain players want to come over here, like our recently signed catcher Kenji Johjima. They televise our games over there because we've had guys like Ichiro, Kaz [Kazuhiro Sasaki], and [Shigetoshi] Hasegawa. It helps us, but it doesn't help us dollar-wise." Available at www.bizofbaseball.com.

86. "Japan: Five New Sponsors and Nine Renewals," *Ballpark: The Official International Newsletter of Major League Baseball*, April 2005, 3.

87. Angelo Bruscas, "Suzuki Signing Strengthens Mariners' Bridge to Japan" and "M's Making Right Marketing Moves," *Seattle Post-Intelligencer*, November 20, 2000, and March 30, 2001; Whiting, *Meaning of Ichiro*, 30.

88. Chin, *Seattle's International District*, 106.

89. According to a survey conducted during the summer of 1995 by the Chinese Information and Service Center and the International District Business Improvement Area, fourteen
of the twenty-nine businesspeople polled opposed the new ballpark, regardless of any possible concessions for the International District. Only two respondents supported the ballpark
without qualification. Other respondents suggested that they would support the project if
new fan-only taxes were levied, or if the team and the city made new commitments to re-
solving issues such as parking, traffic, and pollution. See Dean Wong, "Seattle Mariners and
Community Meet about Stadium," *International Examiner*, September 19, 1995.

90. Soyon Im, "Community's Battle Cry against Stadium," *International Examiner*, July 16,
1996.

91. Ian Dapiaoen, "A Day in the Life: The International District," *International Examiner*,
July 3, 2002.

92. Newsletter, Wing Luke Asian Museum, spring 2003.

93. Elisa Ung and Linda K. Harris, "In Chinatown, 1,500 Protest Stadium Plans," *Philadelphia Inquirer*, June 9, 2000; Frederick Cusick, "Chinatown Residents Breathe Sigh of Relief,"
*Philadelphia Inquirer*, November 14, 2000.

94. John Romano, "World's Eyes on One Name," *St. Petersburg Times*, July 9, 2001.

## Epilogue

1. Timothy Egan, "Seattle, a City Spurned, Heckles a Visiting Son," *New York Times*, April
18, 2001.

2. On the World Baseball Classic, see John D. Kelly, *The American Game: Capitalism, De-
colonization, World Domination, and Baseball* (Chicago: Prickly Paradigm Press, 2006); and
William W. Kelly, "Is Baseball a Global Sport? America's National Pastime as Global Field and
International Sport," *Global Networks* 7.2 (2007): 187–201.

3. "NPBPA Agrees to Play in WBC," *Daily Yomiuri*, September 5, 2012.

4. In a blog post on February 27, 2009, *Seattle Times* columnist Larry Stone wrote: "In the
case of Asian players like Ichiro and Kenji Johjima, who remained with Team Japan rather
than reporting to spring training, they could conceivably not get to Mariners' camp until
March 24, the day after the [WBC] championship game at Dodger Stadium. That would leave
them less than two weeks before Opening Day to be with Seattle—hardly an optimal situation for a team with a new manager and coaching staff" ("World Baseball Classic Fever?
Almost, but Not Quite": http://blog.seattletimes.nwsource.com/stone/2009/02/27/wbc_fe-
ver_almost_but_not_quite.html). See also Ryan Divish, "Ten Things to Watch during Spring
Training," *Tacoma News Tribune*, February 15, 2009. When a bleeding ulcer forced Ichiro to
begin the 2009 MLB season on the disabled list, team physician Mitch Storey cited stress from
the recent WBC as a possible cause. See Larry Stone, "Ichiro Had a Bleeding Ulcer," *Seattle
Times*, April 4, 2009.

5. See Jon Saraceno, "Rodriguez Bobbled Play with Indecision," *USA Today*, January 18,
2006; Christian Red, "Benedict A-Rod Switches Sides for WBC," *New York Daily News*, December 7, 2008.

6. According to the Fantasy Sports Trade Association, approximately 13 million people
played fantasy baseball in 2011. Dan Fost, "Modest Farmer, Managing Mogul," *New York
Times*, October 25, 2011.

7. On the history of fantasy baseball, see Jules Tygiel, "Populist Baseball: Baseball Fantasies
in the 1980s," in his *Past Time: Baseball as History* (New York: Oxford University Press, 2000),
198–222; and Alan Schwarz, *The Numbers Game: Baseball's Lifelong Fascination with Statistics*
(New York: Macmillan, 2005).

8. Alan Schwarz, "No License Is Required to Run Fantasy Leagues," *New York Times*,
August 9, 2006.

9. *Moneyball,* dir. Bennett Miller (2011); Michael Lewis, *Moneyball: The Art of Winning an Unfair Game* (New York: Norton, 2003).

10. Cooper portrayed New York's Gehrig in *The Pride of the Yankees* (1942), and Redford played the fictional Hobbs in *The Natural* (1984).

11. On the history of performance enhancement in baseball, see Howard Bryant, *Juicing the Game: Drugs, Power, and the Fight for the Soul of Major League Baseball* (New York: Viking, 2005).

12. Michael S. Schmidt, "Dominicans Try Shots to Boost Rising Players," *New York Times,* October 25, 2009.

13. Steve Fainaru, "Seeking an Edge with Risky Animal Drugs," *Chicago Tribune,* June 29, 2003; Geoff Baker, "Steroids Part of the Game," *Toronto Star,* May 14, 2005.

14. See José Canseco, *Juiced: Wild Times, Rampant 'Roids, Smash Hits, and How Baseball Got Big* (New York: William Morrow, 2005); and the 2007 "Report to the Commissioner of Baseball of an Independent Investigation into the Illegal Use of Steroids and Other Performance Enhancing Substances by Players in Major League Baseball" ("The Mitchell Report"), www.mlb.com.

15. Geoff Baker, "Buhner: I'd Vomit if Ichiro Got Big Contract Extension," *Seattle Times,* July 18, 2012.

16. Josh Liebeskind, "Ichiro Era Ends for Mariners with Trade to Yankees," MLB.com, July 23, 2012.

# INDEX